IN THE PRESENCE
OF MY ENEMIES

IN THE PRESENCE OF MY ENEMIES

MEMOIRS OF TIBETAN NOBLEMAN TSIPON SHUGUBA

Sumner Carnahan
with
Lama Kunga Rinpoche,
Ngor Thartse Shabtrung

Foreword by Lobsang Lhalungpa
Introduction by Robert A. F. Thurman
Letters from His Holiness the Dalai Lama
and from Professor Thubten J. Norbu

Clear Light Publishers
SANTA FE, NEW MEXICO

Clear Light Publishers, 823 Don Diego, Santa Fe, New Mexico 87501

LIBRARY OF CONGRESS CATALOGING-IN-PUBLICATION DATA

Carnahan, Sumner.
    In the presence of my enemies : memoirs of Tibetan nobleman Tsipon
    Shuguba / by Sumner Carnahan, with Lama Kunga Rinpoche : foreword by
    Lobsang Lhalungpa
        p. cm.
    Includes bibliographical references and index.
    ISBN: 0-940666-61-8 (cloth) : $24.95
    ISBN: 0-940666-62-6 (paper) : $14.95
    1. Tsipon Shuguba. 2. Tibet (China)—History—Uprising of 1959—
Personal narratives, Tibetan. 3. Tibet (China)—History—1951–
I. Lama Kunga, Rinpoche. II. Title.
DS786.C29   1995
951'.505'092—dc20
[B]   94–43886
                                                                      CIP

Translations from the Tibetan: Lama Kunga Rinpoche; Translation assistance: Lucy Du Pertuis,
    Ph.D.; Tibetan calligraphy: Lama Kunga Rinpoche; Photo production manager: Patrick
    James Sumner.

Edited exerpts from "Mystic Nation in Exile" by Robert A. F. Thurman reprinted with kind
    permission from *Parabola* magazine, Vol. X, No. 2, May 1985.

"Prayer for the Happiness of All That Lives" written by Ngorchen Kunga Zangpo, founder of
    Ngor Monastery, fifteenth century. Original translation from the Tibetan by Thutop Tulku
    and K. T. Khechog Palmo, 1967.

Front Cover photos: *Background:* The Potala, Lhasa, Tibet; *Foreground:* Tsipon Shuguba as yasor
    general at festival in Lhasa, wood-horse year, 1954.

Back Cover photo: His Holiness the Fourteenth Dalai Lama of Tibet with Tsipon Shuguba, at
    the Fairmont Hotel in San Francisco, 1991.

Frontispiece photo: *Center:* Tsipon Jamyang Khedrup Shuguba; *Left:* Sonam Wangyal
    (Shuguba's brother) holding his daughter, Tenzing Wangmo; *Right:* Tsering Chodzom
    (Shuguba's wife), at family home in Lhasa, 1956.

Contents

Letter from His Holiness the Dalai Lama

THE DALAI LAMA

ༀ། སྤུ་ལོ་ཁ་རི་ར་ངོ་འཕྱུད་སྐྱབས་ཇེ་ལྷར་བཀོད་མངགས་བགྱིས་པ་
བཞིན། ཅེས་དཔོན་ཕུད་ཁྲུད་འཇམ་དབྱངས་མཁས་གྲུབ་དེ་ཉིད་ནས།   རང་
གི་མི་ཚེའི་ནང་སྐྱེད་སྡུག་ཉམས་མྱོང་དངོས་བྱུང་གི་ལོ་རྒྱུས་བཅོས་མིན་བརྗམས་
བྱིས་འདི་ལ་བརྟེན་ནས་དཔེ་དེབ་ཀློག་པ་པོ་རྣམས་ནས་བར་སྐབས་བོད་ནང་གི་
གནས་སྟངས་ངོ་མ་གང་འཆམས་ཤེས་རྟོགས་ཐུབ་རྒྱུར་ཕན་ཚ་འབྱུང་ངེས། དེ་
ཉིད་ཪོགས་བྱང་མྱུར་དུ་ཐོབ་པའི་སྐྱབས་སྨོན་བཅས། ༡ ༠༤ ཟླ་མས།
༡༩༩༥ ཟླ་ ༦ ཚེས་ ༡༤ ལ།

s I requested at our last meeting in San Francisco, the late Tsipon Shuguba Jamyang Khedrup, former Tibetan Minister of Finance, has completed this autobiography, an undistorted narrative of the events of his life, both happy and sad. From this book readers will obtain a true understanding of the situation in Tibet. With prayers for his swift enlightenment.

June 14, 1995   The Dalai Lama

Letter from Professor Thubten J. Norbu

I am very happy to see ***In the Presence of My Enemies*** as published by Clear Light. This literature is both a chronicle of Tsipon Shuguba's experience and life story as well as a document of the tumultuous recent history of central Asia. It stands as a personal account of one of the greatest continuing tragedies of the twentieth century.

When I first knew of him in the mid-1940s, Tsipon Shuguba was one of the four treasurer-secretaries of His Holiness' government. Everyone respected him because of his position and the quality of his work. I personally came to know him when I was in Drepung Monastery and he oversaw allocation of the provisions for the entire college. He helped me make sure that goods were distributed fairly, that everyone was treated equally well, and that all monks got what they needed. By 1945, we became good friends through our repeated interactions. Then came the Chinese Communist invasion of Tibet. I left the monastery in 1951, never seeing Shuguba again until he came to the United States almost three decades later. His son, Kunga Rinpoche, brought him from Tibet to Berkeley, California in 1980. On a few occasions, while visiting Berkeley, I saw him and quite enjoyed his company. It is so terribly sad that he had to endure nineteen years of imprisonment at the hands of the Chinese, even as hundreds of thousands of Tibetans have suffered similarly, right up to the present day.

This book is an important milestone for preserving Tibetan customs and culture as well as for showing the world community how Tibet and her people have suffered under the illegal Chinese communist occupation.

Prof. Thubten J. Norbu

Foreword

The memoirs of Tsipon Shuguba [transliteration: Shu bkod pa] is indeed welcome. This rare, personal account will help to create a more rounded picture of Tibet, projecting as it does an image of old Tibet — "The Sacred Realm" — which is no more, and of the new one being created by the Communist conquerors in their own image.

Shuguba's story covers a span of eighty-seven years. For over forty years, he was a lay official of the former Tibet government; during most of his remaining years, under Chinese control, a prisoner and, later, a reminder of what his captors dubbed as the "reactionary upper strata."

I have known Tsipon Shuguba since 1940, the year I was appointed monk-official, soon thereafter to join the staff of the "Tsi-Yigtsang," the Dalai Lama's Grand Secretariat at the Potala Palace in Lhasa. We met at numerous official and social functions, and our acquaintance developed into friendship during the weeks we lived and worked together at Reting. Shuguba was the commander of one of two separate military units dispatched to secure Reting Monastery from the rebellious supporters of the former regent, Reting Rinpoche.

I can say without reservation that Tsipon Shuguba was a senior official held in high esteem by many Tibetans, including myself. He was a man of honesty, integrity, competence, and compassion, who served his country well and remained loyal to the Dalai Lama to the end. Despite the long, traumatic years under Chinese occupation, he maintained his natural calmness and serenity, probably because his personality was deeply imbued with spirituality.

The first part of Shuguba's life in independent Tibet stands in sharp and shocking contrast to what he went through under Chinese occupation. Many Tibetans in exile cannot reveal their experiences of those years for fear of reprisals against family members in Tibet. This important account should be viewed against the background of devastation the Chinese have wrought in Tibet, and the rosy picture their propaganda presents to the outside world, always proclaiming themselves to be the "liberators" of Tibet and the wise and altruistic "brothers."

Our native country, Tibet, had many shortcomings, but it was home to a pious and peaceful people, who, on the whole, devoted themselves to Buddha's teachings of nonviolence, tolerance, and compassion. Tibetans respected every form of life and looked upon the different groups of people as a human family.

When the Chinese Communists began occupying Tibet in 1950, they publicly proclaimed that Tibet, as part of the "Great Motherland," would be turned into a Socialist paradise. Like many other things they said, this was just a deception. In reality it meant that by seizing all power and privileges for the ruling Communist hierarchy, they created a paradise for themselves. The slogan had two contradictory aspects: one was purported to be the Tibet Development Program, the other had a more sinister side: development for the Han colonizers and occupation forces. There were only a few symbolic gestures made towards "the ungrateful, troublesome Tibetans." In addition, the "development" had a hidden agenda, namely to undermine the Tibetan community and culture, and simultaneously, sinocise them.

I would like to congratulate Clear Light Publishers for bringing the memoirs of this distinguished Tibetan official to an American audience, and commend Lama Kunga Rinpoche, and the writer, Sumner Carnahan, for her painstaking interviewing and sensitive writing.

Lobsang Lhalungpa

Preface

Jamyang Khedrup Shuguba was educated and literate. Brought to the United States in 1980 at the age of seventy-six, he began — at the urging of his son, Lama Kunga Rinpoche — to write down in Tibetan what had happened to him. The specifics of two decades of intense change inside the homeland had been concealed from Tibetans in exile. Clouded, too, were certain events surrounding the takeover itself. Long before Shuguba's capture by the Chinese and his son's escape to India, they lived separate lives: Rinpoche carried out his duties as vice-abbot at rural Ngor Monastery; Shuguba worked in Lhasa as *tsipon*, one of four finance ministers in the Dalai Lama's government.

Tsipon Shuguba's recounting of his life was prompted by, and gains significance from, the catastrophic events into which he was drawn. Vanity was not the motivation for his telling but rather the need to reconstruct. By the latter half of the twentieth century, Tibetan culture had perfected — in parallel with material developments of the West — what has been described as an advanced "spiritual technology." That progress was thwarted in 1959 when Lhasa was seized, shattering the secular and religious heart of Tibet.

I met Mr. Shuguba in 1984 at the home of my friend Laetitia, who was married to one of Shuguba's sons, Hiroshi Sonami. During a simple Tibetan-style meal of meat dumplings, noodles, and beer, Shuguba sat quietly by while Lama Kunga Rinpoche offered the barest facts of his father's life: nineteen years of imprisonment, his wife's mysterious suicide before her trial, their daughter's tragic death, time spent in a twenty-by-thirty-foot room with nine other men.

I was moved. I wanted to know more.

Eighty-year-old Shuguba spoke no English when I first began visiting him. In the process of exchanging vocabularies, Shuguba's playful miming got me laughing. I enjoyed being with him. One day, I heard that someone was needed to help with the writing of his life story. I plunged into the task of asking questions — a process that lasted ten years.

Mr. Shuguba, an aristocrat, was not a storyteller by inclination, nor an historian. His original tale (translated into literal English by Rinpoche) had been recounted candidly without sentimentality or bitterness, but it lacked elaboration. In order to clarify moments, to excavate the nuances and emotions from Shuguba's experience, I took notes and recorded hours of audiotape over the years, speaking with Shuguba, his friends, and his family in exile. Every recorded interview with Shuguba but one was attended by my collaborator, Rinpoche, acting as translator. The one time I interviewed Shuguba alone, we were in his room. I asked him to describe the things around him. During that session, as at other times, I felt that in spite of our language differences we communicated quite clearly.

On another visit, disregarding the question I had posed, he spoke of a dream he'd had the night before about his wife. That was the last time we met.

During this period I began studying Tibetan classical language with Shuguba's son Hiroshi Sonami (Ngor Thartse Khen Rinpoche), who was then dying of cancer. A highly-respected scholar, former abbot of Ngor, he left Tibet in 1958 carrying his monastery's treasured mandalas to safety. After Tibet's fall, he studied and taught in Japan on a Rockefeller Fellowship. In California in the 1980s he was unable to find work — was refused a job as a clerk in an Asian Studies library. Though I was less than successful with the language, I learned about the integrity and vitality of Tibetan Buddhism from Hiroshi's methods and his dignity while dying. Concerned for the future of Buddhism, Hiroshi devoted his last moments to teaching and translating esoteric Buddhist texts.

Three of Shuguba's sons were recognized *tulkus* — reincarnations of great Buddhist teachers from the past. Before the diaspora, these men would have lived out their lives in monasteries. Shuguba, however, was a secular official, perhaps best described as a bureaucrat. He did his job, he had nothing to hide, no program or agenda. He hadn't been, in any real sense, instrumental in preventing or contributing to the demise of Tibet. He was concerned, as are most people, with living his life, enjoying it. Though possessing keen powers of observation and an articulate intelligence, he couldn't understand *why* some things were happening to him. He appears to have had no interest in taking part in world history. Now, his hapless moments have gained significance beyond the life of the man.

Strictly speaking, this book is not an autobiography. That manuscript exists, and may one day be published as is, in Tibetan. Rather than attempt to clarify and refine the sparsely-worded anecdotes, I chose to bring the story to life for a Western readership, which I assumed might be ignorant, as I had been, of what transpired in Tibet in the twentieth century. Needless to say, all of Shuguba's original recollections have been included, as well as the material gleaned from my interviews with him. And, except for a rearrangement in the order of telling for dramatic purposes, I have remained loyal to Shuguba's idiom and chronology. Most of the lengthy elaborations I added (in Shuguba's voice) were translated back to him by his son for verification. The final manuscript was revised with the benefit of Rinpoche's expert and intimate attention.

Though written with the Western reader in mind, this book remains true to Shuguba's original concern — that "the truth, the facts" about the operation and protocol of his world be preserved.

❀ ❀ ❀

Lama Kunga Rinpoche joins me in appreciation for the people who helped bring his father to the United States and who have helped make it possible to bring this story to light, many of whom are mentioned in the following pages. Special acknowledgment to Lucy Du Pertuis, Ph.D., for assisting Rinpoche with translation and transcription of the original autobiographical material. Thanks to Professor Janet Gyatso, Lobsang Lhalungpa, Judith Skinner, Laetitia Sonami, Robert A. F. Thurman, and the Office of Tibet in New York City for detailed editorial advice and assistance. Thanks to Kathleen Burch, and to Ewam Choden Tibetan Buddhist Meditation Center for encouragement. Special thanks to Tsenshab Rinpoche and Hiroshi Sonami for participating in in-depth interviews, and to Harmon Houghton and Marcia Keegan for their vision and dedication. Grateful acknowledgment to His Holiness the Fourteenth Dalai Lama of Tibet for ongoing inspiration.

Sumner Carnahan

The Potala Palace in Lhasa, Tibet. The former residence of the Dalai Lamas. Photograph © by Marcia Keegan.

Introduction

When His Holiness the Dalai Lama of Tibet had to flee the invading Red Army of the People's Republic of China in 1959, he was followed eventually by over one hundred thousand Tibetans, with many more tens of thousands perishing in the attempt. Since then, those Tibetans who could not get away have suffered genocidal occupation by the Chinese Communists. And those in the diaspora in India, Europe, and America have had to be responsible for the preservation of the entire culture.

The policy of the Chinese occupation forces was described as "genocidal" by the International Commission of Jurists in Geneva. Following Mao's determination to expand the borders of China to include all the former protectorates of the Manchu Empire, the mission of the Chinese generals in charge was to eradicate Tibetan culture and assimilate Tibetans into the Chinese race.

❖ ❖ ❖

Tibet, culturally including the widely-scattered Mongolian peoples, has its own unique civilization, which is not "traditional" in our usual sense of "premodern," but also is not "modern" in the *Western* sense of modern. It is not a "medieval" or "feudal" civilization, as often even its most sympathetic students have assumed. It had its own "renaissance" and "reformation," developed its own form of "industrial revolution." But where the Western industrial modernity is "exterior," i.e., materialistic, secularistic, and aimed at ultimately positive transformation of the world as a physical, external environment, the Tibetan industrial modernity is spiritual, religious, and aimed at ultimately positive transformation of the world as an intersubjective, internal realm of living minds.

Tibet/Mongolia was the only society on the planet in which Buddhism had become completely central, the only fully monasticized society in history. This does not mean it was "pure" or the "Buddha-land," a land where all Buddhist ideals, both individual and social, were fulfilled. No land could ever satisfy the messianic aspirations of the Mahayana bodhisattvas without the entire planet going along, according to the Buddhist view of the interconnectedness of all beings. Tibet showed her implicit awareness of her own imperfection in this sense by seeking in the end to shut out the rest of the violent world. . . .

Tibetans were once a powerful race of conquerors, feared by the T'ang emperors, Muslim caliphs, Bengali and Nepali kings, and Inner Asian princes. In the seventh century, Srongtsen Gampo brought in Buddhism against the strenuous objections of his fierce feudal vassals, and it took his dynasty almost two hundred years to build the first Buddhist monastery. In the tenth through the fourteenth century, Tibet was slowly monasticized, as the nation's warrior energies turned more and more inward to the conquest of the inner enemies of ignorance, lust, and hate. The power of the feudal nobles still remained great, however, and the fortunes of the monastic Orders teetered in a precarious balance with the various dynasties, with foreign powers often involved — especially the as yet untamed Mongols. This was the period of the "feudal, medieval Tibetan society" so many think still existed until recently, due to the combination of Tibet's lack of "exterior modernity," the propaganda of the Chinese, ignorance, and the lack of even a concept of a form of personality and society that existed nowhere else, a form we can suitably call "interior modernity."

Then in the fifteenth through seventeenth centuries, something remarkable happened, something that did not happen anywhere else on the planet. The monastic, spiritually-centered institutions became the secular power, gradually assuming responsibility for government. They took over the management of resources, developing a skilled bureaucracy. During these same centuries in northern Europe, the merchant classes backed secular kings to suppress the feudal nobles, the Protestant ideology destroyed the role of the monasteries by making "interior industry" irrelevant to a predetermined salvation by faith alone and hence irrational, and the unification of the sacred/secular duality was accomplished by the collapse of the sacred into the secular. In Tibet, the monastic Orders employed Messianic and Apocalyptic Buddhist ideas to produce a Sacred King to control the feudal nobles, depriving them of much of their land and all feudal claims over the peasants. The monasteries became the seats of the national industry: the inner perfection of minds and souls through education and contemplation.

The magnificent edifice renowned as the Potala was completed during the seventeenth century, combining monastery, ancestral royal fortress-palace, apocalyptic mystery temple, and bureaucratic administrative hall of government. It symbolizes dramatically the synthesis I have so quickly sketched above.

Tibet's "modernity" is her conquest of the realms of the individual mind through a refined technology of self-perfecting education and contemplation, and her "industrial revolution" of producing powerful and beautiful, benevolent, magical energies to create new spaces of the human imagination, within which invisible horizon, the imaginations of all peoples could flourish. This is not an intellectual game. I mean this in great seriousness. Opening a path of insight toward this social possibility can bring us to the concept of something as important, useful, even essential to us as an alternative modernity; a way of becoming modern that is equal and yet opposite to the one Europe chose; a way of modernity that may complement our own.

This means we have much to learn, especially in the line of ethics, psychology, and philosophy included in Inner Science. We can learn much from books, but more from people.

It is not only a moral imperative to stop the human rights abuse in Tibet and to base our policy there on the principle of freedom and self-determination. It is in our own interest and in the interests of the Chinese to see Tibetans free. We should not just enjoy the spiritual gift of the Tibetans (in exile), ignoring their relative political plight. We should see that they regain their freedom, as a planetary priority, more important than any nation's face-saving or short-term interest, even a huge nation such as China. A free Tibet can do even more for the world than the Tibetans free in exile are now already doing.

Tsipon Shuguba has given us a moving account of the beauty of life in free Tibet, and of the horrendous tragedy of the Chinese invasion and occupation. This life is powerful testimony of the nobility of the human spirit, able to suffer the most devastating experiences and still not lose the essential human qualities of kindness, humor, and generosity. Though often unsettling, it is a pleasure and a privilege to travel with him through his heroic world and difficult times.

Robert A. F. Thurman

Tsipon Shuguba, San Francisco, 1991.

CHAPTER I

A Dedication

*We ourselves always considered that the people who speak
Tibetan and eat roasted barley as their staple food are
Tibetans.* — *Born in Tibet*, Chogyam Trungpa, 1966

I have lived eighty-seven years in this "twentieth century" and have
done things which to this day make me feel ashamed, little for which
I might be proud except to say I survived certain hardships and tried
all the while to speak truthfully.

Living now in the hills above Berkeley at my son's house — the
Tibetan Buddhist center he founded and directs — life might be comfortable again. Flowers bloom year-round, there is plenty to eat and
drink, and our young visitors seem to smile perpetually. . . . I am old and
no longer appreciate pleasures as I once was able. Respectfully called
"Father" by everyone, perhaps I have lived long enough.

In the course of my duties as district governor, army captain, and city
manager, I traveled every region of Tibet. I observed miracles, subdued a
local spirit cult, and arrested the ex-regent. I fired on rebellious monks,
and I fathered nine children. Imprisoned by Chinese invaders at the
height of my career — as a finance minister to the Fourteenth Dalai
Lama — I was forced daily to acknowledge death. I witnessed executions,
heard reports of the destruction of monasteries, learned of the loss of
family and friends. And then, informed of the circumstances surrounding
the deaths of my wife and my daughter, I no longer feared for my own
life. I gained a kind of freedom of mind.

It was simple after that, I did what I had to do. I had no plans.

I hope this book will help people to know of one individual's life —
its ups and downs, the truth of it, the facts.

About my wife: I dreamed of her last night. This dream takes place at Gawo, my mother's family residence — the place of luxurious gardens in the province of Duchung, where I was governor in my youth.

In the dream she appears in official dress, wearing her brocades and jewels. We are in a two-storied house in this dream — strangely, she sleeps on the ground floor while I have a bedroom above. Later in the night she visits. She is asking me, laughing, saying she would like to come upstairs to sleep. Yes, I say to her, you can come.

The last time I saw her I stood with other prisoners on a balcony, my wrists bound. We were on display to the crowd gathered at the other side of a fence across a field. (She and I had not been together since weeks before the firing started.) Families gathered to view the prisoners across this distance. I spotted her with her arm raised in what I took to be a gesture of recognition. Perhaps she was shielding her eyes from the sun. I don't know whether she recognized me. My face was sooted from the fires and gunpowder blasts during the shelling of Lhasa that had lasted nearly a week.

Prisoners were lined up in rows, myself with the tallest to the rear. We all wore the same rough cloth having been robbed of our clothing and our belongings upon capture. Chinese guards held positions among us. I noticed a small grey dog moving freely through the field below, attracting no particular attention. I am almost certain I saw my wife among the crowd, but I cannot be certain she saw me. The Chinese had taken my boots, my long turquoise ear ornament denoting rank, my robe, my sash, my Swiss-made wristwatch, my medicines, bone pills, prayer beads, and the black fedora hat I'd brought back from India. I had no idea on that particular day that I would never see her again, or that these objects I have listed, things useless now, would be returned to me at the end of nineteen years imprisonment.

At first, the men who were captured held to the belief that a mistake had been made, that the Chinese takeover could not be sustained.

❊ ❊ ❊

Recently I met with His Holiness the Fourteenth Dalai Lama of Tibet, Tenzin Gyatso, in his suite at the Fairmont Hotel in San Francisco. This was the first time we'd seen each other since his exile from Tibet over thirty years before.

His Holiness the Fourteenth Dalai Lama of Tibet (left) with Tsipon Shuguba, Fairmont Hotel, San Francisco, 1991.

Feeling strong that morning, I'd put aside my cane, but suddenly, at the sight of His Holiness greeting me from the doorway, I found myself too weak to move. I paused in the hall, my arms supported by my son, Lama Kunga Rinpoche, and a new friend here in America, Peggy Day. I had begun to revive in my mind scenes from the days when Lhasa fell under fire.

For nearly an hour I sat knee to knee with His Holiness talking of people we had known. He had many questions regarding those days when I stayed behind while he with his family and top ministers made their escape to safety, disguised as soldiers.

I have often thought of that morning in the earth-pig year — March 18, 1959, on the Western calendar — when a letter delivered by a monk-official informed me, in the Dalai Lama's own handwriting, that the other ministers and myself were to take positions of generals and attempt to negotiate with the Chinese in order to regain Tibet's freedom. I felt uneasy that fourth-rank officials such as myself and my friend L. T. Shakabpa were to be entrusted with such an important task. We were told by the Dalai Lama's personal note (he was then just twenty-three) that if the Chinese refused to negotiate, we must deliberate profoundly amongst ourselves and come to an agreement about whether to fight or to use other methods of resistance.

The Dalai Lama said he would pray for us unceasingly, but he would be unable to communicate further. It was left to us to decide on a peaceful or a wrathful solution.

At midnight on the nineteenth, the Chinese began shelling the Norbulinga Palace with countless guns and cannons. From left to right one saw nothing but the bodies of animals and people. I knew then that Tibet had fallen, that we'd failed and no longer had a choice. Guns mounted on the hill behind the Potala were fired into the enemy camp. Throughout the city, Tibetans gave their lives — soldiers and civilians alike — fighting for six days and nights against the well-armed Chinese. There were massacres on both sides. Since most of the Chinese artillery was directed toward the Norbulinga Palace, some Tibetans managed to escape from Lhasa by swimming through the pond behind the Potala, climbing up the hill back of Sera Monastery, then crossing the mountain — ultimately to leave Tibet for asylum with the Dalai Lama in India.

For days, Mr. Shakabpa and I were trapped inside the enormous crumbling palace. One afternoon, searching for water, we came upon two friends, monk-officials Khenchung Gyantsen and Lobsang Nyendra, in the act of putting relic pills into a cup of water. Usually people do this only when dying. We questioned them, but they roughly pushed us off. Later it was discovered they drank the relic pill water then shot each other.

At dusk we crawled back inside the temple walls to avoid the incessant firing. Lobsang Tashi — the monk prime minister, his nephew and two secretaries, my servant Sonam Tashi, and some others were hiding there as well, huddled together in a storeroom among bins of spilled grain and split sacks of barley flour. We could hardly breathe for all the dust and smoke. No one spoke, so deafening were the sounds of mortar and brick crashing all around.

Finally, we surmised it was too dangerous to remain. The firing had become more intense and insistent. It was clear the remaining walls could be blown away at an instant. A few tried to sneak through holes in the palace walls to the adjacent park. Some got killed. Mr. Shakabpa and I decided to try to reach the Indian mission. We crossed from fence to fence. Crouching and crawling, we passed countless dead with severed limbs and holes blown open in their chests or faces. On the other side of a wall we surprised two Chinese soldiers in the act of relieving themselves. A third and fourth appeared, pressing their guns to our throats. We carried no weapons. There was nothing to do but surrender. From that moment on, the fate of the land I had known and cherished for fifty-five years was no longer to be my concern.

❊ ❊ ❊

This book is dedicated to the Tibet I knew from the day of my birth in 1904 until the final Chinese takeover in 1959. It is dedicated to all Tibetans, to my father and my mother, to my children and grandchildren, and to my wife, who in life and in death has not failed to inspire my admiration and devotion.

Tsering Chodzom, Shuguba's wife, Lhasa, 1956.

CHAPTER II

Celebration

I was born at noon in the sixth month of the wood-snake year. Summer at Shugu estate in Black Horse Village brought clouds in the shapes of animals and birds from which issued heavy drops that stippled the powdery earth.

On the morning of my birth, strong winds carried desert air from the Chathang province. My mother said my head was nicely shaped and my legs long even then. Since I was the first son born, the abbot of Ngor Monastery was summoned to give me a long monastic name, and preparations were made for a celebration. After the ceremony, guests brought gifts into the room and placed them around my cradle. Everyone kissed me and welcomed me. They complimented my mother on my fair skin and sturdy limbs.

Seated on cushions around a long central table they drank *chang* — Tibetan barley ale, ate *tsampa*, or roasted barley flour, and *momo*, which are dumplings full of bits of dried meat. Buttered tea was served while my father described my troublesome entry into the world.

I had been preceded by three tiny and lively girls.

❋ ❋ ❋

I remember my sister carrying me on her back. I must have been two years old. I caught her long braids and held them like reins as she galloped in a wide curve. Faster and faster she ran, whinnying and laughing. I saw the glisten of her teeth as she looked back at me. I held on tighter, screaming with delight, whereupon she chastised me for pulling her hair. . . .

I was the only son for several years; thus it was decided that I could not become a monk but must go into government service. My long monastic name was shortened to Jamyang Khedrup.

One day in the iron-dog year, 1909, when I was five, a monk-physician wearing a yellow hat came to Black Horse Village from Shigatse, saying he had medicine for smallpox. He gave each of the children vaccinations for the price of two coins. Strangely, as a result of this vaccination, nearly all of the children contracted the disease and many died, including sixty from families on the Shugu estate. I and three of my sisters and my young brother became ill, and the blisters on my eldest sister and my brother never went away and both died.

The blisters on myself and my two other sisters, which had covered us from top to bottom of the body, did go away, and gradually we recovered.

Our parents began teaching us. Mother told us to acknowledge that it was a privilege to be able to read and write: Tibet had been without a written language until the great King Srongtsen Gampo in the seventh century sent his minister to India to devise a script and grammar based on Indian models in order that the Buddhist canon might be translated for us. Each day until I was seven my sisters and I sat on mats with our wooden boards, bamboo pens, and pots of brown ink made from charred barley. We practiced the thirty letters, beginning with the *yigk-go*, sun and moon, and ending with a firm downward stroke. Mother said if we practiced consistently, soon we would be reading from the *Kangyur* ourselves. She told us about the Tibetan Buddhist canon, comprised of 108 volumes, which was so meticulously translated from the Sanskrit it later became a primary source when the originals were lost to fires of India's Moslem invaders.

She unwrapped and held before us a family treasure, beautifully lettered in gold on pages made black by rubbing with Chinese ink. When she replaced the book's carved wooden cover, I asked about the figure adorning its surface. Amitabha Buddha, she said, is the spiritual father of Chenrezig, Tibet's worldly guardian who incarnates again and again in the person of His Holiness.

Our schoolroom was established on the east side of the house beneath a large shuttered window. On warm days the shutters were pushed wide and the sun shone onto the floor, making a bright square in the carpet of yak's wool. I enjoyed watching clouds move against the blue, seeing them as demons or the faces of the deities my mother described. She often reprimanded, "Son, you're not listening!" Still I couldn't resist.

I came to realize later when attending a school run by monks that my mother was not very strict.

My father, tall and booted with a sword at his hip, taught us mathematics and memorization. He swept the sword back as he knelt beside me to decipher where I had gone wrong. His laugh was quick and hearty. He wore a mustache — unusual for Tibetans — and his chin was narrow. These things were considered marks of distinction by the populace, which admired him for his stamina and his skill with the rapier. Mother, too, was well formed, with a full face and clear, steady eyes. Some said she was the loveliest woman in town. Her hands were always scented with blossom.

. . . I didn't know what it was at the time, but one day in my duties as gardener in prison I identified the scent. I was raking up the apricot leaves torn from the trees by an early hailstorm when I noticed conspicuous buds on the rose bushes we had planted to harvest for their hips. Pressing my nose to a blossom, I breathed its delicate fragrance. Mother's face suddenly appeared before me, and vast tributaries of memory were opened, making it difficult for days to keep my attention on the duties at hand.

She was five years older than my father, an intelligent woman, well intentioned, and healthy most of her life. She gave birth to five daughters and four sons. I was the fourth child born of nine.

❀ ❀ ❀

Whenever we had time between studies, my sisters and I played with other children of the Shugu estate. My particular favorites were a boy everyone called Jojo, meaning brother, and a small smiling-faced girl we called Kara, "the green apple," who stayed close by, pretending to be my wife. She and I built a hutch in the rushes where we playacted, doing things we believed were done by grownup married people.

My friends and I ran races. We skated in winter on the thickly crusted stream. In summer, we swam where burgeoning creeks formed pools, and we made picnics near short-lived waterfalls.

❀ ❀ ❀

In the water-bull year, when I was nine years old, the Thirteenth Dalai Lama returned to Lhasa from his refuge in India. My father took me along with him to the town of Phari near the border to receive the Dalai Lama. We stayed with our family friend, Gonpo. Another Phari family had arranged for the Dalai Lama to give the Avalokiteshvara empowerment and initiation in their home. Avalokiteshvara, known as Chenrezig to Tibetans, is the Buddha of Compassion. After the initiation, the Dalai Lama granted an interview, allowing Father and I to sit on a tiger-skin rug bordered by bright gold cloth. I was overwhelmed. I had never seen such a thing. I ran my fingers along the thick black stripes. Until I heard my name spoken, I had almost forgotten I was in the presence of His Holiness. I looked up to see him smiling.

I do not remember what words passed between my father and the Dalai Lama that day, but as we departed one of the Dalai Lama's attendants followed and gave me some leftover cooked rice from the Dalai Lama's personal bowl. Food from the Dalai Lama's bowl is considered to be an especially auspicious blessing. I wrapped the rice in a piece of cloth to bring it home to my mother.

On the way back, we stopped for several days at a friend's house, and I was very careful with the rice ball, showing it to everyone but not letting anyone touch it. I knew how pleased my mother would be with such a gift.

The day we said good-bye to our friends, I forgot the rice ball, mistakenly leaving it behind on their shrine. During the long ride back, I did not once think of the rice ball, but as soon as I saw my mother's face I remembered what it would have meant to her, and I felt very sorry.

When I told her how sorry I was, she said: "It's all right because your intention to bring me such a nice thing was good."

❀ ❀ ❀

When I was ten years old, I was sent to the small monastery in Black Horse Village to study under the abbot, with two other classmates: one from Shigatse and one from Black Horse.

We soon recognized that our precious teacher was very short-tempered. However, my two classmates were never punished, while I alone was punished nearly every day for two years. I often wondered about this. His discipline took the form of deprivations, extra duties, and thrashings. Surprisingly, I found myself growing accustomed to these punishments. I

The Thirteenth Dalai Lama of Tibet, c. 1910.

worked harder at my studies and soon found I had advanced quite beyond my classmates in writing, reading, and grammar. I never complained to my mother of these chastisements, though once, seeing my wounds, she gently inquired if I got along well with my teacher. I assured her that I did.

Our teacher had earlier completed the Five Signs of Knowledge. We knew we were fortunate to have him as our tutor. Completing the Five Signs involves disciplined study in the major areas of Tibetan science: Buddhist philosophy, medicine, art, mathematics, and astrology. The monk must pass a rigorous system of oral and written tests in competition with his peers. Only a few monks reach such a high level of scholastic attainment, and to do so they must also be deemed of estimable character.

Four years later, when our teacher was about to resume his duties as abbot, he became ill and died. I was no longer studying with him, but the news of his death saddened me. I heard from the attending monks that at the time of his departure there were miraculous signs like the sounds of *dakini* bells and drums. It does not often happen that the dakinis — female earth-blessing deities — welcome someone to their land. This firmly convinced me that he was indeed a *bodhisattva*, an enlightened being who returns to earth to help others achieve release from suffering.

❁ ❁ ❁

One day in the fire-dragon year, 1916, when I was twelve, our good friend the Tantric Yogi Weatherman came to Black Horse to perform an incense-burning ritual. He had been asked to do this to protect our early crop from hailstorm damage. He was quite respected in his ability to control the weather. Various magical rituals had been passed down in his family for generations. The execution of these ritual activities was paid for by the community. Everyone gathered to observe and participate as he directed.

He had left his horse saddled in the barn, removing the bridle so the horse could graze. A group of us — my brother, some friends, and myself — sneaked out to the barn, bridled the horse, and I rode off alone toward another town. I was terrified the whole time, but exultant. It was a glorious moment — a beautiful horse, cream-white, dappled grey, with a fine white mane. We flew down the path when a dog suddenly rushed out from a wall and began chasing us. The horse became frightened and took off at a wild gallop across a rocky field. I took a fall and hit hard, splitting my chin. I got a huge cut the size of a mouth, which bled profusely.

My mother was notified by some laborers working nearby. Soon she arrived, the servants following breathlessly. She bound my head and rode with me slowly toward home, holding me in her arms. I had plenty of time to consider my misdeed. My mother treated my cut with herbs and salve and continual prayer. It was three months before I healed completely. The wound reopened whenever I tried to chew or talk. I still have a very clear scar.

❈ ❈ ❈

In the fire-snake year, 1917, when I was thirteen, I entered the upper school, which offered training for government staff. My younger brother and I had been attending the private school at the Potala in Lhasa. I enjoyed my time there; my uncle on my father's side lived nearby, and he was always an excitement as well as a help to us. There were more than a hundred students in the Lhasa school, but because of the conscientious attentions of my parents and teachers who had already taught me well, I was always first or second in the class.

A few years before, four nobles' sons from the school had been sent to England to study language, culture, and science. Among them was a monk-official, Kyenrab Kunsang, who studied geology at Cambridge. When he returned, he chose me and another student to assist him in a geological survey of Tibet. My father had objections and at first refused to let me go, but the persuasive arguments of my mother and my uncle finally won him over. My father was not keen on Western influence of any kind, particularly British. My uncle, however, had very different ideas. He convinced my father that this would be of great use in my future government work. I was thrilled. This was to be my first excursion across Tibet without a member of my family to watch over me.

We traveled for days on horseback, arriving at a place called Om Tashi, where we found some red and green-colored rocks in a cliff. We melted them down, and the pure molten copper was as runny as water. At a place called E Lha Gyari underground water had burst out high up on the mountains, causing a muddy flood filled with all kinds of underground creatures, including a *naga* — a high-born creature whose upper

13

part is human and lower part is snake. (I have been told that the mummified body of that naga can still be seen.)

The land was wide open to the sky, inhabited by herds of antelope and a few solitary holy men who lived in caves. Other places along the way we panned for gold in streams and creeks. We found gold, silver, copper, iron, lead, and a few semiprecious stones. At the time, there was virtually no mining in Tibet apart from surface recovery. Gold and silver used in temples and for jewelry was imported from Nepal.

We visited many famous sites on our journey, and we stayed with wealthy families that treated us royally. At Ganden Chokor Monastery I saw an altar skull-cup from the head of a famous robber. So strong that no one could defeat him, he died a natural death. But before he died, he willed that his skull be fashioned into a skull-cup and given to the abbot. That skull-cup was all of one section, white like a conch, about a quarter of an inch thick. In the center of the forehead, an embossed area the size of a U.S. dollar coin shone with a brilliant light.

To the east of Ganden Chokor is a small river created by a yogi who spent his life there. The day I visited with the geologist and my student friend the waterfall was making the sound of the six syllables: *"Om Mani Padme Hum."* We all heard it and marveled at the miracle.

Upwards from Ganden Chokor one comes upon Shang, where the very famous Kyungpo Naljor lived, a *mahasiddha*, and "root lama" of the Kagyupa tradition. There I saw a *chorten* — a shrine that houses relics — which was twelve feet high. Inside were the bone pills of Kyungpo Naljor. Verses from the *Mahakala Sadhana* were carved into the monastery walls. They had a local history, which I read while visiting.

I don't recall all of what I read, but I do remember this: many years ago, behind the Ganden Chokor Monastery was a bigger monastery called She Dawa. When Kyungpo Naljor was alive, the abbot of She Dawa massed many thousands of soldiers to attack him. Seeing the invaders approaching through a gap in the mountain, the disciples of Kyungpo Naljor asked what they should do. He gave them a handful of needles and told them to place the needles in a line on the roof and to fasten each one down by placing a small rock on it. "Then everything will be all right," he said.

The lama's attendant started upstairs with the needles, but urgent questions of visitors delayed him.

"What is happening?"

"Will we be killed?"

He barely managed to reach the roof as the advancing soldiers stormed the monastery gates. He threw the needles at the attackers, and the needles themselves turned into iron soldiers, who killed the attacking monks one by one.

When the abbot saw that his soldiers were overpowered, he said to his servant: "I am going to die today. Between the inhalation and the exhalation of my last breath, you must cut off my head and bury it by the river under the bridge."

When the time came, the attendant could not bring himself to do what he had been told, so the abbot's death proceeded naturally, and he was reborn as a ghost-devil, who stayed around a long time, bothering villagers and causing human and animal deaths.

The villagers were so concerned they visited a famous Sakya lineage holder, Dagchen Rinpoche, and asked him to do a fire ceremony to burn the ghost. There was trouble. The crafty ghost transformed itself into a hoard of mice and attempted to escape.

Dagchen Rinpoche's wife caught them one by one, saying, "Evil is here! Away. Away." She threw all into the fire. Since that time, the ghost caused no more problems.

❊ ❊ ❊

Black Horse Village, where I spent most of my youth, was so named many years ago by the powerful Panchen Lama, Palden Yeshe, while he was making an offering to the black-faced local deity. His prayer to the deity went thusly: "To you, the grand Lord, the very glorious black man who rides on a black horse," and the village was named accordingly.

The Shugu estate of Black Horse Village under the Shigatse District in western Tibet was comprised of three sections: Black Horse, a farm of seven and one-fourth *don*; Akang Village, a farm of four don; and Polhagawo Village, a farm of three don. A don is a measure of land equivalent to two *kang*; each kang is equal to sixty *rukhay*. One rukhay amounts to the quantity of land that can be sown with a single bushel of barley. The two larger farms were beautiful lands of mountains, valleys, grasses, rivers, and trees. Over one-third of the area was used directly by the estate owners, who took the name of the estate as part of their surname. Hence, I became Shuguba, or man of the Shugu estate.

On the remainder of land lived about thirty *miser*, who were taxpayers and stewards of the land, and thirty *tuchung*, peasant farmers, living with their families. The miser had large holdings, and many were able to ensure themselves of a high standard of living. In exchange for land use, they supplied a portion of their harvest as tax, and also supplied laborers to the estate. If they owned as much as one don, they could provide one soldier and supply food, clothing, and money for him. Then they would be free of taxation in terms of seed.

Tuchung each had four rukhay of land that they worked themselves, and they paid for its use by supplying labor to the estate. Miser and tuchung land use, as ours, was obtained through inheritance.

Land division was based not on actual size but on productivity, which was influenced by altitude and other factors. Generally, one don was equal to the amount of land that can be sown with 120 bushels of barley. But in the lower central valley, in the Lhasa region — which was much more fertile — a different system was used.

The Ngor Ewam Choden Monastery was tied to our family and to the land by intimate and complex connections. The monastery was reduced to a pile of rubble by Chinese soldiers during the "Cultural Revolution." Established in the fifteenth century, Ngor housed hundreds of monks in four lama residences, called *labrang*. The Thartse Labrang lineage, to which our family contributed, originated with the Drangtipa lineage holder, who was one of the Nine Original Wise Tibetan Scholars. Succeeding lamas were important scholars and meditators of the Sutra and Tantra traditions. At the time of the great abbot, Jamyang Rinchen Dorje, in the 1800s, the Drangtipa lineage was in danger of dying out. Himself the last of the line, this great abbot was concerned with maintaining an unbroken continuity of lineage, so he suggested to his young nephew, Shabtrung Namkha Sangpo, then vice-abbot, to renounce his monastic vows in order to marry and produce an heir.

Not daring to reject the wishes of his uncle, the young man left his monastic post and moved to the estate called Pegya, which already belonged to the Thartse Labrang, having been awarded to its treasurer during the Nepali-Tibetan War for his excellent management of military transport. The size of this estate, with house, river, and fields, amounted to one don. Having received deed to this property, the young man settled there with his new bride, daughter of a married lama from a small neighboring monastery outside Black Horse Village. After ten daughters, a son was born to them, and Namkha Sangpo sent this son back to his uncle, to carry on the lineage. This young monk later became abbot and was renowned as a superior scholar. He was a former incarnation of my son, Sonam Gyatso, now known as Hiroshi Sonami, who was abbot of Ngor from the age of fifteen.

According to Namkha Sangpo, earlier and even greater than the Nine Original Wise Tibetan Scholars were the Six Scholars of Tibet. Since he had given his only son to the monastery, he wanted to find someone of the other lineage to marry one of his daughters. He sent a special aide to the Lhasa area to search for anyone who could claim an unbroken line from one of the Six Scholars. He found such a man; his name was Chung Nay Sangpo, a distinguished gentleman, elder brother to a prominent government minister whose family descended directly from one of the six stainless lineages. This tall, soft-spoken man was forty-two years old, living at his family's home in Lhasa. Chung Nay Sangpo found the terms of the marriage attractive. A dowry of fine clothing and sturdy horses was sent to him as he traveled the long road to the Pegya estate to meet his fourteen-year-old bride.

The two married and soon produced a daughter, then a son, who later became vice-abbot of the Thartse Labrang. A second son was born and a third. The second son, Rinchen Wangdu, was my father.

My grandfather, the tall, quiet man I have described, assumed the post of treasurer at Thartse Labrang. From time to time he could be seen traveling about the area in the act of readjusting debts. Returning home after a lengthy excursion, he passed through the tiny village of Dedrok late one night when a stray dog jumped at his mule. The frightened mule bolted, and my grandfather fell from its back. His foot caught in the stirrup, and the mule dragged him along, badly injuring his head. Though dying, he managed to return home that night on the back of his horse. The mule was never found. My grandfather died a few weeks later, at the age of fifty-two.

When my father was sixteen, in the water-horse year, he married a beautiful young daughter of the Shugu estate, who had recently arrived to visit her uncle. Lhawang Putri, my mother, was herself of the lineage

Ngor Monastery, 1956, before destruction by Chinese Communists.

Ngor Monastery, 1980. The monastery was destroyed by the Chinese during the "Cultural Revolution."

of a great eighth-century Buddhist translator, Chockro Lhuyi Gyaltsen. She was twenty years old at the time of their union, which brought about the merging of the Shugu and Pegya estates of the Thartse Labrang of Ngor Monastery.

❀ ❀ ❀

My father's heroics fighting against the British were well known. I had often been told how fortunate I was to have been born his son. I had little understanding of politics, little desire to know. I was unaware of others, caring more for the games of challenge and chase. One spring day, I noticed a strange discomfort in myself as I heard my father's voice dismissing my mother from the room. He sat before his children and spoke quietly.

"From the time of the iron-dog and iron-pig years," he said, "the number of Chinese soldiers in Tibet has increased until now more than ten thousand Chinese troops are stationed here."

He told us this was a dangerous moment in history, more serious than the recent British invasion, more disturbing than the Nepali invasion a half-century before.

"China is an immense land mass, crouched low around us to the north and east," he gestured with a sweep of his arm. "Its people are intelligent, indomitable, greedy, and capable of great cruelty."

We had not yet studied geography. We knew only that their language was strange and their uniforms unattractive.

"Recently," Father revealed, "Chinese soldiers in Lhasa threatened the Dalai Lama's life."

Young as we were, we understood how serious this was. (The Thirteenth Dalai Lama had only recently returned from six years of exile in Mongolia.) My father said it was important now for every Tibetan to conduct his person with courage and with wisdom.

He didn't intend to frighten us, he said, but he wanted to make certain we understood things would be different for a while. We were to be constantly on guard, to be conscientious and helpful and do exactly as we were told. I felt a pang of fear.

Then he told us more: "Two weeks ago, the Dalai Lama's advisors successfully escorted him out of Lhasa at night, disguising themselves as a band of merchants. When the Chinese discovered His Holiness was gone, orders were given to pursue him — soldiers were dispatched with the command to bring him back dead or alive. A young man named Dazang Dadul, born to a poor peasant family of arrow-makers, was a favorite of the Dalai Lama because of his energy, resourcefulness, and clever ways. Dazang Dadul — nicknamed 'Clear Eye' — so distinguished himself in service at the Potala school, he had been asked to travel with the Dalai Lama in exile through Mongolia. But when His Holiness took flight this time, Clear Eye remained behind. Anticipating the Chinese response, Clear Eye took command of a small band of soldiers and civilians, and with but thirty-four rifles among them, at great peril to their lives, they held at bay a superior enemy force in excess of two hundred. For two days straight, they kept the Chinese from crossing the bridge, thereby saving the Dalai Lama's life."

My father told us to memorize the details. He said it was important that men like Clear Eye be remembered for their courage and intelligence, not just as a reward for their honorable actions, but to serve us as a guide. As of tomorrow, we would begin taking our lessons from our young uncle, a monk of the Thartse Labrang.

"Now, go outside and play."

My sisters and I gleefully ran off, not knowing that father had already volunteered for soldiering against the Chinese. He left early the next morning without saying good-bye.

❀ ❀ ❀

Two months later a son was born. Now there were seven of us: two small boys, myself, and four girls — my oldest sister and my nearest brother having died of smallpox.

During the Dalai Lama's absence, the Lujun combat division of Chinese foot soldiers continuously occupied Tibet. At first we saw them in Shigatse wandering the streets in groups of three or four. Then my mother refused to take us with her. She did not like to leave the estate and would only go into Black Horse Village in the company of a single trusted servant. She did not know where my father was. The Tibetan government had appointed two men to organize a Secret War Department: one, a secretary monk-official who had been appointed general, and the other, an accounting minister from Lhasa, Mr. Norbu Wangyal Trimon — father of the girl who was later to become my wife.

The southern part of Lhasa was completely occupied by Chinese. On the north side, Tibetan soldiers held the Potala, the Jokhang (Lhasa's main temple), and the Sera and Ganden monasteries. And at Drepung Monastery a few miles outside Lhasa, the biggest monastery in Tibet, one college became traitorous and allied with the Chinese. The Tibetan Parliament was still able to meet each Thursday in the Potala or on the roof of the temple, largely due to the persistent and loyal efforts of Minister Tsarong. (Two years later, Tsarong was charged with treason by dissenting ministers, who had him dragged to his death down a long flight of stone steps.)

The Tibetan government had successfully solicited many soldier volunteers — including my father, a respected veteran at thirty-two, as well as eight other noblemen from our area. They traveled to the Namling District at night, several days ride, and there my father was appointed leader of all volunteer forces. This was a tremendous responsibility. He could not consider declining. Under his leadership, volunteer forces fought the Chinese at Shigatse, Panam, Katong, and Gyantse. They were able to defeat the Chinese at each. News of these battles, and of their casualties, reached us in the form of rumors. We were unable to communicate directly with my father as the success of his activities depended on surprise and secrecy. His soldiers were equipped with swords, slings, axes, and spears. What few rifles, cannons, and pistols Tibet had gained from the British and the Chinese had been put to use by the regular military forces. My father's troops moved quietly and killed swiftly. He wore a turban on his head made of a silk shirt from the Thartse abbot, which protected him from bullets. Soon everyone praised his victories in song:

> *The Lujun soldiers are like herds of sheep;*
> *The man from Shugu is a wolf in their midst.*

Later, my father was asked to protect the Potala park in Lhasa. Alongside my future father-in-law, he fought triumphantly at the Battle of the Turquoise Bridge, where the Chinese were driven out. With the surrender of the Chinese ambassador in 1912, the fighting in Lhasa was finally over, and my father made plans to return home.

CHAPTER III

Householder

I n 1917, the fire-snake year — near the end of my tour with the government geologist — I received word from my father's younger brother, Khenjung, asking for my quick return. With apologies to my teacher, I returned to Lhasa.

Largely due to my uncle's efforts, I was soon awarded a *shabdo* staff position with the government for the ceremony of the Dalai Lama's procession to the Norbulinga, just outside Lhasa. I and a friend, Shalungpa, were appointed guards — each of us stood over six feet tall. Our duty was to help keep order in the crowds during the long procession out to the summer palace of His Holiness.

My uncle had arranged all the necessary transport and servants for that special day. My friend and I, as officials of the Tibetan government, were stationed with the secular authorities. Though youths ourselves, we wore the traditional garb of dignitaries, heavy brocade with elaborate beaded belts, sashes, and jewelry, with the addition of hats that were flat like a pancake and tied under the chin.

We thought these ceremonial costumes laughable, and whenever we caught sight of each other we were overtaken with mirth. Yet this was a serious occasion. My uncle had said it would be an auspicious way to begin my career.

I continued my studies in the government school, where we were primarily taught to write letters and do accounting. My uncle devoted much of his time and money to making arrangements for a significant government post for me. He requested a position for the Duchung District in western Tibet, which then was granted.

The honorable position of governor was given to me in part because my father had fought well in two important campaigns. I received a personal letter from the Thirteenth Dalai Lama announcing my promotion, and in the water-dog year I arrived at Duchung District to assume all the former governor's duties. His huge house and elaborate furnishings were transferred to me, along with all his responsibilities. I was seventeen.

Surrounding the walls of this enormous governor's house were one hundred miser farms of various sizes. In ancient times, the famous scholar Duchungpa introduced a new mathematical and accounting system into Tibet. The top floor of the four-pillar, eight-beam house I was to inhabit contained shrines belonging to that scholar. The flooring was of *aka*, a type of cement stained various colors and polished so thoroughly it takes on a translucent appearance like marble or glass.

On the floor in front of an image of Manjushri — highly regarded in Tibet as slayer of ignorance and arbiter of true knowledge — there were finger marks worn into the cement said to have been made by the scholar's continual manipulation of pebbles, potsherds, and colored pieces of bone with which he performed his computations. Because of his diligence in front of that statue, the image spoke to him, suggesting that he publish his mathematical findings in a book. He then revised eight chapters of the old texts, and his new edition became known as the *Duchung Mathematics*, containing weights and measures, multiplication tables, percentages, and other things. The government published this book, which was used thereafter by Tibetans of all ranks.

Duchung Dzong, the governor's house in which I was to live and work, was located in the middle of a wide plateau built on a rocky hill above the village. The word *dzong* refers both to the district and to the fort itself. Inside the house fresh water flowed from a well. The miser families of the government provided the principal income of the district. Seven bushels of barley were collected from each don in the district. Each year as well, four hundred bushels of barley were put aside — taxed from the five subsections of the district — for the government storehouse, and whatever was left over became my profit. Twice a year, summer and fall, my assistant and I went from village to village to collect the harvested revenues.

I enjoyed my position as governor very much, but because I was so young, I regrettably spent most of my time with my assistant, two secretaries, and the youths of the prominent families of the village doing nothing but drinking chang, gambling, singing, and dancing with the young ladies of the district. I particularly enjoyed playing *mahjong*, in which we betted heavily, and also a game called *sho*, similar to dominoes. I was fond of drinking at any hour. News of these activities reached my family, and less than two years after I had taken the post as governor of Duchung, my family began plotting a remedy.

My uncle in Lhasa was being transferred to another district, far away in eastern Tibet. Before he left, he invited his mother to Lhasa to stay at Yuthok, his recreation house. During her stay she did many religious practices such as prostrations to the Buddha Sakyamuni at the Jokhang Temple, circumambulations of holy buildings, and visits to other temples of His Holiness. She also asked the Dalai Lama's accounting minister, Mr. Norbu Wangyal Trimon, for his elegant eighteen-year-old daughter to be my bride.

PRICE OF THE BREAST

Lhasa is the nation's capital and largest city built at a moderate elevation of 11,000 feet, with a population of around 70,000. I had first come to Lhasa at the age of twelve to stay with my uncle and attend the government school in training for becoming an official staff member. At that time, my uncle and Mr. Khenrab, another official, were sent to the western province to collect taxes of wool and salt. On their way back they stopped at the Shugu estate, and Mr. Khenrab (a relative of my wife's family on her mother's side) asked on their behalf for my eldest sister to be engaged to Minister Trimon's son. He then informed Minister Trimon that this suggestion was agreeable to my family. My sister was sent to Lhasa to marry the tall youth, Shalungpa.

After school each day throughout that year, I stopped at the Trimon place to visit with my sister and her husband. Shalungpa and I quickly became friends, always managing to get into trouble. My sister was good-natured. She ignored our pranks. It was in her house, soon after I'd returned from geological surveying, that I first set eyes on my future wife. I learned that her name was Tsering Chodzom. She was twelve years old, and I was thirteen.

Unknown to me, my wife's mother was already making plans for our future. She began sending the two of us off to do the marketing and other such errands. She was pleased to see that we enjoyed each other's company.

There was at that time no physical intimacy between us. We were each shy and awkward, though sometimes when alone together, Tsering Chodzom would press my arm and stare excitedly into my face. Once in jest I kissed her, but she pulled away. I didn't see her for days.

She possessed a lively mind and was quick in speech. She always had very clear bright eyes readily given to merriment, though she had a serious side as well. She was daily involved in prayers and prostrations. She had taken it upon herself to begin the preliminary practices which involve one hundred thousand full prostrations; one hundred thousand recitations of the Triple Refuge; one hundred thousand recitations of a purification mantra — the Vajrasattva; one hundred thousand symbolic offerings (creation of mandalas), and other practices, including contemplation of the five subjects:

1) the rare privilege of being able to receive Buddhist teachings in a human body in this lifetime;
2) the impermanence of life and everything else;
3) the causes and effects of *karma;*
4) understanding the nature of suffering;
5) the necessity for devotion.

Her family considered these activities exceptional for a girl of her age.

Later, when my grandmother visited the Trimon family to ask for their daughter in marriage to me, her mother did not respond immediately, even though she had had the same thought in mind for years. Instead, she asked the Thirteenth Dalai Lama to do a *mo,* or divination, to determine whether or not the marriage might succeed. The Dalai Lama's divination was auspicious. However, it included a warning that there would be some physical difficulties at first, eventually to be resolved. He said that the union would be fruitful.

On the basis of that judgment, the Trimon family decided to allow Tsering Chodzom to marry me.

In 1923, I arrived in Lhasa for the New Year's Festival, staying on with my grandmother at my uncle's house. My father soon arrived from his Payling estate without my mother, who was busy preparing things at home. My bride's father was then stationed in eastern Tibet, so he and his wife could not be present.

The engagement party was to take place at my bride's family home. This celebration is called a Nyen Chang: *nyen* means "good relationship," and *chang*, of course, is beer.

An appropriate wedding date was set, an agreement reached and written up on paper. A very special chang had to be brewed and offered to all the guests, even beggars who might drop in, as much as they could drink. And if this special brew turned out to be good-tasting, it was considered a favorable omen.

The engagement party involves great expense for the groom's family, which must provide the food, drink, and gifts such as wheat, tsampa, salt, and silk for all the bride's family and friends, including the gift of a sum of money which depends on the bride's esteemed value. This sum is termed the "price of the breast," to be paid directly to the bride's mother — even if she is no longer living — as payment for having fed the young girl.

My wife was not unusually pretty in the face, but she had good character, a striking posture and bearing, and an attractive personality. She was charitable and kind to all. I valued these qualities in her, and I was extremely fond of her family. My wife's father also valued her special qualities of character. She was his favorite he once told me. He considered that she had "dakini" aspects. The dakinis are considered by many to be guardians of secret Buddhist texts as well as the protectors of the earth and all mankind.

A BUCKET OF MILK

The ceremony in Lhasa took place at my uncle's house. Everyone we liked and all our relatives in Lhasa were invited. We wore traditional wedding costumes — an elaborate headdress for the bride with a lot of heavy jewelry provided by her parents. My parents, too, provided items of jewelry specially purchased for the occasion. Songs were sung and dances performed loudly — designed to overshadow the crying of the bride. My wife, however, did not shed a tear.

After the initial ceremony, we stayed on a few days in Lhasa, then we returned to the estate house at Black Horse in order to celebrate there with friends and servants.

Along the way from Lhasa, receptions were held at two other places. Twenty to thirty people journeyed six days in caravan first to Shigatse — Tibet's second largest city — where we spent three days at the Udu house of my relatives. The bride was received with a reception; then we traveled to Payling for another celebration, and finally arrived at Black Horse

Village, where we were given an extensive traditional wedding reception, the events of which were held in tents in a large field.

Since we had been officially married in Lhasa, the ceremony was cut down a bit. Still, all our relatives from miles away were invited, all our friends and their servants, as well as a few of the villagers. We celebrated at my family's estate house for a month at the beginning of spring.

A traditional aspect of the ceremony was performed in the main house, in the big hallway. My mother, dressed luxuriously, stood on the stairs with a bucket of fresh milk in her hand. Inside the bucket, she had placed ornaments of gold and silver and numerous precious stones. My wife and I ascended the stairs to meet my mother at the top. My mother handed the wooden bucket, full of milk and jewels, to my bride, placing it in her left hand. Covering the bride's hand with her own, my mother then pulled up the bucket, supporting the hand of the bride all the while. This activity is symbolic of prosperity and the wealth of many healthy children to come. It is auspicious, bringing both the wealth of children and ordinary wealth, for the new bride and groom.

After the event, the bucket of milk and jewels is placed in a special storage area where the material wealth of the bride and groom will hopefully someday accumulate.

When this event was over, we proceeded to the large hall. My father and mother were to sit on one side opposite myself and my new wife. Then began the wine ceremony in which specially-dressed young ladies bring wine to everyone. A group of young men do a dance while singing, similar to what is called "tap dancing" in the West. After the dancing, we offer tea, food, rice, and *droma*, which is something like small sweet yams cooked in butter.

During the month-long celebration at Black Horse Village, every group of relatives that came to celebrate had to provide one day's food and entertainment. Each tried to outdo the other, which is why, if you have a lot of relatives as we did, these festivities continue for a very long time. While the celebrations are in progress, no one need attend to their normal duties.

During our month-long celebration, the very famous Tibetan drama teacher Kyormolung Gegen Migmar Gyaltsen, a friend of my father's, arrived with his daughter and a troupe of thirty to perform. Tibetan drama was very popular, provided by lay troupes such as this, whose historical dramas were sung and spoken in turns by the versatile members, who also accompanied themselves on cymbals, drums, and stringed instruments.

Our wedding tradition requires that the first night the young couple spend together they find, drawn in wheat or rice on top of their bed, a huge swastika, covered by thick white velvet cloth. The bride and groom are supposed to sleep on top of that swastika for the night. This symbol confirms the continuity and stability of the marriage. It is the forward-flowing swastika similar to the beneficence symbol in use by America's native peoples.

After the month-long celebration was over, my wife and I returned to the Duchung District, where I had been governor for the last two years. There, a celebration was enacted by the villagers, who received my wife warmly. The secretaries and prominent families of the district also entertained us in their homes. We lived happily in Duchung for two more years.

My wife and I stayed most of the time in the eastern part of the district, living in a large house that once belonged to my mother's family called Gawo Nangpa situated in a pocket of mountain greenery — a fertile place of grasses, flowers, and abundant trees. Every morning at dawn the mists came down from the mountains shrouding the house. Deer, musk, foxes, and many kinds of birds frequented the surrounding woods. Inside the house were large shrines in offering to various deities, and its library held the *Kangyur* — the official collection of all the teachings of the historical Buddha, Sakyamuni.

In the summer, we stayed at Gawo, where we spent time by the river, swimming and picnicing, rambling through the resplendent park. For important government work, I always returned to the dzong. In winter, we lived at the dzong — the district governor's house. My private life at Duchung and Gawo was extremely pleasant. Every day alive was mainly an enjoyment. Shelter and everything were taken care of; we didn't have a worry. Food was provided by staff members — three delicious meals a day.

Gawo was famous as the home of a well-loved minister of the Seventh Dalai Lama's time. His stone castle was nearby, which we often visited.

My wife and I were inexperienced when we married. And though I had spent the last two years drinking and trifling with the ladies of my district, no one had managed to reveal much of the truth about herself. When we married and began spending our days and nights together, we discovered for ourselves the ways to give happiness to each other. There was affectionate tenderness between us. For many years, we were eager to please each other and entirely satisfied with our life together. I have heard it said that though a man notices a diminution of sexual interest in a woman after five years, a woman may feel the ongoing attraction for one man throughout her life. I don't know if that is so.

My wife's kind and conscientious character made her cooperative and solicitous as a wife. She made certain my favorite foods were prepared, and she attended me cheerfully. She was considerate and gentle. I fear in those early years I took advantage of that quality in her, being sometimes short-tempered and harsh when she did not deserve it. Years later I began to understand how much more a woman suffers than does a man — the pain women silently bear from their monthlies and in childbearing, and how much they grieve at the loss of children and loved ones.

Recently, I learned that my wife was asked for by another. My cousin — the venerable Jetsun Kushola, a recognized tulku and highly-revered married lama who now lives in Seattle, told me her own grandparents had asked for my wife to marry one of their sons. They were too late. My wife's family had already given permission for her to marry me.

My wife and I got along well in those early years when I was governor. We rarely quarreled. She was not involved in my work directly, but she was sympathetic and helpful to my assistants and secretaries, and to the villagers when they came to us with their problems and complaints. There was always at that time a closeness and sincere affection between my wife and myself. She was of estimable character, she was loyal and respectful to me, and not intent on forcefully changing my ways.

Many joyous years were to pass before my wife began to live with my young brother as wife and bore him a child. I could not harbor any resentment. She had already given eight children to me. Also, there is a practice in Tibet of polyandry: a woman may marry with her husband's brothers if she wishes, and if the family deems it wise. I know that my wife had long been fond of my brother, Sonam Wangyal, and that she loved him well though he was twelve years her junior and had had several girlfriends but no other wife.

During those years, when my wife and my brother together managed the family estate at Black Horse Village, I was away, serving as city manager in Lhasa. Often, I spent days and nights at the house of my mistress and had been doing so for a while. When the time comes, I shall speak more of this.

CHAPTER IV

Mistakes

Let me now return to the water-pig year, 1923. I was nearing the age of twenty. My wife stayed on alone at Gawo while I traveled to Lhasa at the government's request to participate with other young staff members in horse racing, shooting, and archery contests as part of our New Year's festivities.

After the appearance of the state oracle in trance — when New Year's predictions are given — the athletes are directed to gather on the Barkhor field for wrestling, weight lifting, footraces, and riderless horse racing. Finally, come the shooting contests in which I participated.

These shooting contests are a popularly attended event held outside Lhasa on a vast plain set with tents and booths for spectators. Wearing armor, we mounted our favorite horses and one at a time galloped past the hanging target to shoot into the bull's-eye with our matchlock guns. The guns were then exchanged for bows and arrows, and another target was approached. Finally, a third target was aimed at with a spear. All of this was accomplished while riding on horseback at breakneck speed.

I stayed in Lhasa at the house of my wife's older sister and her husband. They took good care of me. For four months prior to the events, my friends and I — along with many other young men — practiced riding and target shooting with our guns, arrows, and spears. We also practiced long-distance archery from a standing position. On the first day of the fifth month of practice our skills were tested in the area south of the Norbulinga Palace. The Thirteenth Dalai Lama came to watch, along with his Cabinet, Parliament, and all the high-ranking officials of the government, who acted as judges. There was a preliminary rehearsal-exhibition; then two days later the performance took place before the public as part of the lengthy New Year's celebration.

Though I was out of practice, having neglected this training during my governorship, I hit the targets, placing twenty-sixth out of a field of sixty contestants. On my return to my district, my secretaries and assistants gave me a congratulatory reception. Every afternoon and evening during that spring and summer we enjoyed parties involving games of archery.

TWENTY-FIVE LASHES

Soon after harvest, a man named Pemba traveled with his partner from Sikkim to Duchung to purchase grain from us. A shepherd reported that those men had shot his dog. I ordered the villagers not to let the Sikkimese go until the matter was settled. But by the next morning the two men had escaped.

Not knowing what to do, I ordered that twenty-five villagers be whipped — twenty-five lashes each. After this was accomplished, the villagers were very upset, and they reported it to the customs official of Gyantse, who was then popular with the people. Since he was also a close friend of the Dalai Lama the villagers thought he would report the incident to the government, and the Dalai Lama would in turn reprimand me. But the customs official replied that he couldn't do anything, and he advised them to go straight to Lhasa to report it themselves.

As soon as I heard what they were planning to do, I wrote a report directly to the Dalai Lama in Lhasa explaining the incident as best I could, saying that if the villagers came to report it to Parliament, I would personally appear to state the facts of the case.

I don't know why, but the villagers hesitated in reporting to Lhasa. The twenty-five who had been whipped ran away. I believe they were afraid to come back for fear of further punishment. Gradually, however, they did return, and I gathered them together to apologize, saying that I had been unable to make a clear decision about the Sikkimese; that I should have seized the culprits myself immediately instead of delaying; and that it was the Sikkimese and not the villagers who had deserved reprimand.

The misunderstanding was finally overcome, and I was able to control the unrest in the village. It seemed to me for a time that no one bore a grudge.

FIRST BIRTH

At the end of my four-year term as governor, a lower-ranking official came to take over. We were soon good friends, and I invited him, along with his friends and assistants, for a month-long celebration at Gawo.

At the official close of my term, my wife and I returned to my wife's parents' house in Lhasa. Her father, Minister Trimon, had also just finished his term in eastern Tibet. All the governors are replaced about the same time — this is a process known as *tsidru*. We arrived in Lhasa a little ahead of her father, but soon he appeared with his sons, and we had a wonderful reunion. That same year, my wife gave birth to our first child, a boy. I was twenty-three, and she was twenty-two.

For three and a half years we had been having difficulty conceiving a child. No one knew why. My mother told us that there is a special place to visit called Pomo, a nunnery not too far away, and people go there if they are expecting a baby or would like to have a baby. There is a banner inside the temple at Pomo, and on this banner people stick pins, needles, and finger rings. It is a tradition at Pomo that after you have prayed you shake the banner a bit — both prospective parents must do this — and what falls on the ground indicates whether or not a child will be born, and what sex the child will be. We shook the banner, and one large needle dropped.

My mother told me later it was a good sign and that a big baby boy would be born sometime soon. If a ring falls, she told us, that means a baby girl will be conceived.

After visiting the nunnery, we did conceive a son. My wife had a dream about a nice large round cloud in the sky, and inside that cloud there was a big baby boy who came down from the sky, then entered into her. This dream occurred while we were living at Duchung around the time he was conceived. He was born in Lhasa.

My wife often had very clear dreams that interpreted the future or prophesied things to come. One time she had a dream about her husband — that her husband was sleeping with another woman. She had that dream.

She never tried to increase her enthusiasm for dreaming or to

33

attempt to improve her dreams, but occasionally, unexpectedly, a dream would come to her. Whenever she had a dream and told it to me, I wrote it on my calendar. We had a history of her dreams recorded there.

The day my first child was born, in the fire-tiger year, it was springtime and the birth proceeded comfortably. The midwife was my wife's sister, and the birth occurred in the inner room of my wife's apartment at her parents' house. My wife was not well, however, and so we stayed on in Lhasa for a month before returning to Shugu estate with our son, Sonam Paljor. Our nurse was good with him. My wife fed him from the breast for a while, but soon we stopped that and began feeding him boiled cow's milk in order to protect my wife's health. We returned to Gawo and lived there for more than a year.

LU DING ESTATE

In the fire-hare year, 1927, I was promoted to sixth rank as governor of Hray District. The former governor had let the district to someone else for a year, and when the time came to change governors, I met with that man and sorted out all the records of assets and debts and he handed everything over into my charge.

Hray was close to our hometown so we could go back and forth. My second son was born at Payling, one of my family's homes. The second son was born approximately two years after the first in the earth-dragon year.

The district of Hray was divided into two sections. An earlier Dalai Lama had commissioned the upper part to a monastery. Its dzong, located on top of a high hill, had a complete library with many precious works, as well as images and shrines of great antiquity. Both the upper and lower houses were well kept. I stayed mostly in the lower part of the district, spending my time, except for the autumn month of tax collecting, near the dzong at my Lu Ding estate house.

Lu Ding was beautiful in summertime, with wide green meadows whose herds produced plentiful meat and excellent dairy products for us to eat. My secretary there was married to the daughter of a relative of my grandmother. His family was very kind to us, and we visited often with them.

Every day, two butler-housekeepers came to meetings at my office.

Trak-Yerba, hermitage near Lhasa, c. 1945.

The heads of the village also came to meet with me about taxation and other important matters. Annually we held a large meeting on financial matters at which the taxes for the whole area were inventoried and the books balanced. The local miser provided food and paid for the expenses of the village leaders attending this meeting.

The Hray District provided more than one hundred monks for the Norbu Chokorling Monastery located on the other side of the mountain. This monastery each year invited the district governor and his people to their own elaborate New Year's Festival. Behind my Lu Ding estate, on the other side of the hill, was the Turquoise Cave, so named because Padmasambhava, the founder of Buddhism in Tibet, was reputed to have found enormous chunks of turquoise there. I visited that site many times. The first time I visited, I discovered a yogi from the Dotra Chusang Monastery meditating there. Though at first he appeared to be deep in meditation, he greeted me kindly and took the time to teach me a long song of the famous sage Milarepa. Though it is said Milarepa harmed many people early in life, through sincere remorse and dedication as well as the hardships he suffered, he later became one of Tibet's greatest saints. The song begins:

Wandering the plain of the six states of being,
Taking up illusory bodies of birth, death, and bardo,
Passing through cities of bardo and dream,
I have traveled the narrow road between existence and rebirth.

I have lived over and over in hell regions,
Been tormented by neurotic hunger and thirst,
Experienced the miserable stupidity of animals,
And merely tasted the lives of gods and men.

Now, by chance, I have obtained human life.
In youth I employed evil powers and came to regret it enormously.
I then went to Marpa, best of men, and guided by that great saint
My human existence was made meaningful.

The monk's song made an impression on me. I returned to the cave the next day to visit him, but he was gone. I did not encounter another living person in the cave on any subsequent visit.

Generally, each of the governor's assistants was assigned to a different area to collect taxes during summer. Mainly we asked for various types of wool and butter. Each village we visited received us with generous provisions of food and shelter, and my private servants were also given gifts of wool, butter, and cheese from the villagers.

On a mountain in the upper valley of the Hray District stands a monastery, a tantric college, said to have been established by the venerable sage Sherab Senge. A holy stream called "Goddess of Logyonma" originates there in a very small cave, and it flows right through the monastery, providing hundreds of monks with fresh water for their daily tea as well as for their horses and other animals to drink. This stream never runs dry. Each year the tantric college uses this water to produce pills of great medicinal value called "pills from the Tantric College of Hray." Sometimes the water overflows, which is considered to be a bad omen.

The monks there were known to be initiates of advanced practices transmitted orally from ancient times, teacher to disciple. The villagers were in awe of them. While I was governor of Hray District, the water overflowed once, flooding the courtyard of the college. At the time the flooding was reported, I thought nothing of it, but later, when dismissed in disgrace, I remembered it and understood that it may have had special significance for me.

The venerable Sherab Senge was attended by a devoted benefactor named Dongkar Hrakba, who dearly loved to drink chang. Let me tell you the story. Once Lama Sherab Senge said to his benefactor, "Whatever you want I will give to you," and the man replied that he wished nothing more than to drink chang all the time. The lama told him to take a jar of fermented barley, close the top tightly, put a spigot on the bottom, and simply open the spigot whenever he wanted a drink. The lama made him promise never to open the top.

As long as that devoted man lived, and for two generations after, there was always enough chang for all who wished to drink. Finally, the bride of a newcomer wondered about this inexhaustible jar into which one need never pour water, so she pried open the top and seeing nothing inside but writhing white worms, she screamed out of fear.

From then on, no chang flowed from the jar. But the family kept it as a relic, and even today because of its power nothing ever goes wrong when people in that family make chang. Their chang is the most delicious in the area.

Many sights and attractions exist in the Hray District. The high mountains nearby contain therapeutic hot springs; Vulture Hot Spring, for example, specializes in the healing of broken bones. Visitors come each autumn to take the cure. There is also a rocky peak pitted with deep tunnels said to have been made by crystals and diamonds, which are believed to travel through rocks in the same way that worms bore their way through apples.

A ruined monastery called Tagar lies to the east, abandoned hundreds of years ago. If one looks through the cracks in nearby rocks, one sees all kinds of visions. And if one blows through the hole in a certain square stone, a loud sound is heard, similar to a conch shell but much louder. It can be heard throughout the valley. There are many large silver stones in that mountain which have never been mined.

SHAME

When I was governor of Hray, I did not pressure the villagers nor make any disturbance. Our third child was on its way. Our friends and family visited often. My brother, Sonam Wangyal, still a very young monk, was studying to be a doctor nearby at Tashilhunpo Monastery in Shigatse. We enjoyed his visits. He was kind and devoted to both of us. My wife and I were happy, and there were no more health problems.

One miser had a field of one kang which he was too lazy to irrigate and farm. Thus the tax due from that field was uncollectable, and it had to be borne by the other miser families as an extra burden. I was not clear about what to do. One day I ordered one of the wealthier families, the Rangpang Pesurva family, to take care of this one kang field for me, in order that the other villagers did not have to pay the extra tax on it. Not only did this family refuse to obey me, but they persuaded several others that I was harsh and unfair. These disgruntled people reported the matter to Lhasa.

One day a high-ranking accountant named Trogawa arrived from Lhasa to investigate the complaint. Although this official supported my case, my opponents in the Rangpang Pesurva family had secretly sought backing from another high-ranking accounting minister. The case was finally decided against me, using circumstantial evidence of my incompetence and cruelty. I lost my post and was forbidden to work for the government again.

I transferred the governorship of the lower dzong to my replacement — a man named Gyimepa who was sympathetic toward me, which only made matters worse. I gave the upper dzong back to the monastery.

It was a sorrowful day for my wife and family when I left the Hray District in disgrace, returning to my family home on the Shugu estate.

Tibetan plain, near hermitage at Shalu, c. 1930.

CHAPTER V

Border Exile

The red-black hairs of my horse's mane stiffen with the cold. Over-looking the valley at Phari, I descend a rocky path, recalling the time I visited years ago with my father to receive the Thirteenth Dalai Lama. We had traveled for weeks in caravan. I was allowed the honor of sitting before His Holiness on the tiger-skin rug. . . .

The town is clouded with smoke from domestic fires. I am without servants, without friends.

Hope deceives, they say, but fear paralyzes.

I pray to my divine protector Manjushri to give me strength to accomplish the tasks I have been assigned as a low-ranking customs offi-cial in a border town — the region of rough nomadic peoples.

It is the iron-sheep year, 1930.

This journey was not accompanied by many pleasures. I left my wife and my family the morning after receiving official notice of my appoint-ment here. Any delay would only make matters worse and perhaps weaken my resolve. We are to be separated for an uncertain time. . . . Fol-lowing the line of the trail down into the village I see the vendors closing their stalls. Smoke pours out from the lowest houses, which have been in shadow for hours. A steeple of rock protects the town on the northeast from ravaging winds so forceful that a man may be separated from his horse, so bleak that the snow turns instantly to vapor, collecting only in protected valleys such as this. . . .

There are few springs, fewer bunches of grass. Husbandry consists of tending nearly-wild sheep that range over vast distances. These herds are followed by nomads with their tents and a few pack animals. Chomolhari, and her sisters, glisten in the distance. . . .

Traveling through this region years ago with my father, these hazards seemed an adventure, everything new to my eyes. It was spring. I noticed the tiny white flowers crushed by our horses' hooves. . . .

I dismount to prostrate to my deity. My boots sound hollow on the polished earth. Palms together touching the top of my head, my forehead, and the region of my heart, I lie face down on the bleached dirt feeling a desuetude of sorrow. . . .

I settle into my rooms at the customs house. The house is maintained by the district governor, who I soon discover was a friend and admirer of my father's.

For ten sheep-loads of salt I am to collect three *sho* (coins); for one sheepskin, five *gar*; for one goat skin, two and a half gar. I keep detailed records and send the fees I collect from the nomadic traders, enclosed with the "tea and salt" office seal, to the central government the first month of every year. For ten loads of baking soda I collect two and a half gar, and for five mule-loads of limestone, three sho. Smaller fees are collected for other items brought in from outside, across the pass.

I am to be well acquainted with these nomads during the course of my duties. Their swarthy complexions are kept shining by daily rubbing with lavish amounts of sheep fat. Their faces are broad, the teeth stained or broken, the eyes sunk deep into pockets of flesh. They are a strong people. They can go days without water and seem to need very little to eat, though when I am invited to join a family for a meal I am amazed at how quickly they consume large portions of jerkied lamb or enormous bowls of the steaming blood of fresh kill. The women are stern with me at first, but soon I discover I can make them laugh by moving my eyes a certain way.

Phari is the only town they know. They travel vast distances to arrive in time for the market. They never complain of their lot but seem instead to thrive on hardship. Though they treat me kindly and respectfully, as do other families of the village, I am isolated by my own sense of remorse. . . .

MIRACLES

One summer while traveling to outlying regions in the course of my duties, I paused for a few days at hot springs in Shay Village, which was formerly used by the great Panchen Lama, Thubten Chokyi Nyima. At this time the Thubten Monastery in Shay Village was home to Lama Gyabun, a reincarnation of Yamantaka, who had horns on his head.

I was curious to meet this lama. I had heard of him from my wife. She went frequently to the nunnery as a girl to engage in fasting and for retreats. She had received teachings from powerful lamas. When we were first married and living at Gawo, she encouraged the villagers in their religious practices, and she was patient in instructing them. Later in life, the path of advanced Vajrayana was opened to her, and she was initiated into the practice of Yamantaka, a great Tantric discipline.

I went to see this famous lama and received the "long-life empowerment" from him. But since he wore a hat the whole time I couldn't determine if he, too, had horns as I had been told. I asked him to remove his hat so I could see. When he did I saw that the ridges of his temporal bones, what we call "shape of elephant trunk," protruded as far as the width of a thick pencil.

This respected lama had made an extensive retreat during which he recited one million mantras with which he empowered certain black and white pills. He gave me two envelopes full, saying that the black ones are good for general infection and the white ones for *rahula* sickness, or stroke.

Years later, when traveling to the Chamdo region, my friend's servant happened to fall ill from a stroke so I gave him one of the white pills. It took effect; he recovered and was well enough to go home with us. This gave me confidence in the pills, and I always carried a few with me, except during the long years of imprisonment. I have since located my original package (which had been kept at my niece's house with some photographs, papers, and books), and I have them with me now. The effectiveness of such pills is due to the empowerment of the lama's mantras, his meditative concentration, and the blowing of his breath onto them.

One day, traveling from the village of Shay, where I had some business to attend to, I decided to go home to Black Horse Valley. I left a representative to act in my place at the town of Rinchentse to the north, where I had lately set up my post. I traveled south, alone, and stopped for a while at the Buru Hot Spring, which was once the special hot spring of the Panchen Lama. In this spacious valley the wind never blows, and the sweet-smelling grasses are soft as down.

I stared into the pool with its heated currents. A mist about as thick as a hand floated above the pool, covering its surface nearly to the edges.

I thought of my mother and the way she patiently taught me

43

techniques to keep my thoughts from wandering. I knew my mind was restless as a colt — its sudden lurching starts were to blame, in part, for my current predicament. I'd better learn to rein it in — something I knew well how to achieve with my horses.

The healing breaths of these waters allowed room for a spring of hope to arise in me. I saw that wherever I lived and whatever my duties, I must accept them gracefully. Dozing for a moment with my head pillowed by a tuft of the *chungshi* herb, I felt restored. The medicinal value of that herb is one reason people come to the spring.

I drank a bit of the water and later bathed myself. Soon I felt the benefit to my chronic stomach ailment.

A while later I traveled up the valley to the cave in which King Gesar is said to have meditated the last years of his life. There is a small round pool, which is fed by a cool underground spring; it never dries up, never freezes, and the surrounding grass is always new.

When I returned to my home village, having been away for over a year, there was no one to greet me, no fanfare, no admiring glances from the ladies I had known. I was a lowly customs official. My family home appeared deserted but for the servants and my old friend the Tantric Yogi Weatherman, whose horse I once had stolen. He seemed elated at my unexpected arrival and told me that my mother and my brothers had gone to visit my wife in Lhasa. Father, though retired, had been sent to investigate a scandal in the eastern provinces. My uncle was in Lhasa as well.

The Tantric Yogi Weatherman, whose name was Ngachang Tashi, had stayed on to keep the weather, there having been little rain that spring and the young barley shoots might easily be damaged by hailstones.

I assisted him with his rituals. Then I persuaded him to return with me to the wonderful hot spring at Buru, several days' ride. I did not have the inclination to show my face in Lhasa, thinking it best not to advertise my wanderings. Ngachang Tashi went with me to visit the cave in which Lotsawa used to meditate. On the way we encountered a terrific hailstorm, but my friend's activities seemed successful in redirecting the lumpy violet clouds.

My friend returned to Black Horse Village, and I traveled on alone to the lower valley of Shayzik on the way back to my post. In ancient times the Mahasiddha Guru Londsay lived there, appearing to all as an ordinary hunter. Let me tell you the story of how the famous translator

Trubu Lotsawa came to the area one day to investigate what kind of person Guru Londsay was, having heard great tales of this simple hunter's extraordinary powers. On arriving, he inquired of Guru Londsay's wife where the master had gone. She replied that he was off hunting but would soon return. Presently, Guru Londsay was seen just as she predicted, carrying his bow and arrow, leading his two female dogs. Slung across his shoulders was the carcass of a deer.

The translator, Trubu Lotsawa, thought that Guru Londsay would bow and pay respects to a man of his own high reputation. But when the meeting actually took place, the scholarly man could not bear the power emanating from Guru Londsay, so he came down from the throne where he had seated himself, motioned Guru Londsay to sit upon it instead, and settled himself on the floor with the guru's dogs. He asked the guru to explain the source of his power and confidence. In reply, Guru Londsay sliced open his own chest with a knife and revealed a mandala of Chakrasamvara.

Seeing this mandala, Trubu Lotsawa immediately begged for teachings. But the guru only smiled, saying, "No, my friend, you have come to me with the wrong attitude, intending to investigate my authenticity rather than to learn from me. However, I see that in the future you will contract a serious disease. At that time, come to me and I will help." As soon as he finished speaking, Guru Londsay spied a deer out the window. He leaped up from his throne and hurried off after it.

Sometime later as the story goes Trubu Lotsawa became ill with leprosy, and the treatments he tried were of no avail. Finally, remembering the promise of Guru Londsay, Trubu Lotsawa went back to visit him in the lower valley of Shayzik. He explained his predicament. The Mahasiddha Guru then stuck one of his hunting arrows into the ground, and water surged forth.

"Why don't you take a bath here," he said to the suffering man. When he did, he was relieved of the leprosy. Thus the pool was named "Leprosy Pond," and even today if one takes the time to bathe in that pond conditions of leprosy and other skin ailments can be alleviated. The local people carry home water from the pool in jars.

In the monastery of Guru Londsay at the lower edge of Black Horse Valley one can see a statue of the guru with his bow and arrow. Beside the statue are the stuffed bodies of his two female dogs.

. . . I now follow the river upland. Far off to my right are the Nyenchen Tangula, the "spirit of the expanse of great fear" mountains, defining the extreme edge of Chathang province, which opens as a high dry steppe broad as all of India. How large is the country of Tibet? I can't say in terms of meters or miles. My father said with pride after the departure of the British Younghusband Expedition, "Tibet is ten times the size of Great Britain!" Some say a man can cross Tibet in a day flying in an airplane at the height of Mt. Everest. I have been told that the goddess mountain, we call Chomolungma, now houses a secret Chinese military installation with underground tunnels for the storage of weapons.

. . . It often took us weeks to travel from Black Horse Village to Lhasa, stopping as we liked to do to visit friends and family along the way. A caravan of yak or mule or men riding horseback may travel for eight to twelve months the long distance from Lhasa to Beijing. Not many horses exist in Tibet these days. The Chinese carved roads from our paths. Dust clouds roll out for miles across the Kyichu plain whenever a convoy of trucks arrives or departs from our capital city. The streets of Lhasa, in which pigs and lambs once foraged, are now coated with tar. I saw these things myself before leaving Tibet forever, traveling a Chinese-made road in a Chinese jeep driven by a Chinese soldier.

. . . I sit quietly now while my horse drinks from a stream that flows from a spur of rock in the foothills of the "spirit of the expanse of great fear."

Traveling home to Black Horse Valley after nearly a year in border exile had taken me several weeks. But this return trip seems to pass more quickly, perhaps because I do not look forward to arriving. In fact, I require a renewal of determination to return at all. Summer has ended. The sun early quits the sky. Nights are cold. I camp sheltered by giant boulders, or beneath trees bearing dwarfed walnuts. The established campsites are best, because of their stone fire pits and the chance of finding dried dung from earlier caravans. Removing my provisions from their leather sacks, I rehearse a speech I must give on return to a trader, or recheck my calculations of fees. In that way my mind is kept occupied.

Always I pray that the man I left in my stead proves as faithful and canny as he seemed. I invent a test to ensure his honesty, devising to complain that taxes collected from a certain sector have not yet arrived in Lhasa. If he apologizes, I'll know he is negligent. But if he says in fact that the tax is not yet due, I'll reward him for his conscientiousness.

Some nights I am invaded by memories. Rather than fight these fantasia I give in, systematically attempting to recall the details of an afternoon, or an evening at Gawo . . . my wife knitting a sweater, laughing in the firelight. I am telling her of a recent vexation — the foolishness of one of my assistants becomes an amusement for us. Tomorrow . . . we've invited the district manager, a few friends, for dominoes and dice. An archery contest. My butler is as skilled as I. We enjoy a heated competition. I observe him coming under the influence of intoxication. He is losing, and as punishment must drink more chang. . . .

I sometimes neglect to erect my small tent and sleep instead in the open, wrapped in blankets and rugs. My mind is not given to speculation on the nature of the dome above our heads or what lies beyond. But one moonless night, looking up, I am astonished to see a meteor of such size and brilliance I cannot help wondering what it portends. . . .

I have two horses with me — my steadfast blue and a cream-beige, which was once a trademark of my family. This allows me to ride steadily, giving each horse, though not myself, some rest. The incessance of this activity, the seemingly endless expanse of light-bleached rock and dusty earth, drive from my mind the insistent longing to see my wife, which if I had given into it would have caused me to turn around and head in the wrong direction.

My horse and I seem nearly alone in these distances. One evening I see an enormous herd of wild yak. By day I glimpse a few gazelles keeping pace alongside me.

The strength of my horse erodes my sense of isolation.

The nomadic peoples of the region, whom I've encountered twice on this journey, live by selling meat, butter, cheese, and wool. Yak provide them with all these things, and with their food, shelter, clothing, and other materials as well. Yak dung is their fuel; ashes are spread on yak hair bunting to keep infants dry. Elaborate tents woven of yak's wool are carried wherever they go. Sometimes I am certain I see one pitched off in the distance . . . but then it is only an outcropping of rock.

Tibet has no great excess of population, which is perhaps why so many deities have chosen to live there. Some say it this way: The gods have come from the center of heaven to this heart of earth fenced round by snows.

The centers of population are grouped around two converging rivers

A view of Shekar Monastery, Chumbi Valley, c. 1930.

— the Tsangpo and the Kyichu — each in its separate valley. To the north, the immense dry spaces are home to horrific deities and to the spirits of the unquiet dead. Foreign men looking for minerals enter that region. Nomads return from there loaded with salt, soda, and borax, which are traded in towns like Phari for butter and meat, or sold to the Nepalese. Most Tibetans do not choose to go there, knowing that the winds and cold are so strong there can be no protection, no escape. Wild herds feed on the scanty grass, lichen, and such, or on each other as do the fox and the bear. There are no fences in Tibet. All herd animals are carefully tended by their keepers — farmers or nomads — who depend on the safekeeping of each creature for their livelihood.

In Lhasa, where I spent much of my life, amenities are common. Warmth, the beauty and luxuriance of well-decorated women, the splendor of the Potala and other sacred places. Lhasa is the city of God. To the east are ragged ranges and enormous rivers such as the Drichu, the "river of yak cows," also called the Yangtse. Far off is the Kham region of broken peaks and scarred valleys. Still farther lies Amdo from whence arise the largest of our men, drafted to be warriors or bodyguards for His Holiness. Beyond Amdo is China.

I passed through the Nagri region on my return to the village of Phari in the Chumbi Valley. I passed "the mountain of the legend of three ages" and stopped again at Thubten Monastery in Shay Village. I was surprised to find the famous horned lama was away. His monk-attendants were gracious, however, and offered use of the lama's personal library wherin I encountered a narrative of the life of the Sixth Dalai Lama of Tibet, which told of his trials and misfortunes. I was unable to depart until I'd read the tale entirely. I've always found stories about the Sixth Dalai Lama intriguing. He was said to have been unsuited for his office, said to have loved many women, as well as having a fondness for gambling and drink. Some say that bliss is a sign desire has temporarily dissolved, but if you grow attached to bliss, it, too, may become an obstacle. Indeed, I am familiar with the many love songs attributed to him, and will speak of that later. There is a mystery surrounding his forced exile and the time and the conditions of his death.

The Secret Biography of
the Sixth Dalai Lama of Tibet

The birth of the Sixth Dalai Lama took place when it was deemed time to bring the Dharma teachings to the Chinese and to the people of southeastern Tibet. His family descended in an uninterrupted line from the Celestial Realm of Clear Light. The child was kept at home for over twelve years after the death of the Fifth Dalai Lama, who had advised it wise to hide his premature death until his successor came of age. Desi Sangye Gyatso, regent during this time, was diligent in carrying out the Fifth Dalai Lama's final instructions, ruling the country in secret until the child could be brought to Lhasa to do so.

At the age of fifteen, in the fire-ox year (1697), Gyalwa Tsang Yang Gyatso was brought to Nangkartse, where he became a monk under the teaching of the Panchen Lama, the living emanation of Amitabha Buddha. His religious name and title were bestowed upon him, and he was enthroned in the Potala.

For many years he studied the Vajrayana precepts and the commentaries on Tantric texts. He also received instruction for the *Kye-Rim*, *Dzog-Rim*, and *Lam-Rim*, and he spent three years intensively studying the treatises of the Fifth Dalai Lama with his personal tutor Gelong Jamyang Dragpa.

During this time, Desi Sangye Gyatso put constant pressure on the tutors to thoroughly teach the youth. The teachers in turn became worried, for their pupil was restless and inattentive, known at times to walk out of the room in the middle of a lesson. One time, the venerable Jamyang Dragpa followed after him carrying the text, imploring him to please pay attention.

Only then, out of compassion for his tutor, did the young Dalai Lama return to his lessons. Later he is said to have commented: "Throughout my life I have known both happiness and sorrow, the heights and depths of *samsara*. I regret now having strayed so far from the Dharma in my youth." Remembering his past misdeeds, he struck his own head with his fist and tore at his hair.

Internal dissension increased between Desi Sangye Gyatso and a minister of the government, Lhazang Khan. Lhazang Khan criticized Desi Sangye Gyatso for having ruled in secret for so long, and he wished to disprove that the young Dalai Lama was the true reincarnation.

By the year of the fire-dog, 1706, relations between the two had grown worse, requiring the emperor of China to send two lamas from China to help negotiate. Before the lamas arrived, Lhasang Khan assassinated Desi Sangye Gyatso. This brought jeopardy to the life of the young Dalai Lama, and the two Chinese representatives saw clearly the need for him to escape.

Lhasang Khan approved, and at the age of twenty-five, accompanied by two representative lamas, the Sixth Dalai Lama began his journey to China.

The party headed north along a path which led eventually to the Black Sea. A messenger from China greeted them with a note from the emperor, scolding them for not performing their duties and telling them that the Dalai Lama could not continue into China for there was no one willing to provide support for him. The representatives were terrified, fearful for their lives. In desperation, knowing that he had the power to do so, they asked the Dalai Lama if he could die or disappear so as to relieve them of their suffering.

The Dalai Lama told them, "According to your agreement with Lhasang, I must travel to China if only to see the emperor's face. This I must do."

The two representatives grew more fearful and prepared to commit suicide themselves. When the Dalai Lama heard of their plan, he became concerned, saying, "I would be unable to live knowing of your suffering. Give me time to think of a solution." With these words they were able to continue on.

While camped, the local people came to see the Dalai Lama. He decided that in order to fulfill the wishes of the representatives, he must perform magic and pray to the Triple Gem. Upon so doing, he received direction from Mahakali telling him to disguise himself in a yellow woolen robe with a red brocade robe beneath it dotted with gold coins, a yellow hat, and Mongolian boots, and to carry Buddha's Bone Pill (a relic the size of an egg), a red sandalwood rosary, and an important seal. He should also carry a dagger on his belt.

Thus clothed he walked from his tent and called for his attendants and the two representatives. He gave them blessings and advice, and to their great dismay he parted company with them and walked on alone in a southeasterly direction in accordance with the words of the goddess.

As he walked, a dust storm arose, shaking the corners of heaven and earth. Dust formed in torrential clouds, and the Dalai Lama became lost in the storm. Sparks of fire appeared in the distance. Following these sparks of fire he was led to a woman wearing the clothing of nomadic peoples. He followed her until she disappeared and the dust storm abated. The Dalai Lama found himself alone in the midst of an immense dust-filled basin barren of all life. He walked on.

The next morning he arrived in a valley with grass-covered mountains on either side. Unaccustomed to walking, he became thirsty and exhausted. His feet were covered with blisters. Lying down to rest, he thought to himself: "High rank ends in grief, gathering ends in dispersion, and accumulation ends in emptiness."

The nature of impermanence made him sad. He thought that perhaps the reason for his isolation was so that he might work harder in his practice of the Dharma to purify past omissions and ignorance. Realizing that his problems were created by the Triple Gem in order to teach him freed his mind.

He continued to journey down a wide highway. While traveling he met a group of merchants returning from Xining. The Dalai Lama was extremely desirous of tea but having had no experience at begging he found himself too shy to ask. He could do nothing but sit quietly near the group. After a while, an old man in the group came over and asked him who he was. The old man offered him tea, but the Dalai Lama had no cup. Another man poured the tea into a huge, black wooden bowl, and the tea was again offered to the Dalai Lama, who accepted it gratefully. Since he had never before experienced drinking from another's bowl, he could not help feeling repulsed by the dirtiness of the vessel. Although this thought came to him, he nevertheless drank the tea and found it most delicious.

While the Dalai Lama drank, the merchants observed him. After talking amongst themselves they looked more carefully at him. They whispered to each other: "This person is no ordinary human being. The beauty of his body goes beyond the human and reaches toward the realm of the gods."

They insisted upon questioning him as to his destination and from whence he had come. He did not know what to tell them at first, but decided to say that he had been traveling with other Tibetan monks and during an attack by robbers he had become separated from his friends.

After saying this he thought ruefully: "Now I have told my first lie." The story, however, aroused much sympathy from the group, particularly from one old man named Bande Kyab, the leader of the merchants.

As the merchants reloaded their mules they asked the Dalai Lama if he would like to travel with them. He said yes he would like to do so, but his feet, blistered and swollen, were too sore for travel. The merchants had extra yak so they gave a yak to him with a wooden saddle upon which to ride. However, this saddle caused an increase in pain. The older man, the leader Bande Kyab, took off his woolen upper robe, folded it, and placed it on the saddle to provide a buffer to the wood. He also made a stirrup out of rope so that the Dalai Lama could rest his feet. At last, the Dalai Lama was comfortable.

During the long journey, the Dalai Lama found himself tending the yak, something completely new and quite interesting to him. He thought to himself how funny it was that he was helping these merchants tend their yak. A fondness grew up among the men toward this strange being, and although he tried to talk to them they could not understand him very well.

The group met other travelers along the way, and soon the Dalai Lama felt the need to change into more humble clothing so as not to attract so much attention. One day, a monk wearing an old yellow robe met up with the merchants. The Dalai Lama asked him if he would consider exchanging clothes. The monk looked at him in disbelief. The Dalai Lama proceeded to divest himself of his garb in order to convince the monk of the sincerity of the offer. No one could understand why he would want to give up his clothes for those of a poor monk.

Eventually, the Dalai Lama felt the results of drinking from a dirty cup and wearing the filthy clothes of the poor monk. He became extremely sick, and sores broke out all over his face and in his mouth. After some days he recovered most of his strength.

One day the group could not decide which road to take — the one leading north or the one leading south. The southern route was much shorter but entailed the crossing of a great river. Being undecided still, they asked the Dalai Lama if he knew how to perform a mo, and although he already knew the answer to their dilemma he pretended to perform the divination for their benefit. He told them that the river was covered with ice.

Upon reaching the river they found his foresight to be true, and they crossed with ease.

The travelers finally reached the town of Arig, where the old man, the group's leader, lived. He and his wife showed great devotion toward the Dalai Lama. They asked him repeatedly to spend some time with them. He stayed two months, reciting the Vajra Chitica Sutra and teaching them the law of karma. They had recognized him as the precious Dalai Lama but vowed to keep silent. When the time of parting grew near, he left them with the fringes from his scarf to wear as protection cords. The old woman gave him a woolen robe and a new pair of boots as well as supplies of tea, butter, cheese, and other gifts. He was careful to take only those things that were necessary.

On parting, many tears were shed. The old man and his son traveled for a day with him before saying their good-byes. He blessed the old couple and their son, prayed for them, and continued on alone.

In the seventh month of the year he journeyed toward Tsarong Valley and after many weeks arrived at a place called Torge, completely covered with forests and fruit trees. At this time, in the province of Kham in eastern Tibet, people were dying of smallpox, and many towns were uninhabited as a result. Here, at Torge, the Sixth Dalai Lama, too, became ill, as the sores of smallpox spread all over his body.

Having by this time exhausted his supplies of food and drink and being unprotected from the weather, the sufferings of hunger, heat, and cold added to his misery. For days he lay under a grape arbor. During this time, he was unable to move even the slightest bit—not even to open his eyes. He was unconscious with fever most of the time, awakening periodically to pray for help from the Triple Gem. He thought that perhaps his sickness would somehow eliminate the smallpox plaguing the town and purify the accumulation of bad karma present there.

Ten days passed. The sores filled with pus, and his clothing stuck to his body. Insects covered him, feeding on the suppuration. His pain worsened. He fell unconscious.

Finally, he regained consciousness and could move his arms a little. He struggled to reach some of the grapes over his head and managed to get a few into his mouth. Only then did he feel a tiny bit of relief.

Twenty days later the sickness finally passed, leaving his body weak from hunger and his legs too feeble to carry him. He thought, "Although

I did not die from smallpox, I will surely die of hunger if I do not find something soon."

At that moment, a crow flew overhead, dropping a piece of meat from its claws. He managed to swallow this meat, and he felt a little better. He knew that he had to get to town soon.

With the aid of a walking stick, he slowly began his journey, taking very small steps and only a few at a time because of the shaking of his legs. On the way, he found some fruit trees which bore ripe red berries. He ate some of the berries. He soon discovered they were poisonous.

He experienced terrible pain in his intestines and once again felt himself approaching death. But because one cannot die unless one's karma is exhausted, the Dalai Lama found himself still to be alive. The pain was incomparable with any suffering he had yet encountered. It was so intense that even later in life, if he thought of that experience, he again felt the intensity of that pain. When the pain subsided a little, he was able to sleep.

While dreaming, he saw a young man, dressed in a yellow robe, asking who he was. Then he heard a voice say that poisonous food should not be eaten. And another voice said, "A person who can change poison into medicine will not be affected by it." At which point the voice broke into laughter and continued:

> *Although the fruit be poison,*
> *One possessed of a strong mind*
> *Can turn the poison into nectar.*
> *Now your body is purified and burns*
> *With great bliss. Celebrate,*
> *And prepare to go.*

Ceremony at Samye Monastery, c. 1930.

CHAPTER VI

Return of the Threat

When the iron bird flies and horses run on wheels,
the Tibetan people will be scattered like ants
across the world, and the teachings of the Buddha
will come to the land of the Red Man.
— Eighth-century prophesy of Padmasambhava

In the iron-sheep year, 1931, at the age of twenty-eight, I was appointed butter lamp manager at Samye Monastery, taking over the post from the retiring official. Samye was built by an early Dharmaking, Trisong Detsan, with the help of an Indian abbot, named Bodhisattva, said to have attained the age of 999 years.

In the innermost shrine of the main central temple, called Tsang Khang, there are images of the Buddha Sakyamuni and of eight great bodhisattvas. In the main congregation hall there stands an image of Padmasambhava made during his lifetime in the eighth century, and an image of the 999-year-old Indian abbot. The main chorten is three stories high. Beside it are temples representing the sun and the moon and the four continents and the subcontinents of earth.

The king's ministers had built great chortens of different colors: white, yellow, and blue. A wall of chortens surrounded this whole large area, and outside this wall were many other temples, including the three built by the three wives of the Dharma King.

My duties as butter lamp manager entailed providing butter for all the lamps in the various temples, as well as other supplies for the three great annual festivals: Monlam in the first month, the birthday of Buddha Sakyamuni in the fifth month, and the descent of Buddha from Tushita Heaven in the ninth month. A representative of the Dalai Lama came to Samye Monastery to work with me during festivals.

I had performed my duties faithfully at Phari so that when this position at Samye became available my uncle was able to speak to the Dalai Lama's ministers on my behalf. I knew this position would offer a test of my maturity. I took it to heart, never allowing the smallest detail to escape my notice. The job was well done.

It is difficult to work out an exact corollary between the Tibetan calendar and the one used in the West. First, our lunar year consists of twelve thirty-day months — which adds up to three hundred and sixty days — so an extra month is added every third year and may be inserted any place among the twelve which is considered auspicious for that particular year. The next difficulty arises because the real lunar year has only three hundred and fifty-four days so a certain number of days must be left out each year. There are squares on our calendars with no number but only the word *chod*, meaning "cut off." That day for that particular year no longer exists. Also, in order to avoid an unlucky day, an auspicious date may happen twice. That particular date repeated in two consecutive squares will be offset by chods elsewhere in the year.

Toward the end of each year a new calendar is worked out by the state astrologers. Consequently, no one knows what the next year will contain until it has almost started. Therefore, it is often difficult to plan festivals accurately, as the dates — particularly for the New Year's Festival — are not known much in advance. The Monlam Festival usually occurs somewhere during mid-February to mid-March on the Western calendar. Our months are numbered instead of having names, but the days of the week are named after the planets as in the West.

Our calendar has always been based, since the ancient days of King Gesar and perhaps before, on a great twelve-year cycle. Each year is named after an animal: mouse, ox, tiger, hare, dragon, snake, horse, sheep, monkey, bird, dog, and pig. In the eleventh century, a sixty-year cycle was introduced by combining the names of the animals with the five elements: wood, fire, earth, iron, and water.

Our new year begins officially as Losar with the rising of the new moon March or February, depending on when and where the extra month has been added that year. Monlam begins on the third or fourth day of the new year, depending on whether or not there was a missing day at the beginning of the year. This festival celebrates Buddha Sakyamuni's triumph over the evil spirits who tempted him during his meditations.

On the morning of the Dodechemo celebration at Samye, the state oracle of the guardian spirit, Tsimar, held his ceremony on top of the pagoda. The butter lamp manager's duty was to offer to the oracle tea, beverages, and a white scarf, a *kata*. In return, the oracle gave a protection thread and blessings. This event occurred at dawn. Everyone from the monastery and surrounding villages and farms came out to watch. The oracle dedicated and blessed all the roof decorations that had been carefully installed in anticipation of the event. And he carried in his hand the Great Seal of Padmasambhava. Although one particular oracle was a fat man, he jumped and ran about wildly without falling off the roof, without seeming to get exhausted. I was convinced that he had indeed become Tsimar.

Another state oracle was a very old woman. In trance, she came down from the roof, danced wildly for many minutes, and then climbed back up onto her throne without help from anyone — seemingly without fear — though she was blind. Once I consulted her privately. When I handed her a kata, she smiled, asking if I could stay for good at Samye. I explained that after three years I would probably be stationed back at Lhasa. She told me that I would face certain difficulties, but in the end I would live a long life.

Another time, she and her daughter came to visit me in my office, bringing a pot of tea which turned out to be exceptionally delicious. She had come to me because a man in the village told her I was able to cure cataracts. I felt embarrassed. I assured her that I didn't know anything about medicine but that I did know a little about prayer, and I would pray that her blindness might be cured.

A while later, the monk templekeeper came to me to ask my assistance in writing a government report because he couldn't do it properly himself. I saw the fear in his eyes. He was a young monk, much younger than I. He was afraid of being deemed inadequate to the task, afraid of failure. I was extremely overburdened with work at the moment and considered this request a nuisance. Suddenly I recalled the face of the blind old oracle lady humbly asking for my help and the ultimate futility of her request as I had nothing to offer but my prayers.

Now I interpreted that visit from the blind lady as an indication that

Rock at Samye Monastery with Guru Padmasambhava's footprint.

I should help this young monk any way I could; indeed, that I must help anyone who comes to me with a request for which I am qualified to assist.

THE EVIL ONE

Behind the temple of the local guardian spirit Tsimar there is a large empty structure called the Ükhang, or "breath chamber." It is believed at Samye that here the local spirit gathers the soul, or air, from the last breath of all nearby dying persons and feeds off this air. No living person steps inside that chamber without dire consequences, not even the abbot.

Once, in curiosity, I approached it alone at midday, the "hour of the horse."

The heat of the sun poured down upon me as I neared the chamber, yet I detected a foul odor and felt a cold breath seeping out from between the bleached rocks. Shamelessly, I hastily turned back. A man had died the night before — a poor villager trampled by a mule. His body had been flayed upon the rock outside the village, cut into pieces by the servants of death — strong men whose lot in life is such thankless butchering. His heart was thrown to the first circling crows, which have precedence over the vultures and other scavengers.

The man's burial had proceeded according to custom. Only high lamas, as a rule, are allowed cremation. Other monks and laymen of stature are generally taken to remote mountain sites and given more elaborate rituals to speed their souls through the various afterdeath states. A few are buried. But a poor person has only this efficacious dispersal to look forward to.

The naked corpse is placed face down on the rock by six sturdy men. The limbs are severed. The hair and scalp torn from the skull. The intestines separated from their cavity and set aside. Thousands of birds stand by, well trained by these men. The birds do not move toward the corpse until summoned by a whistle.

While the deceased is being consumed, one of the men might pluck out a bird's long white tail feather and offer it to a child. Every part of the corpse must be disposed of. The bones are crushed and mixed with the intestines, which have been laid aside. This mix is now offered to the scavengers, which have again retreated to a distance of some yards waiting for their summons. After everything has been eaten, the hair is burned, and only then do these hardworking men sit down to eat and drink chang as a reward for their labors.

I witnessed such a burial as a child. Afterwards I suffered intense pain in my scalp, and I was unable to eat meat for many weeks in spite of my father's warnings that I would not make a good soldier if I let fears overwhelm my mind. He said fear is useful if you can control it. It had been his idea to make my sisters and I witness the event. Watching how the dead are disposed of is considered to be instructive. All Tibetans believe that keeping our final end in sight is essential for spiritual growth. Firsthand knowledge of death is viewed as an antidote to foolishness — an essential step on the path to wisdom and compassion. Often we celebrate the death day of our revered saints rather than the birthday, believing that the death day is the day of liberation.

As I made my way back down the path from the "breath chamber" I wondered whether I should instruct my children as my father had instructed me. I knew my wife would have an answer. I trusted her judgment on spiritual matters. She had by that time completed the first two steps of the preliminary practices of the Vajrayana.

Soon my wife would be joining me at Samye, but only for a visit. Lodgings inside the monastery were not adequate for a family, and although I was a lay official, tending the butter lamps is considered a sacred duty and must be attended with fullness of mind. Generally, it is carried out by a much older man.

The New Year's festivities at Samye were scrupulously observed. As elsewhere in the homes and monasteries of Tibet, special pastries are cooked — *khabse*, of several varieties each about a foot long. These delicacies, made of finely ground flour, honey, walnuts, and cooked in butter or oil, are offered to any monk or official who visits. Barley and wheat are sown in pots and placed on the altars two weeks ahead of time. By Monlam the shoots have sprouted in intimation of the coming spring. Special chang is brewed, a bowl offered to each visitor.

In every Lhasa home, on New Year's Day, a pinch each of the newly milled wheat then the tsampa flour are thrown into the air (taken between thumb and forefinger). Each is then tasted. Similarly, freshly-brewed chang is sprinkled into the air with the fourth finger and a drop taken on the tongue. The head of a sheep, lavishly decorated with colored butters is ceremoniously placed on the family altar. On the last day of the old year, everybody spends the day in prayer to expel evil from the house, from the government, and from each of the monasteries.

62

Each year at the end of Monlam, the 108 monks of the Tantric College of Samye perform a ceremony during which they construct images made of barley dough. Each member of the Dalai Lama's family, his Cabinet ministers, and the Dalai Lama himself are represented. These images are then burned to get rid of the negative things that are bothering people. This ceremony is called *sorpen.*

Afterwards, on the floor in front of the Chokang courtyard in Lhasa, near a willow tree and between the stone-carved pillars, a dice-throwing contest takes place with the abbot of Samye and a person who dresses up as the personification of evil, called Lukhong Gyalpo. All the faces on the Evil One's dice have the same number, but the abbot's dice has different numbers. A judge records the throws, identifies the winner, and reports it to the Dalai Lama. When the Evil One is named loser, he scrutinizes his one-numbered dice and screams, recognizing that he has been cheated. He is then banished to the Ükhang. He crosses the Kyichu River by coracle and travels toward Samye. When he reaches the monastery, he must sleep seven nights alone in the Ükhang. The Evil One wears a shawl made of a goat skin turned inside out. His face is painted half black and half white, and in his hands he carries a black yak's tail.

People of the town believe that touching that yak tail is very inauspicious. It is part of the Evil One's job to try to make people come into contact with the evil tail. He jumps about, appears and disappears, and chases after young boys and girls, trying to lash them with it.

The person who plays the role of the Evil One is usually selected from among laborers who service the Potala and who live beneath the hill where the Potala stands, in the area called Shobe Nangtsen. Because of the power of the local spirit at Samye, and because this person has to sleep alone in the terrible breaths of the Ükhang chamber, he tends to live a short life.

The back of the Ükhang has a very small window placed way up high so no one can see in. It is from this window that the bad smells — seeming always to surround the place — are said to issue forth.

THE EAT NOW! FIELD

Many years before, my uncle Khenjung was sent by the government with another man to establish new taxation procedures for salt and wool. They stopped at Black Horse Village to ask my father to let them take me along. He agreed, and we traveled during that year through the Shang Shung region. I must have been eleven or twelve years old. Eventually, we arrived back at my uncle's house in Lhasa, where they left me before traveling on the great distance to Ngari.

I remembered having passed the famous cave of Padmasambhava, his crystal rock cave high up on a mountain. At that time the path was considered to be, by my uncle and his friend, too steep to climb. During the time I was butter lamp manager at Samye, I made extensive pilgrimages in the area. On one such pilgrimage I again passed the path to the cave. This time I stopped.

Having tethered my horse to an old willow near the stream, I traversed the narrow slope climbing into the sun. The fertile valley lay below in shadow. The air was unusually still as I stood before a cool dark opening in the rock, which the workings of many hands had polished.

The cave's entrance glistened like metal; the rock beneath my boots was smooth as a mirror.

I entered the crystal rock cave and laid an offering upon the altar. Numerous prayers were placed upon it, each held down by a smooth round stone. One such paper contained the "Song of Impermanence," attributed to Milarepa, ending thus:

> . . . *like the streaming river Tsangpo*
> *Nothing is still even for a moment.*
> *Like the twilight between day and night,*
> *Life itself swiftly fades.*

Returning to the light, I saw the immense fields of grain below, nutlike seeds ripening among the chaff. I listened to the tsa tsa sound made by the grain in the wind.

I recalled a story my mother told us as children, about how we came to know the ways of planting and harvesting grain. The mating of a bodhisattva-monkey and a beautiful local demoness produced many offspring. The demoness complained, "Though we must be grateful for the bounty of so many healthy children, my husband, still we have nothing to eat!" Whereupon he gave seed and planted the field from which erupted robust crops of barley and wheat that sprang up in an instant then ripened before their eyes.

The bodhisattva-monkey said to his wife, "Eat Now!" Thus the field was so named.

WHITE MEDICINE GODDESS

After three years at Samye I finished my term. In the wood-pig year, at the age of thirty-one, I was restored to my former sixth-rank status and appointed governor of Namdzong District in the central region of Tibet. I took over the position from the previous governor, who had finished his four-year term. Upon receiving notice of my new appointment, I traveled to Lhasa with horses and servants. My family made preparations for the journey to our new home.

The fort at Namdzong, situated on top of a very rocky hill, was the former palace of King Gesar. Nearby is a holy mountain associated with King Gesar's aunt, Namen Karmo, the White Medicine Goddess who guided him and to whom he prayed. Inside the mountain lives an evil black poisonous snake.

Also associated with King Gesar's aunt, one finds in an upper valley of the mountain, the Holy Nectar Stream, which becomes milk-colored on the night of the full moon of the fourth month. Every year the Panchen Lama sent someone there from the Tashilhunpo Monastery to collect some of that water.

Nearly a year before my appointment, on the evening of the thirtieth day of the tenth month of the water-bird year (December 1933), His Holiness, the Thirteenth Dalai Lama, died at the age of fifty-eight. The suddenness of his death was a great surprise to all, though many said he himself predicted it the year before in his political statement, now known as his "last testament."

No one suspected the seriousness of the illness that prevented him from appearing before the Upper Tantric College on the morning of the twenty-fifth. One monk reportedly burst into tears at the sight of the "throne audience" — the Dalai Lama's ceremonial robe had been placed upon the throne as a substitute for his actual presence.

The public and laymen in the government only learned that the Dalai Lama had been ill the evening his death was officially announced. Twenty-four hours of continuous prayer were invoked. At the Potala, ritual drums sounded, and butter lamps were placed on the roof. Selfishly, we hoped that his return to this world would be swift. Prayer flags and other decorations had to be taken down from all the houses in Lhasa, and everyone dressed in traditional mourning clothes. Aprons and jewelry were removed. There would be no singing and dancing. Only the slow mournful beat of the *damas*, which issued unceasingly from the roof of the Potala.

The spirit Chenrezig, Bodhisattva of Compassion, did not reappear in human form for nineteen months. Since a Dalai Lama generally assumes full political powers at the age of eighteen, we were to be without direct spiritual and secular guidance for nearly twenty years.

During this period of instability, control of the government was officially shared by two regents: the by now infamous Reting Rinpoche and the elder Taktra Rinpoche, known as "the tiger." This was a time of great trial for Tibet. Difficulties arose or were increased between the following contenders for power: the young Reting Rinpoche; the Panchen Lama (with ties to the Chinese); the Lonchen Langdun (prime minister); the Kashag (four top council members) under the leadership of my father-in-law Trimon; and lay official Lungshar, among the forces for reform, having spent time in England in 1914 studying systems of Western government.

THE RED IDEOLOGY

The Thirteenth Dalai Lama's personal assistant Kumbela had gained much power during the Dalai Lama's life. Kumbela was charged with murder, and though the charges could not be sustained, he was imprisoned and his property and his family's property were confiscated. Later, an uprising in the Kham District caused scandal inside the Kashag. Meanwhile, Lungshar's authority was growing. News of these uncertain events traveled Tibet in the form of rumors (often severely distorted) and songs sung in the streets. I did not confer directly with my stepfather on these matters as I was not experienced enough to be taken into his confidence.

This was an extremely difficult time. The Kashag attempted to reestablish its authority, having not been often consulted by the Thirteenth Dalai Lama, who valued the advice of those closer to him. The young Reting Rinpoche was a favorite. The Thirteenth Dalai Lama once gave Reting Rinpoche his personal divination book. Nonetheless, when Reting was chosen by the assembly using divine lottery, opposition to his appointment persisted long after his installation on the eighth day of the first month of the wood-dog year (January 1934).

A prophesy circulating widely was believed to have important implications. It warned that a chorten without a head would come to Tibet. Of the several factions vying for power months after the Thirteenth Dalai Lama's death, it was generally agreed that none had a strong enough leader to keep Tibet united. Each group accused the others of dishonesty and wrongdoing. It seemed chaos might break loose. Various approaches and propositions were made in secret by dissenting parties in opportunistic alliance with the British or the Chinese.

My wife was carrying our child. Leaving a friend to substitute for my duties, I traveled with my wife to Lhasa, where our fourth son, Kunga Gyurme, was born. We lived in rooms off the south corner of the courtyard of my wife's father's house. We had heard rumors of the troubles he was having, that Lungshar had plotted to discredit him. The day we arrived Trimon was not to be found. Tsipon Shakabpa reported that Trimon had departed early that morning wearing his amulet box and taking its cloth traveling case. Only if you are going on a long journey do you take the traveling case. Clearly Shakabpa was worried. Later, we discovered that Trimon had gone straight to Reting Rinpoche to complain of a threat on his life. He stayed for a while at Drepung Monastery to gain protection. The warning had come from Kapshoba, a young lay official with well-known ambitions. Many people became suspicious at hearing of the source. There seemed to be no end to the intrigue and counter-intrigue. Each new event boded poorly for our time.

Meanwhile, my son's birth presented my wife and myself with our own difficulties. Kunga Gyurme was born as the morning sun rose. Its reflected rays touched the top of his head — a good omen. But he was weak and unable to nurse. Then he became weaker still from a childhood illness.

At the time, the sons of Sakya Dolma Photang (of the Royal Sakya family) came to Lhasa and stayed at a friend's house. I invited a younger Sakya prince, who was also a lama, to give the *kago* blessing for our baby. He did so, but warned that the child might not survive. After he left, my wife took the baby on her lap and cried. The baby was silent.

We invited our guru, the Thirteenth Dalai Lama's younger tutor, who was old by this time but wise and alert. Trijang Rinpoche came to us immediately. He joked with us, saying, "If you give me this sick baby, I will make him live." I replied, "If you make him live, I will give him to you." He performed a secret ritual alone with the baby. Outside the room, we prayed and dedicated our offerings. When the baby and our guru returned from the other room, the baby's eyes were open, and he was able to nurse. He also ate some tsampa in tea. My wife was very happy. Afterwards, the child grew stronger, and the danger of death seemed to have passed.

I didn't forget my promise to our guru. He was grateful and said that we might send this child to be a lama of any school, it didn't matter which one. He named the baby Lobsang Kunga Gyurme. He is the one who brought me to America.

My wife conceived again while we were visiting Black Horse Valley. We had left the robust Kunga Gyurme in the care of my sister in Lhasa. Her own children were already grown. She adored him and promised to take good care of him, which she did. She asked me to send her wool, so I stopped in Tsang province, across the river from Shigatse, and bought one hundred female sheep and sent them back to her, paying with grain from our stores.

In 1936, the fire-mouse year, my first daughter was born, Ngawang Chodron — a tiny creature with delicate lips and a fierce cry. My wife stayed on with the baby girl at Black Horse Valley, but I returned to Lhasa. Minister Trimon had remodeled his entire house. I moved into a new apartment of eight rooms, with my own horse stable on the northeast side of the courtyard. Trimon had survived the skirmishes that ensued after the untimely death of the Thirteenth Dalai Lama. By this time, the new Dalai Lama had been located, under the clear direction of Reting Rinpoche, who received a vision from Lake Lhamoi Latso. The treacherous Lungshar, as well as his competitors Kumbela and Kapshoba, found themselves for a while residents of the same government prison. Lungshar was treated most harshly because of the black magic mantras discovered in his boots: "Harm Trimon Norbu Wangyal." Lungshar was also charged with plotting to overthrow the government. He was suspected of being a Chinese sympathizer.

Trimon seemed exhausted. He explained to me that the words of the Thirteenth Dalai Lama's "last testament" were filled with grave foreboding. The testament said, in part:

. . . this present era is rampant with the five forms of degeneration, in particular, the red ideology. In outer Mongolia . . . monks were forced into the army; the Buddhist religion destroyed, leaving no trace of identity. . . . In the future, this system will certainly be forced — either from within or without — on our land that cherishes the joint spiritual and temporal system. If, in such an event, we fail to defend our land, the holy lamas, including "the triumphant father and son" [the Panchen Lama and the Dalai Lama] will be eliminated without a trace. . . . Moreover, our political system, originated by the three ancient kings, will be reduced to an empty name . . . and my people, subjected to fear and miseries, will not be able to endure day or night. Such an era will certainly come! . . . Our political stability depends on the devotion of the ecclesiastic and secular officials and upon their ability to employ skillfully every diplomatic and military means without any possibility of regret or failure. . . .

Lungshar was punished by mutilation — removal of his eyeballs. All his property was confiscated and his progeny forever barred from government service. The mutilation was accomplished ten days after Lungshar's trial — using the ancient technique wherin the smooth, round knucklebone of a yak is placed upon the temple, bound tightly with a leather strap, and twisted with a stick at the top of the head until the eyeballs are pushed out from the sockets. This punishment had not been used in Tibet for a very long time. Lungshar survived his four-year term of imprisonment and was released into the care of his son. He died a year later.

He is reported to have said that as painful as his punishment had been, and as fearful and extended his imprisonment, it had one benefit: He was able to complete one hundred million *"Om Mani Padme Hum"* mantras.

MY FATHER'S PASSING

The fire-ox year, 1936, at the age of thirty-three, I was promoted from sixth rank to fifth rank as a city manager in Lhasa.

The Tibetan ranking system is fairly simple, the lowest rank is seventh and the highest rank is third; members of the top council, the Kashag, are third-rank officials. However, there are other positions of equal rank that have no number, titles such as *dzasa* and *darhan*.

Promotion to a higher rank doesn't happen simply because a number of years are spent in government service. I am certain that my uncle and my father-in-law made influence on my behalf.

My closest colleague was a high-ranking monk-official. For my promotion ceremony, my family was required to provide all the beverages, tsampa, cookies, and rice. My new secretaries and butlers introduced themselves and congratulated me.

The next morning my colleagues and I paid our respects to the Parliament members who sat together at the Potala. Later, at the inauguration of the entire fifth rank, my new colleagues and I sat in the fifth-rank file at the big government ceremony, and later that evening my relatives stopped by our house to congratulate me. The Trimon family and my sister gave me a party that lasted several days during which there was much feasting, drinking of chang, music, and dancing. The musicians were chosen by my father-in-law Trimon, who had always been fond of music.

My office had joined recently with the Construction Office in responsibility for remodeling the Norbulinga, the Potala, and the main temple at Sera. All these activities, including the completion of the Thirteenth Dalai Lama's chorten (in which his remains were to be entombed) were urgently needed. Reting Rinpoche had revealed to the Tibetan National Assembly the details of his vision at Lake Lhamoi Latso, the lake traditionally used for such divination, ten days journey from Lhasa.

According to his directions, the search party had located a young boy in Amdo. The boy amazed the monk-officials during their examination of him. Each time he was presented with a choice between the former Dalai Lama's articles and matching duplicates, he chose the originals. He cried out when they pretended to be leaving. He said he wanted to "go home, to Lhasa!" The lay official Kheme broke down in tears upon first meeting with the child so certain was he that they had found our new Dalai Lama. Everything had to be completed and made ready for the enthronement of the child, which would take place in a few years.

We were kept busy remodeling the main entrance to the Norbulinga, the Dalai Lama's rooms on the roof of the main congregation hall at Sera, and the *pembe* walls (painted tied bundles of straw, stacked evenly) of the roofs of Drepung and the Tantric Colleges. We also had to restore the *pemgyen* — large medallions set at intervals along these walls. In addition, we constructed a new house for the Dalai Lama's parents at the Norbulinga Palace.

That same year my father died of rheumatism. He had been many years retired from service as military captain and advisor, and he spent his days overseeing the workings of the Shugu estate. He had been successful at amassing great wealth in terms of herds and stores of grain, and had been fortunate in his dealings with the traders along the border.

For his funeral service I gave tea and gifts to twenty thousand monks in the monasteries around Lhasa and asked them to do prayers for him. For seven days we attended services for my father under the direction of our guru, who continued doing prayers according to the custom for a total of forty-nine days.

My father's body was cremated and his ashes encased in an urn Mother kept near his bed for a year, making ritual offerings and saying prayers to his deities at the altar she had created for him. A favorite prayer — written by Ngorchen Kunga Zangpo, founder of the monastery to which our family was intricately linked — was printed on small scraps of paper by the government printing office in Lhasa. These prayers were kept in our amulet boxes, the remaining thousands distributed to the winds on a mountain pass above Shigatse by my brother.

My father had grown disenchanted with events since the death of the Thirteenth Dalai Lama, whom he particularly revered. My father trusted in the words of prophesy from Padmasambhava, and though he had no idea how those words would come to pass, he was nonetheless convinced during the last years of his life that Tibet was on a disastrous course. My father had in his youth made a pilgrimage to the sun-medallion lake, Tso Mapham, "The Undefeated," with its dark partner shaped like a crescent moon. He hoped during his lifetime to see return of the glistening ribbon Ganga Chu — connecting waters which ebb and flow with the seasons and years. The Ganga Chu, we were told, had been dry for nearly a century — an omen boding ill. Tso Mapham, it is said, was once a divine paradise at the foot of Mt. Kailasa, the sacred mountain shaped like a chorten, which is often depicted in the center of mandalas, representing the legendary Mt. Meru, source of the four great rivers and center of the universe.

My father said that the ancient lake, fifteen miles across, and the

71

sacred mountain, were once engulfed by fir trees, flowering shrubs, and the singing of countless birds. The great sage Milarepa, after his conversion, wrested the mountain from the Bonpo high priest in the eleventh century, claiming it as a Buddhist sanctuary. This was accomplished during extensive battles of wit and sorcery during which it was reported that Milarepa was transferred instantly to the top of the mountain by merging his life energy with that of the last rays of the sun.

My father said that the land surrounding the mountain and the lakes is now barren, but what few plants remain are healing herbs, also used for incense offerings. There are still many foxes, *kyang* grazing nearby, and vast herds of antelope. The animals living near the mountain are sacred. They are never hunted for their skins or meat.

Father alone, among family and friends who traveled together to the region for a month-long stay, made the meritorious thirteen circuits of the mountain. An entire circumambulation along the path takes no less than twelve hours at a brisk pace, being around thirty-two miles in length. He regretted not returning to the region later in life, as he had intended, to walk on the *nangkhor* path that passes two tiny lakes — the waters of the first being black like tea, the waters of the second being white like milk. This inner route, close to the sacred mountain itself, is open only to those pilgrims who have first completed thirteen circuits on the longer outside path.

I traveled near the region on my journeys with the geologist monk in my youth. It was our intention to investigate the river sources. My teacher had learned in England that the area was indeed, as legend stated, the source land for the four great rivers that water all of the Asian continent: the north-flowing Senge Kabub, or Mouth of a Lion; the south-flowing Mapcha Kabub, Mouth of a Peacock; the east-flowing river Tamchock Kabub, or Horse-Mouth; and the westward-flowing Langchen Kabub, Elephant Mouth.

However, I was called back to Lhasa by my uncle to enter government school, and my journey in the sacred lands was cut short. I had thought to return one day. My wife and I discussed this as a possibility when our children got older. But it never came to pass.

As it was, I was burdened with duties in overseeing the activities of the Jokhang, Lhasa's main temple. All supplies had to be ordered and dispersed; I had to keep accurate accounts of everything and manage all the workers, who kept the temple operating on schedule. These duties were shared by three of us.

Every evening we made a complete tour of the area, to be sure all the butter lamps were out and the guards properly stationed. Meanwhile, the construction and reconstruction of various buildings was under our management. We had to visit those sites during the daytime to ensure proper conduct among the workers and to investigate whether the building was proceeding according to the elaborate plans developed by the Dalai Lama's architects.

AN APPEARANCE OF MAHAKALI

One day, during the New Year's Festival of 1937 when I was on duty at the southern entrance to the main temple, a fire occurred on the north side. I immediately rushed to the place and found smoke everywhere. I could not locate the source of the flames.

I sent my assistant off to the temple of the goddess Mahakali to pray for the protection of the Jokhang. When the people circumambulating the main temple saw the smoke, they brought buckets of water from the fountain, and eventually the flames were smothered.

Later, investigating the source of the fire I found that it had started in the Kurso Khang, where fabrics for temple decorations were sewn and stored. During the festival, that area had been used night and day for frying huge cookies in great tubs of boiling oil. Hot oil from these tubs had dripped down into the basement, where bamboo and lumber were stored, and some sticks had caught fire. My office had earlier decided against renting that area for cooking purposes, but the head cook did not heed our instructions. He and his staff had gone ahead and cooked there anyway. The fire damaged two stories of the Kurso Kang but not the main sections of the temple.

Those who had decided to cook there were staff members of the Regent Reting Rinpoche. When he sent his investigators to find out the reason for the fire, I told them it was caused by the insubordination of two officials who were under direction of the regent's treasurer — a different staff from officials such as myself.

The regent promptly dismissed the responsible officials, and because everyone was extremely busy with their regular festival duties and didn't have time to find replacements, secretaries and abbots were called in to complete the work of the cooks who had been fired. In addition, four officials were punished with fines of five ounces of gold to be given to the National Treasury toward rebuilding the damaged rooms. The officials who were fined were the following: 1) Gi-gyeb, son of the regent's treasurer, who was general manager of the Monlam Festival; 2) a receptionist from the Upper Cabinet of the Potala, who was responsible for watching the comings and goings on that side of the temple; 3) myself, who was on active managerial duty that day at the temple; 4) a monk-representative from the college of monks living at the Potala.

During the same festival period, we lost a gold butter lamp, which was stolen from the altar of the main temple. This was a serious offense. All were intensely questioned. The manager of the altar keepers, Gon Nye Bon, always slept outside the main entrance. He said he had recently witnessed a young man in the characteristic garb of a pilgrim from Amdo taking a scarf from off the altar. When he called out to the thief, the boy escaped through a side exit, and the manager was not able to determine if he had stolen anything else. My secretaries located and questioned the boy, but he insisted he had not stolen the lamp. He had taken only the scarf as a blessing to bring home to his mother.

He told us that he knew a man named Nangma who had bragged about selling gold to Nepalis. Maybe that man was the thief. We asked where we might find him, and he directed us to a local tavern.

Nangma was arrested and brought to my office. I recognized him as one of six former temple janitors I had known. When he was young, he had been a very good monk-student at the Chogen Gego, part of the Potala School which I attended. Later, when he gave up his monk's robes and became a layman and janitor, he kept his previous name.

As soon as I saw his face I remembered him and how much trouble he had been as a janitor, though there was always something about him I liked.

When I asked him if he had taken the gold chalice, he said no. I asked where he had gotten the gold he sold to the Nepalis, and he told us that he had stolen an apron of gold from the tomb of the Fifth Dalai Lama and sold that to the Nepalis.

This seemed impossible. There were always people around the tomb in the daytime, and at night it was closed.

He replied that he had entered from the back door of the Potala, in the courtyard of the monks which he knew so well from his former days as student. He entered the tomb by climbing up the wall to the main window. He had done this at night, opened the window and entered the shrine, then climbed back out the way he had come in.

Tegun was altar keeper for that temple. He was informed of the theft and severely reprimanded. Both Nangma and the boy who had reported him were whipped many times. Neither confessed to the theft of the chalice. Nangma confessed only to selling the gold from the Fifth Dalai Lama's tomb. The other admitted only to stealing the scarf, and he was released. We were left in doubt about the theft of the chalice.

Gon Nye Bon, the altar keeper's manager, offered to replace the chalice himself as his punishment for not keeping a watchful eye on the temple. Still the mystery disturbed me. I wanted the satisfaction of having the thief caught and punished.

Later, I visited Nangma in prison and asked him again about the chalice, offering to shorten his sentence if he could provide clues to the whereabouts of the true thief.

He continued to deny that he had stolen the golden chalice, but he confessed to a number of other crimes, including the many times he had stolen butter and tea from the temple storage house when he was a janitor there. I asked him how he had gotten into the storage rooms because the main door was always locked and sealed with wax. He told me that he had opened the lock with a cotton-needle.

I didn't believe him, but later when I brought a lock to him he demonstrated his technique. I asked him how he had opened doors without breaking the seals, and he said in the early mornings when he arrived for his tour of duty he noticed that a seal had sometimes fallen off and lay unbroken on the stone floor. He kept those seals, and after he had broken in, he put a fresh one in place of the one he had broken.

One day, in the temple of Mahakali at the end of the double stairway, Nangma had seen a naked lady suspended in the air. He knew that Mahakali was angry with him. He quit his job as janitor and lived off the money he had made from previously stolen things.

Finally, Nangma was released from prison, and though I attempted to counsel him several times, believing he was a good man inside — truthful in speech though dishonest in deed — I was unable to prevent him from further thievery.

75

Eventually, he was killed, falling from a rope at the Potala while attempting to break into a treasure room.

CEREMONY

I was one of four Lhasa city managers, or *nyertsang*. The other three city managers were: 1) a monk-official named Choden Tar; 2) another monk-official named Tsuden Nyima; 3) and Chang Nyoba, a lay official such as myself. Under us there was a secretary named Tara Wa, three butlers, a house manager, and several janitors and other workers, altogether making twenty people in the department.

Lords, upper-class people, and ministers of the government gather together on the fourth day of the sixth month. The wives of Cabinet members attend or send their representatives. Early in the morning of that day, my department was responsible for putting new butter in the butter lamps of all the temples of Lhasa and in front of the image of King Srongtsen Gampo.

We set up altar offerings early in the morning, before the temples were opened. Seats for all the dignitaries were prearranged according to rank in a large hall reserved for such purposes. Elaborate offerings of tea, rice, and dates were prepared and placed near each seat.

Paysoma, lovely young serving women, were hired to serve the specially-made wine. They first filled their own cups to the brim, lifted up their hands, and together sang "Lhasa, the Glorious Religious Center of the World," which lasted some time as it had many verses. After that, and before tasting the wine themselves, they served it to all the dignitaries.

Another duty of my department during these festivities was to wrap in yellow brocade a huge clay wine container decorated with silver that had actually been used by the king in the seventh century. It was shaped like a horse's head. It was over a foot tall and quite heavy. We filled it with wine and took it to the Gesan Podong in the Norbulinga, where the young Dalai Lama was living with his family. We paid homage to His Holiness and symbolically offered the wine to him, receiving his blessing upon it.

That morning, all the Shukor and Tsekor, high lay and monk-officials making up the two bodies of the government came to the ceremony and received blessings from that special jar, each drinking a part. Then the rest of the wine was plentifully offered to the ordinary staff workers.

76

The jar was refilled continually until the workers had their fill, drinking of it by using their own bowls, which they habitually carried with them inside the folds of their chubas.

After the official blessing, we traveled to the Si-lun, a department consisting of two prime ministers, a monk, and a lay official. We exchanged katas with them and served them wine, offering blessings from the nectar of that great king's jar, which is said to be at least fourteen hundred years old. Then we went into the Ka-lun, or the Cabinet office, which was located in town, not at the Potala. We offered blessings to the Cabinet members.

Later that day we went with jars of the blessed wine to all the friends of officials and to the heads of aristocratic families. We also offered blessings of wine from the jar to the general public at a special bier that was set up outside the gates of the Jokhang.

After the festival is over, the jar is again filled with wine and wrapped in cloth and left to sit in the temple of Srongtsen Gampo on a special tray at the back of the temple until the next year. Although the jar has never been damaged, has no holes or cracks that can be detected, nectar leaks from it during the year. But no matter how much leaks out, the quantity remaining inside is never reduced.

King Srongtsen Gampo believed the lake in front of the Jokhang Temple to be sacred. He threw his ring into the water, where it remains to this day. The temple was built at the edge of the lake; it is an immense temple. Inside is the sacred *Jo* — an image of Sakyamuni Buddha with a crown of jewels and vestments of gold depicted in the "adorned, enjoying body" state of enlightenment.

According to custom, at the time of the fall harvest in the fertile Kyichu Valley surrounding Lhasa, farmers take grain from their fields three times to officials for testing to find out if the grain is ready to be harvested. Two monks and two lay officials from Lhasa are appointed to officiate at these harvest activities. Many believe that the Potala is at its most splendid this time of year, bathed in a golden light filtered through splinters created by the threshing of the grain.

At harvest time the year before the Fourteenth Dalai Lama was enthroned, the harvest was particularly good all over the valley and in the Tsangpo Valley as well. I was among the officials appointed to take charge of the harvest celebration. We were to wear blue Chinese silk robes with red woolen overcoats. We carried special inlaid knives and tea cup cases, and there were unusual earrings of many-colored jewels and tassels to wear in addition to our ordinary ones.

Our hats were swathed in gold ribbon and had other decorations and medallions of precious metals. Our boots were of felt and leather — custom-made and rainbow hued. Our horses wore special saddles from which were suspended a number of fine ornaments. Eight horsemen carrying *tankas* picturing the Wheel of Life headed the procession from the hill of the Potala down to the Jokhang and through the streets of Lhasa out onto the field, at which time the games and contests were inaugurated. The head of the Jokhang Temple carried garments for the Sakyamuni statue, as well as a garment made by the wife of King Srongtsen Gampo with pearls the size of beans sewn into the cloth. All the while approximately two hundred monks from the Miru College played their instruments while walking and bearing banners. This procession made one complete circumambulation around the city of Lhasa and the gleaming Potala.

That year the Regent Reting Rinpoche was visiting the Dalai Lama's family. Together they watched everything through binoculars from the Potala. At sunset, the procession left the small village of Langru Shega and proceeded through several other towns until it slowly returned to the main road in Lhasa. The people lined the roads to receive blessings from seeing the beautiful robe of the Sakyamuni statue, which was only displayed at this time of year.

The members of the procession dismounted near the Jokhang. We gathered together once more in our offices for tea and freshly brewed chang, and then we returned to our families.

And so ended the harvest festival in the years before the Chinese takeover.

MAD DOG

Let me tell you here the story of the woman who came to be known as Mad Dog.

I was living alone in my father-in-law's house in the special apartments he had arranged. My younger brother was at Black Horse. My children were with my wife at Black Horse, or with my sister in another house nearby.

Sonam Wangyal, Shuguba's younger brother, in Lhasa, c. 1950.

My younger brother, Sonam Wangyal, had been a monk at Tashil-hunpo Monastery in Shigatse. He studied diligently and learned both medicine and mathematics, passing his exams with the highest honors. Then, according to the wishes of the Thirteenth Dalai Lama, he had been drafted and trained for the special forces as a Tibetan doctor, under the tutelage of the Dalai Lama's personal physician. After the death of the Thirteenth Dalai Lama all of these "soldiers of the aristocracy" were dismissed and allowed to return home. From that time, my brother had stayed at the Black Horse Shugu estate to take care of our parents. When my father died, my brother became overseer.

Since he was still young, my wife and I discussed the arrangements of a marriage for him. He was eleven years my junior and had spent the majority of his years in a monastery. My mother felt that we should leave the choice of a wife to him, but when my wife discussed the matter with her parents, they replied in a characteristically protective manner: "If there are two brides in one family at one estate, you will not be comfortable."

There is a tradition in Tibet that the wife of an elder son may become wife to his brothers. This was a conservative approach to family harmony and served a purpose. If a wife was barren or property needed to be retained, occasionally polygamy was offered as a remedy. Polyandry, however, was much more common and was generally included as part of the written marriage agreement. In accordance with the suggestion of her parents, my wife became my younger brother's wife, and went to live with him at the Shugu estate. My wife and I had eight children at the time:

Sonam Paljor, a son, born in the fire-tiger year in Lhasa
Sonam Targye, a son, born in the earth-dragon year in Tsang
    (Beling estate)
Yeshe Tenzing, a son, born in the earth-snake year in Tsang
Yeshe Thondup, a son, born in the iron-sheep year at Shugu estate
Sonam Gyatso, a son, born in the water-bird year at Shugu estate
Lobsang Kunga Gyurme, a son, born in the wood-pig year in Lhasa
Ngawang Chodron, a daughter, born in the fire-mouse year at
    Shugu estate
Nyima Chuzom, a daughter, born in the earth-tiger year in Lhasa
    (She was the last child born to us but soon died.)
At the Shugu estate my brother had several girlfriends but no wife.

He had fathered a son, Nyudrup, with the wife of a friend, and had earlier conceived a son with our family maid. That son was later recognized as a reincarnation of a great scholar, a *geshe* from the Tashilhunpo Monastery.

A child born out of wedlock was generally received into the family of the woman who gave birth to it, particularly if the woman was married and had no children of her own. However, for a young and unmarried girl, bearing a child before her wedding carried a stigma. Nuns were particularly susceptible to censure for this cause. Though many indeed remained celibate after taking a vow, some did not. Those who conceived often resorted to unorthodox methods for attempting to prevent the birth. My wife said she knew of instances in which a newborn infant had been abandoned in the crevice of a rock near a path with the hope that villagers would find the child and adopt it before it died. The appearance of mysterious infants was accepted as a gift from the gods and the origin of the infant never investigated.

My brother was kind, thoughtful, and humble. Though he was not robust nor particularly vigorous in form, his character made him attractive to women, who felt his sympathies strongly and admired him for his learning and his lively intelligence.

During this period while I was city manager in Lhasa, I enjoyed very much having my brother visit. Though he was conscientious in conducting his duties and never shirked from them, he often played tricks on me, attempting to get a laugh. I was in my late thirties, he a young man — about a head shorter than I. Agile and energetic, he retained throughout his life a youthful temperament. My wife had always been particularly fond of him, since the early years of our marriage when he visited us at Duchung Dzong with my mother.

When he visited me in Lhasa, we'd go out at times to visit friends or attend a gaming event. As we walked the streets, I often lost sight of him when he suddenly turned down an alley or paused midstep to help a beggar on the path. He carried his medicine bag with him at all times. He could not pass a sick man without stopping to do something for him. He had no feelings of shame or fears about getting dirty or sick from contact with these beggars. He would stoop to attend a man on the ground covered with oozing sores — a terrible stench rising off the person. Even when he was quite young and had just begun his studies, his brothers and sisters benefited from his prescriptions. Once he cured my mother of a tumor in her neck, and he helped my wife with her childbirth pains. He was a good doctor, trained in traditional Tibetan medicine.

One evening in spring we were out walking when my brother wandered off suddenly. I peered into a courtyard but did not see him inside. I continued on alone since we had an appointment to keep. Eventually he arrived at the home of our family friends, and he told us this story: A young woman had called to him. She led him into the inner chamber of a house. He could see she was limping, and though he carried his medicine bag, she did not at first ask him for assistance but took off all her clothes and lay down upon a narrow bed. He told her that he had noticed her damaged ankle, and she said she did not now want his medicine but that is indeed why she had first called to him. He helped one of her friends last week, she said. He said no, it wasn't he. Then he asked her to put her robes back on. He told her he was a monk who had taken a vow of celibacy, which of course wasn't true. He said it only to frighten her.

The young woman began to cry furiously. He comforted her, covering her with her garments as he did so. Then he pressed her wrist and found her pulse shallow — fast and irregular. On examining the ankle he discovered it was whole, not bruised or broken. He surmised that she had been pretending. He gave her some pills to calm her heart. He said good-bye.

My brother's face was flushed. He seemed agitated as he spoke. We could see that this experience had been an uncertain one for him. He said he felt drawn to her from the moment he saw her beckoning. A lovely face, quite young, but afflicted. He soon discovered she was infamous — Mad Dog was her nickname. It seemed everyone had a story to tell about her.

My brother had arrived in Lhasa the week before to provide witness at a court case involving some village matters. This was an involved drawn-out affair. There were many conflicting accounts. My brother's testimony was heard several times over the course of the weeks. Many villagers were involved with what seemed to be a massive deception. Meanwhile, he fell in love with Mad Dog.

When the court case was concluded in favor of the estate, my brother stayed on in Lhasa, living in apartments with Mad Dog. We all grew concerned for his sanity.

I chanced to see him in the market one day, and he seemed confused, though he insisted he was extremely happy. He said nothing about her then or about her exploits, which were mounting in the eyes of the town. A song was heard in the streets about the pair:

> *The gentle doctor from Shugu estate*
> *Has taken on a demon he cannot shake.*

My wife was extremely disturbed and distressed by this affair. We worried, too, for her sanity. Mad Dog was indeed a beauty. Some said she'd come from Amdo near the birthplace of the Dalai Lama and that her parents lived there still, believing her to be dead.

Others said she was part Chinese and had journeyed to Lhasa from a small town near the border.

My elder sister, married to Shalungpa, Minister Trimon's eldest son, resolved to break up the relationship. She threatened Sonam Wangyal, warning him of the shame he was bringing upon our family and to the minister himself. Finally with these words she was able to persuade our brother to break off with the woman and return home to Black Horse.

It wasn't easy. He went back with Mad Dog several times. Eventually the young woman held onto some of his things — gold earrings and other possessions. She continued to write to him after his return to the estate, begging him to come back to her.

My brother told us he believed she was a dakini. He said she always wore a bracelet of tiny bells on her wrist and a circlet of chain on her ankle. She gave half her earnings to the Sakya School. He described how he had tried to persuade her to abandon her destructive livelihood, but no matter what he said or offered her, including marriage, she persisted in her evil ways. He had hoped for a son she could give to the monastery.

No one knew truly where she had come from. One of her friends said that Mad Dog herself was the illegitimate daughter of a nun. The wildest tale had it that she'd been born out of wedlock to a Nepalese princess and a Tibetan monk, and to avoid having to strangle the infant at birth, the nursemaid journeyed with her across the Himalayan border only to perish in the wilds herself, whereupon the ailing child was taken in by nomads.

One morning my brother found her sobbing upon her bed, her head and neck covered with wounds and her arms badly bruised. She had received rough treatment from a *dopdop*, a warrior-monk in the service of the Potala. There was nothing to be done, she said, refusing to reveal his name.

Sonam Wangyal's wife, Tseden Drolma, and Sonam Wangyal, Lhasa, 1955.

My brother eventually returned her letters and made no attempt to retrieve the items he had lent her (or that she had stolen from him). Later we learned she had died. He was again living at Shugu with my wife, who had by then conceived a daughter by him, who died in miscarriage.

My second eldest son, Sonam Targye, had early on married a girl from the Omolung estate in Shigatse, who quickly bore him a girl, and a second one, then twin boys who died at birth. Soon after, Sonam Targye, who had been generally unhealthy most of his life, died at the age of twenty-five at our estate home. Our family guru saw the column of smoke rise up from the cremation fire toward the east. He said my son would be reborn a human being.

Three years later, other relatives gave birth to a child who one day declared that he wanted to go home "to Tanak" (Black Horse) of the "Shugu estate," which indicated that he might be the reincarnation of my second son. He also said a few days later, "I have a white horse and a yellow hat," and he listed various other belongings of my son who had died.

When this boy came to Lhasa to meet me, it was clear to me that he was indeed the incarnation of my son. I attributed our good fortune to my brother's proper conducting of the funeral and to his good influence on our guru.

Soon after the funeral of my son, my brother was married to my son's widow. A healthy daughter was born to them, and my wife returned to stay with me in Lhasa. This daughter eventually married, and she lives to this day with her family on a tiny farm at Black Horse. My brother was a good father and cared well for his children.

My brother used his skills at medicine and mathematics to keep the estate workers happy. He did well keeping the accounts in order and was helpful to my two sons at Ngor: Sonam Gyatso, who was to become abbot of the monastery having been recognized a tulku, which is a reincarnation of a famous lama or saint from the past; and Kunga Gyurme, who later became vice-abbot and was also a tulku.

While I served as city manager during the years 1936 to 1940, I was building a new house in Lhasa. I asked my wife for advice in planning the design of our new home. By the iron-snake year we had finished the first floor and were just beginning work on the second. Then I was appointed fourth-rank assistant to the governor of the distant province of Chamdo, and the work of building was halted. The house was left unfinished, never to be completed.

Servants with two of Shuguba's horses, Lhasa, 1956.

CHAPTER VII

The Far East

Khampa traders wear a dirk at the hip and a thick tassel of red braided into the hair then wrapped about the head. As we near the settlement, dark-faced men on vigorous white horses ride out to greet us. Each man wears a gold wristwatch, sometimes two or three.

Soon we are greeted by an official assembly — assistants to the minister and monk-officials. A cry from atop a rise — "Ki-ki-ki-so!" I sense the taunting mockery in their welcoming call. . . .

In the iron-dragon year, 1940, the Minister Nangjungpa was appointed governor at Chamdo in the province of Kham, which is the far eastern region of Tibet, bordering China. Before he and his fourth-rank assistant left Lhasa for the arduous journey nearly a third of the distance across Tibet, the minister dislocated his foot and asked to be dismissed from duty. I was chosen by the regent as a replacement.

I halted construction on my house, and in August traveled with my wife, my daughter, and a son along the main road out of Lhasa — the Shung-lum road. We moved swiftly; still we journeyed sixty-one days, crossing twenty-seven mountain passes on horseback with yak caravan.

Kham is the second province of Tibet, the first being U-Tsang, the central region in which two holy rivers, the Tsangpo and the Kyichu, meet. Kham lies far to the east; the sky is immense with domed clouds and forked lightning often in the distance. A traveler crosses several 18,000-foot-high peaks and crosses wide plateaus of juniper, spruce, and cypress. The leopard, the monkey, the wolf, and the bear roam these regions. Overhead the solitary eagle soars followed closely by the noisy crows which inhabit every part of Tibet — hailed always as a good omen, particularly when they appear in pairs.

My wife and daughter collected the iridescent feathers of pheasants my butler occasionally shot for our meat. We bathed in pools in the Nguchu, which flows south through Burma to empty into the Indian Sea.

On the way to Chamdo we visited several monasteries. I was surprised that people in most of these monasteries believed in the local spirit Shugden, as well as Mahakala and his consort Mahakali. When my small party of family and servants passed through the Hlo region at the other side of the sacred mountain, I was apprised of a strange situation: the monks in the Shi-tam Gompa near the dzong, approximately three hundred in all, were engaged in an unusual rebellion.

One day when all the monks had gathered in the great hall, several young monks pretended to be possessed by the local spirit Shugden. While they were thus "possessed" they accused the abbot and the head of the prayer leaders, as well as their monk-guard and several older teachers, of disloyalty to the monastery, of cheating villagers out of their money, and of breaking vows. These were serious accusations.

Eventually, the accused people were dismissed by the young monks, who then chose replacements. Later, when the villagers invited ten or twenty of the young monks into their homes to read aloud from the *Kangyur*, as was their custom, some of the monks again pretended to be possessed by the spirit. The monks told the villagers that certain of their possessions had evil powers or curses cast upon them, and that those items must be given to the monastery for purification rites. I gathered this information from reliable sources among the villagers.

The Minister Nangjungpa's son was governor of the Hlo Dzong area. When I arrived in Chamdo, I gave the Minister Nangjungpa, who had arrived shortly before me, all the details about the Shugden cult in Hlo Dzong. Replying that his son and wife were very devoted to Shugden, he paid little attention to the rest of my report.

The proper date for our first working day at Chamdo having been set according to custom and proscribed by government astrologers, we performed the required ceremony, exchanging scarves with others who worked there. We seated ourselves according to rank and position and were served the traditional tea and rice.

Invited to this ceremony were the secretary of the Kashag, the monk-officials, and the many lay officials governing the large region of

Kham. The local abbots and officials and their assistants welcomed me. Other heads of monasteries in the region who were unable to attend sent their congratulations.

Since there was not then much danger at the border, every Sunday we were allowed a holiday from work.

The mountains were beautiful at that time of year with clouds boiling up in the distance and the scent of autumn-blooming wildflowers. In pools and small lakes water lilies blossomed, and long-legged birds roosted.

The Khampa women are quiet and hidden, except during games of dice when they grow vituperative. The men, as I described, are fierce and warlike, independent-minded, and swift to battle. Many Tibetans, particularly those living in Lhasa, mistrust and fear these men. My father often said they are the backbone of Tibet's strength: Their loyalty must be courted and maintained for the survival of Tibet as an independent nation.

I remembered his words whenever my dealings with these quick-tempered people became difficult, and I avoided many unnecessary skirmishes that way.

At this time, the Minister Nangjungpa, my immediate superior, suggested that I didn't seem to have a proper place to stay. I had been living with my family in one small apartment of a larger house owned by an elderly couple. He encouraged me to look over the nicest houses, mostly occupied by large families. I did not want to force anyone to move out because I knew they might make me regret it later. I looked around and when I had decided on a house I liked, I left a message with the family.

The next day a man from that house came to my office and suggested that since moving out would be extremely difficult for his family, perhaps he could build me a house instead. I accepted his plan, and construction began immediately in an empty lot to the back of his house. They built for me at their own expense a one-story house with two bedrooms and servants' quarters, to which my family and I moved, remaining there for the duration of my stay. My wife and children were with me, except for a few months each year when they visited Lhasa.

RAHULA

One afternoon while riding in the hills above town, I paused for a moment to rest on a flat rock in the sun. For a long time I watched the shape-shifting motions of a cloud off in the northeast. The sky was otherwise clear, and this large cloud had attracted my attention. It looked distinctly like a dragon whose head and neck were turned toward its tail. Smokelike curls issued out from all along the length of the dragon's back, and the gaping mouth slowly opened then closed while the head detached itself from the body. Then, the head floated off toward the west.

This seemed a bad omen. I returned home and said nothing that night of my concerns to my wife, but during the night I dreamed that from a great distance I heard the sound of a buzzing wheel. The sound moved swiftly toward me. The sound struck into my chest, and my whole body went numb. I realized that I had been hit with the rahula sickness — stroke or heart attack.

I prayed one-pointedly to my root-guru, Manjushri, until he appeared beside my head and subdued the buzzing sound. When the sound died down, I woke and felt some difficulty in breathing. I pinched myself hard but felt nothing. I awakened my wife, and she comforted me until I fell asleep again.

The next day we called in a local doctor who had a good reputation. He came right away. After examining my pulses, he told me it wasn't so bad, that the numbness would go away in a few days if I took his medicine.

He told me that rahula was indeed passing through the area, but since I had been alert and remembered my guru, rahula hadn't harmed me. Furthermore, he said, now that I knew him and would be in his care, the rahula sickness would not come to me in the future. I began to feel better. I think the reason I was saved was mainly because of my guru's kindness and blessing in response to my prayers.

Things were quiet in the region at this time. There had been some trouble here around the time of the Thirteenth Dalai Lama's death, but my stepfather and others of the Kashag had been able to control the rebellions. However, one knew that this was a touchy situation and that trouble might spring up again at any moment — the Khampas were, as I said, independent-minded and had a history of problems

90

with the Chinese starting decades before when the Chinese attempted to dominate the region. Through intervention from the central government in Lhasa on their behalf, independence was retained. But many Khampas were dissatisfied with the taxes levied them and with their treatment at the hands of Lhasa authorities.

Chamdo remained an important army post, but some officers there were known advocates of Khampa independence. This local sentiment for autonomy was a temptation to the Chinese, who maintained control through the years over part of the Kham region east of the Yangtse.

Sundays I invited friends and officials to my house. My wife made sure we always had fresh pastries and lots of chang to drink. When the guests arrived, they were served eight different dishes, and soup for lunch, with chang and tea. For dinner we often had several more dishes, including fresh or dried meat. Between meals we played mahjong and dominoes, and we gambled with dice. All day long we drank hot buttered tea — we had our pick of the best coming in from China. About four we were served Indian-style tea and cookies. After dinner the guests returned to their homes, and my wife and I, exhausted, went to bed, to arise quite early, for the next day was a busy one at my office.

POSSESSION

Each day, I went first thing in the morning to Minister Nangjungpa to inquire after his health. Then I walked to my office through the streets where vendors displayed their baskets of incense, flowers, and tea. The heady aromas merged with the stench of sheep being slaughtered down the road. Chamdo was important for the wool trade and also maintained a well-staffed salt office.

My duties as assistant to the governor were to oversee all important transactions and manage the various lay officials. I maintained an attentive ear for trouble spots and would investigate complaints directly if they were not soon resolved.

Each morning at my office, the first thing I did was look over the reports of the previous day's business. Then I divided the upcoming duties among staff members at a general meeting.

One day a report came in from a place two days' ride from Chamdo.

At the Sagang Gompa a few monks were again claiming they were possessed by the local spirit Shugden. They had badly disturbed the local farmers, threatening them and stealing possessions. On hearing this report, I felt certain this was due to Minister Nangjungpa's earlier neglect of the same problem in the Hlo Dzong.

One morning fifteen people — three monks who dressed up like the spirit Shugden, one lama, one prayer leader, and ten other monks — arrived at Chamdo Monastery. They broke down the doors of the Chamdo Labrang storehouse, tore out the bookkeeping documents and poured ink on them, smashed the furniture, threw glasses and cups out the window, and cut up the cushions and carpets with knives. Then they departed. The Minister Nangjungpa ordered the monks at Chamdo Labrang to arrest these men.

The next morning while I was eating lunch with my colleague, Kenchung Thubten, the monk-official in charge sent a messenger to tell me to come right away to the monastery. There in the courtyard I saw a monk tied to the pillar of the storehouse, twitching his hands and feet, rolling his eyes, pretending to be possessed.

When I went to the office upstairs to ask what had happened, the monk-official who had summoned me said that the monks had come again from Sagang and caused a disturbance, and that whatever they had broken should be replaced.

Then he arranged tea and did an offering on the altar to the deity Shugden. I had some peculiar feelings about that offering. However, I said, "Don't worry, we'll go to the main office and talk to the governor." On the way out we saw in the courtyard several of the mischievous monks being whipped, strung up by their feet, wailing loudly.

We told the Minister Nangjungpa what was being done, and he cried out, "I told you to arrest them, not to beat them!" He dismissed us both angrily.

Immediately afterward he called me back into his office and said that I should tell the Chamdo Labrang to transfer the prisoners to the dzong in town. I was to interrogate them thoroughly and give him a full report.

The fifteen were brought in and questioned. The four main instigators were given two hundred lashes each. Their normal human screams proved that their so-called possession was fake. Also, a local spirit will usually not stay too long in a human body. Never as long as three days. Many monasteries have an oracle who becomes possessed by a local spirit in order to execute certain rituals or provide prophesy in times of trouble, and these oracles are recognized by the state. But a spirit does not possess several people at once, and never had I heard of one inciting men to such destructive actions.

During the investigation, the men told me that at Nyingmapa Monastery on the way to Chamdo they had destroyed a thirty-foot statue of Padmasambhava and forced the local residents to give them food. Four of the main instigators were given additional lashes and were sent away to four different dzongs to be held until a trial could be arranged.

One of these men was Lama Lamrim, whom I had met in Lhasa years before. He was usually a very good monk, restrained and intelligent. He confessed that here in eastern Tibet he had become "like an old dog running with a pack of young hounds," and had gone against the principles of the Bodhidharma. He asked to be allowed to go to a hermitage retreat. Due to the sincerity of his remorse, we accommodated his wishes.

The ten young monks had been deceived by their leader, who initially told them only that there was a teaching in Chamdo, not that they would be doing destructive things.

The main instigator of the group, the prayer leader, was apparently highly-revered among the Sagang monks. He had become influential with a band of youths, who seemed devoted to him. He had convinced them along the way of the truth of his claims of possession and incited them to join in, saying that the spirit Shugden was angry with the Chamdo Labrang and wanted to demonstrate this anger. The monks had apparently gone beyond his expectations. Many truly believed themselves to be possessed by Shugden during their most violent moments.

The four instigators were sent to military prison, and the ten young monks were transferred back to the Chamdo Labrang and held there until a decision could be made. Eventually they were found innocent and allowed to return to their own monastery. However, the final decision from Lhasa was that the Sagang Gompa must stop worshipping the evil spirit Shugden. This was not easy to enforce.

One day in Chamdo a devout yogi with long hair named Tsentra Lama visited me and told me that he felt strongly that this devil worship was doing a lot of harm to the teachings of Buddha in the eastern provinces. According to prophesy, he said, a reincarnation of King Trisong Detsen will overcome the rebellion. He said, smiling at me, maybe this is that time.

Suddenly there was a rumor in Chamdo saying that eight hundred Chinese cavalry were on their way to Tibet.

When I asked the yogi about it, he said: "Last night I dreamed that on top of the roof of Derge Monastery was a man with a black hat holding a knife and waving a cloth around with his right hand while many crows perched on the ground nearby. This indicates no immediate danger for us."

Our problems with the Chinese had started, of course, many years before. Though the life of the Sixth Dalai Lama was unusually short and tragic, it is believed he was ultimately purified by his suffering. However, the Seventh Dalai Lama went unrecognized by a portion of the populace, which felt that he was not the true reincarnation, having been chosen before the Sixth Dalai Lama's death was certain.

At the time of the enthronement of the Seventh Dalai Lama in 1720, four high government ministers from Tsang province, and three high ministers from U province had severe political quarrels. Because of these hostilities between Tsang and U provinces, the country was in turmoil, and the Manchus were called in to help. They sent their ambassador, the Amban, along with five hundred soldiers, who they claimed were there to protect the Dalai Lama. These forces were tolerated, and the Chinese ambassador post was retained and increased by two. There were always at least two Ambans in charge of a garrison stationed in Tibet from 1728 until 1912, when the Chinese were driven out in the Battle of the Turquoise Bridge at which my father fought victoriously.

It has been said that Tibetans descended from the Mongol tribes — a warlike conquering people who had many gods and a religion of magic ritual called "Bon." These tribes swept down from the north. Thus, we are not related in terms of heredity or in political history directly to the Chinese, but we do share some aspects of religion with them since many Chinese are followers of the Buddha.

94

Legend describes a time when Tibet was not yet populated. An even-tempered, spiritually-minded monkey and a fierce lusty demoness alone inhabited a mountainside: she in her cave at the bottom of a gorge; he in a house built of rocks at the crest of a hill. The monkey was intelligent and also very compassionate. After repeated nights of laying awake listening to the lonely cries of the demoness far below, he descended the mountain to make his peace with her. They mated ecstatically, each achieving *nirvana*, whereupon the demoness conceived six children, who comprise the six original tribes of Tibet.

These six tribes gradually inhabited all the various regions of Tibet and lived without disagreement until the time of the Fifth Dalai Lama, when the warring Red Hats, an older sect, and the Yellow Hats, the reform movement, each called in Mongol troops to help defeat the other. The Yellow Hats were triumphant. The current Dalai Lama is a member of that sect. Many nations have attempted to gain control of our land, but none has succeeded, until the Chinese.

In 1933 or so, after the death of the Thirteenth Dalai Lama, Tibet allowed a condolence mission from China to enter, which again established an embassy in Lhasa. I believe this was the first stage in our downfall as a nation. We were never after able to relax our guard, fearing that the Chinese again planned to append our territory.

The Chinese soldiers rumored to be traveling toward us in Chamdo posed a potential threat even though it was known that sometimes these smaller bands were simply robbers. In this case, my yogi friend had been correct. The Chinese troops stopped at Yelung Monastery and surrounded it with their guns. The monks attempted to fight back with what little ammunition they could muster. One man and his son were the bravest Sakya monks. They fought all day until they ran out of ammunition. The soldiers broke through the doors, killed the father and his son, took all the horses and cows and some grain, and went on to attack Lhari Bonsang Village, which was then under control of the king of Derge, named Chagur Thubten.

The king of Derge happened to be near the village, hunting in the forest. The Chinese soldiers did not see him as they passed. They destroyed the houses of that village, robbed the villagers of their wealth and possessions, then finally went home. The lord returned to his devastated populace. He reminded them that this situation had occurred because of the previous time when local people stole three hundred mule-loads of Chinese merchandise being carried back to China by unprotected traders. He told them that the soldiers were taking their revenge.

THE RETURNING THREAT

In the water-sheep year, 1943, the Minister Nangjungpa made plans to depart. His three years of duty in Chamdo were over.

Meanwhile in Lhasa, the Chinese ambassador from Chiang Kai-shek's regime was staying in the house of Kyetupa. His bodyguard, also a Chinese, murdered a Tibetan soldier. When the Tibetans tried to capture the bodyguard, the ambassador blocked the door and wouldn't let them in. Some shots were fired from the embassy roof, but Tibetans did not fire back.

That night, the Dalai Lama, then just eight years old, called the minister of defense and told him to protect the Chinese ambassador. Without considering this information, the Chinese ambassador sent a telegram to Beijing, and Chiang Kai-shek responded by ordering ten thousand soldiers each from Szechuan, Yunnan, and Xizling provinces to be sent to Tibet. The generals of two of these provinces did not obey. But Mar Tushi from Xizling ordered four thousand cavalry soldiers to cross the border, making their way toward Lhasa.

Although our tour of duty in Chamdo was over, this incident prevented our returning home. The replacement was unable to depart from Lhasa because of the danger. However, the headstrong Nangjungpa left Chamdo without permission. He appointed a temporary replacement, Kanje Tenzin Chopel, who complained that taking care of the post alone would be impossible for him. He asked that I be appointed to stay with him. Although I had already received permission to return to Lhasa, I accepted the position because of the perilous border situation.

My colleagues and I asked for one hundred soldiers as bodyguards from the "Cha" Battalion, which we trusted. Military divisions were labeled by letters of our alphabet: this was the sixth. Though the government told us they would be sent soon, Nangjungpa intercepted them on his unorthodox return to Lhasa. Inexplicably, he gave them permission for an extended leave to their home in the north.

On the nineteenth day, Lieutenant Tsering, who had been stationed with his three hundred soldiers in Chamdo, announced that he was making plans to return to Lhasa with his garrison. Meanwhile, in Chamdo, a Chinese spy sent a message to China saying the minister and his soldiers had gone back to Lhasa leaving only sixty workers in Chamdo. His message was not intercepted, but a servant reported its contents to me.

A few days later my friend, the young Mr. Shakabpa, captain of the "Cha" Battalion, arrived with his men, saying that two thousand Chinese soldiers had descended upon Nangchen. Since a few of his soldiers had defected, having followed the absurd advice of Nangjungpa, he said we must draft villagers to act as our bodyguards and to protect the immediate borders and the bridge at Riwoche. Altogether we collected one hundred men.

In the village of Markham a captain named Charikpa also requested reinforcement from the central government because civil war had broken out in the Litang province of Tibet. It was a confusing situation.

The central government sent three hundred *yumak* — untrained militia drafted from villages. At Chamdo, Captain Rudok was ordered to protect the area with his soldiers. We were also able to bring back the division of Lieutenant Tsering, who had started for Lhasa two days previously. Then, another officer with one hundred soldiers from the "Ga" Battalion arrived, and we drafted one hundred thirty yumak from the village of Kanjo, ordering them to protect the borders. We also drafted three hundred more yumak from around Chamdo and trained them.

Altogether we had four hundred yumak from Chamdo, and eight hundred more from Trayap who were told to be prepared to fight. In the meantime we received news from a merchant of Kyiguto that two thousand Chinese soldiers on horseback, each with another horse at his side, had marched at dawn into the village of Kyiguto. That night the soldiers disappeared, and it was feared that they were heading for Chamdo.

At the proper time on the proper date, determined by mo augury, we held a ceremony at a field on the east side of town. Our soldiers shot at targets, and a government representative gave the winners katas and twenty-five *tsang* each. I was dismayed that most of the soldiers couldn't hit anywhere near the targets. Then there was a contest between the officers, who succeeded generally in hitting their targets, made of piled-up stones.

The government representative hit all five targets with five shots, and everyone cheered. After that, I used five bullets and also hit all five targets. Other staff members were able to do it as well, which greatly astonished the spectators. It looked to be an auspicious day, clouds forming in the east.

The next day we ordered the manager of the ammunition storehouse to clean and ready the arms. In the battles of Lujun, many years before, Tibetan soldiers had captured ammunition from the Chinese, which we now distributed to soldiers of the "Cha" and "Ga" battalions. The guns were powder and flint muskets, which the soldiers were at first afraid to use. After days of training, some learned to use them quite well and were able to hit the targets. Later, these same soldiers adapted easily to modern weapons, which were much quieter and easier to fire.

We drew up a map of the region on cloth, which we demonstrated to the entire group, explaining our position.

One day, coming in on foot from the direction of Nangchin, an old beggar arrived in Chamdo wearing new boots. He was immediately arrested by our men, who considered him a spy. They didn't find any secret letters on him, or any other incriminating evidence, except for the boots, which he said he had removed from a dead Chinese soldier he encountered near the road. The soldiers released him, believing his story. Even so, he turned out to be an assistant to a real Chinese spy. He was Tibetan but lived in the region controlled by China. His master had died along the way.

This beggar managed to attempt a message to the Chinese, saying to come quickly, for Tibetans were attempting to block all the borders. His message intercepted, we were given a few extra days to prepare.

About this time we learned that Reting Rinpoche had resigned in order to pursue a life of religious study and contemplation. This news came as a surprise. The wise old monk Taktra, whose name means "tiger," was asked to replace him. A respected man, but aging, Taktra had formerly been junior tutor to the Dalai Lama.

There were many stories about how the young regent, Reting Rinpoche, had forsaken his vows of celibacy with the beautiful wife of his young half-brother, and with another married woman named Namkye Tsedron. Everyone believed strongly in the regent's magical powers. It was widely known that he was a master of higher levels of Tantra.

The Thirteenth Dalai Lama had been greatly impressed with the young lama's powers when they first met at Reting Monastery many years before. Later, the regent correctly divined the birthplace of the Dalai Lama's new incarnation from his vision at Lake Lhamoi Latso. But many in Lhasa felt that Reting Rinpoche would be unable to properly transmit, one year hence, the "novice" vows to the young Dalai Lama, which included the vow of celibacy.

I heard from my sister that posters in Lhasa criticized the regent for being unfaithful to his own vows. Monks are encouraged to take vows of celibacy. But they must not take the vow unless they are certain they can keep it. Breaking a vow is considered to be worse than not taking the vow at all.

Soon, however, Mr. Shakabpa, captain of the "Cha" Battalion, sent a warning message to the Chinese soldiers, who were reported to be in Nangchen Village relaxing and tilling fields as if they planned to stay. Mr. Shakabpa asked us if we thought an offensive attack should be launched against them, but we said not to attack but instead come help us protect our region.

Two months later a new governor, Yuthok Dzasa, arrived in Chamdo. The substitute representative stayed in Chamdo and prepared, while I and other staff members went a few miles along the road to receive Yuthok Dzasa and report on our defense preparations. The new governor said that indeed the danger was very great in this area, but he was pleased at the good job we had done.

We learned from him that the trouble was the result of the central government's refusal to allow the Chinese to build a trade road through the region. The Parliament had allowed individual traders to pass through Tibet on pack animals, by first informing and gaining permission of the regional governors. But the Chinese had disobeyed in many instances and had continued with their preparations for building a road. Hence, the number of soldiers sent in scattered groups to

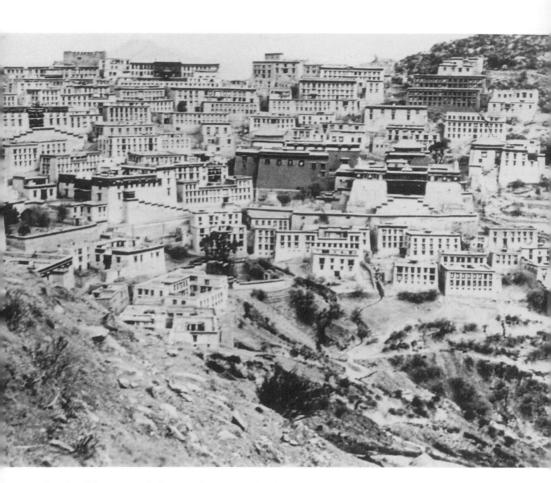

Ganden Monastery, before its destruction by Chinese soldiers. Photograph courtesy Office of Tibet.

Ganden Monastery, after its destruction subsequent to the 1959 Chinese takeover. Photograph courtesy Office of Tibet.

various villages west of the Yangtse River seemed to be in defiance of the truce signed by local officials with the Chinese.

The day after the arrival of the new governor we had a formal reception for him with a full military salute, after which we were served tea, rice, and fruit in a big reception tent set up on a field. We gave all our responsibilities to the new governor and his aides. The governor proceeded in a careful manner, asking a lot of questions, taking notes. Because I and my assistant were related to the new governor, we stayed on for one more month to help him. There was no further trouble with the Chinese soldiers during that time.

In the fifth month of the water-sheep year, 1943, I traveled with my wife, my son, and my daughter back to Lhasa. On the way we stopped for a few days with Mr. Shakabpa, now stationed at Riwoche Village. In the monastery I read from the *Tripitaka*, written in gold and bound Tibetan style with two planks of sandalwood each carved with one thousand tiny Buddhas. In one library books on one wall were piled to the ceiling so high they seemed ready to crash to the floor.

According to legend King Gesar had seen these walls of leaning books and had shot an arrow into the stack which held them up like a nail. It's true that though the books appear to be falling, they never do, and one can still see the arrow sticking in the wall.

The monastery also has some of the clothing that King Gesar wore, his walking stick which he used as a hobbyhorse, and a wool felt hat he wore as a child.

We proceeded on our travels. It was early summer, and the rivers were high; the waters tumbled over rocks along the path. Each day we witnessed violent lightening storms. These storms were brief, and when the sky again cleared aromatic herbs released their fragrances.

The captain of the "Cha" Battalion had sent some boatmen along with us for a time to make our return journey smooth. When we came to the banks of a boisterous stream, we boarded *coracle* boats. The boatmen took us across first, then our animals and belongings.

Coracle boats, which are large and ride high in the water, are strong and stable, constructed of willow branches covered by dried yak skins. My children played with the spotted frogs they discovered along the moss-covered banks. Then we descended into the valley, traveling north between massive peaks until we reached the divided waters, where we proceeded west toward U Tsang province and on into Lhasa.

We had crossed many passes and still had innumerable hills and valleys to traverse during the long passage home. In the evenings we camped outside the confines of a village; my wife would recite from texts she had memorized. We counted falling stars or traced the involutions of the smoke curls from our fire, hoping to detect our fate.

Finally, we saw the banks of the Lhasa river, the Kyichu, which becomes enormous in early fall. We had been traveling for months, and I had been gone from Lhasa three years. We were gladdened at the sight of the golden haze that characterizes the area. At Ganden Monastery we paused, and my cousin gave a small welcoming reception. We boarded the ferry, passing on into Lhasa.

THE CREAM-BEIGE HORSE

Many things had changed in Lhasa. A new minister had been appointed to replace my wife's father Trimon, who had retired. Surkhang was his name. His wife came from the Yuthok estate. He told me about his family, and we happily discovered we were related. At Trimon's house we met him with his wife and sons and my sister. My sister's sons came to visit me. They were almost grown now, and I met a few other new additions to the Shugu family. Those first few weeks in Lhasa were a busy time.

One day we had an interview with the new regent, Taktra, "the tiger." Later that day we met with the Parliament and the Cabinet members to give our report.

I was relieved to hear that the former governor, the headstrong Nangjungpa, had been discharged by Taktra from his previously-held Cabinet post because of his insistence on returning to Lhasa without government authorization.

The Fourteenth Dalai Lama invited me for an interview. He was then still a boy. I received the blessing of tea and rice, and he told me of his gifts for my family.

When the cream-beige horse was delivered, I was overcome with gratitude. I rode the cream-beige horse every day. My family had been admired for their breeding of such horses. We had given one years before to the Dalai Lama's stables.

This was an elegant ride, a very good horse, a horse with noble bearing.

Later, when the horse died, the Dalai Lama gave me another. This one was a specific type of horse I liked very much — an unusual horse, rare even in Tibet, called a *toma*. The color itself was called "toma," meaning a dark blue-grey. But the tips of each hair on its body and the tips of its mane were red. This was a favorite horse of mine. I took special care of it, checking often to make sure it was given proper treatment.

CHAPTER VIII

Calumny

During the next few months I met often with the young Dalai Lama at the Potala. I was impressed with the clarity of his gaze. Once each day I was required to visit the Potala on official business. Every other day there was a meeting of the Kashag at which the Dalai Lama made his appearance. I was again acting in the capacity of city manager, but the new trouble with the Chinese in the Kham region made my opinions and observations of use to the Cabinet. Often I saw the Dalai Lama passing in the hallways. He was kept busy. His brother helped him with his studies, and also helped him to relax, though occasionally they got into a bit of mischief.

Before my duty in Chamdo, I had managed the building of the Yupshi Sarpa, the new palace residence for the Dalai Lama's immediate family. The Dalai Lama's parents had owned a small farm in Amdo. They seemed to adapt well to their new surroundings. We had nearly finished construction by the time I left, and the new family had arrived and been installed. Still there were a few details to complete. Myself and two other lay officials were currently at work on it under the direction of the Dalai Lama's father. He was exacting about what he wanted done.

One day when I was at the Yupshi house, I passed an inner room which was a storehouse for the Dalai Lama's mother's jewels. A window had been broken; bits of glass littered the floor. Investigating further, I found that the Dalai Lama's mother reported to her husband that a thief had come into her room. Carefully, the contents of the room were examined, and it was found that no jewels had been taken. There were some muddy footprints on the floor with broken bits of glass. The Dalai Lama's mother expressed her fear that the thief might return.

At that moment, the young Dalai Lama came to comfort her, and he assured her that there was no thief. By his presence, she was greatly calmed. He said there must be another explanation for the broken glass and the footprints. He promised to look into it himself.

Later, we discovered that the Dalai Lama's brother had been playing, pretending to be a thief. And though he had moved the jewels around he had not taken anything. The Dalai Lama did not report on his brother but smoothed the matter over graciously.

By this time my wife and I had conceived six sons and two daughters. The first son had been born in Lhasa in springtime of the fire-tiger year, my wife's sister helping with the birth. . . . I remember waiting anxiously in the hall until her cries changed to exhausted sobs. . . . We stopped off at the Shugu estate, where my mother was staying, to proudly show her our new baby.

We retained, throughout many of the subsequent births and early upbringing, a good nurse whose name was Ani Lakpe. She did wonderfully in caring for our children. At first my wife tried feeding from the breast, but later boiled cow's milk was used. Each birth proved more difficult than the last. We spent a happy year at Gawo before I was transferred to the Hray District where I stayed four years, traveling back and forth between the estate and our family home Payling, where our second son was born, in the earth-dragon year.

My younger brother was then at Tashilhunpo Monastery. I spent a total of eight years in governorships of the Tsang province. My wife took care of our home; she was an expert at making carpets and weaving cloth. Mornings she spent in prayer. At night we sat around the fire in the kitchen talking over the day's work. Quite often we were alone, and happy to be so — completely at ease in each other's company. Friends occasionally stopped in. Summers were spend outdoors in the extensive park surrounding the house. My wife served chang on folding trays. There was much heavy betting. I was never very good at games of chance, often losing large sums. My wife never complained in those early years. She enjoyed seeing us happy: my butler and longtime friend, the village chief, joining in, and the district manager. . . .

During the years she was giving birth and caring for our children, my wife continued her spiritual practices. When our fourth son was born, I was assigned governorship of the Panam District. I left a representative there and spent most of my time in Lhasa, where I had been called to work. The fourth, fifth, and sixth sons spent their youths in monasteries. All three are recognized tulkus: Yeshe Thondup, now called Tsenshab Rinpoche, lives in Switzerland, a Sera lama. Sonam Gyatso, who changed his name to Hiroshi Sonami in exile in Japan, was Ngor Thartse Khen Rinpoche, and my sixth son, Kunga Gyurme, was Ngor Thartse Shabtrung until the Chinese takeover in 1959.

Just before the birth of our fifth son, my wife had a dream about a stranger: A monk from the eastern provinces of Tibet arrived late one night knocking loudly on the door. He departed after leaving an urgent message, "In this house is born a lama who must be well cared for." This dream occurred just before Sonam Gyatso was born.

I will tell you how it happened that the fourth son was recognized. Yeshe Thondup was born and raised in Lhasa. My wife began to worry at this time about our having too many sons to care for. She reminded me that we were not very wealthy as a family. What were all these boys to do when they became men? We had not enough property to give each of them. She decided that our fourth son must become a monk, so she gave him to her brother, who was a monk-official at the Potala.

Soon it became apparent that Yeshe Thondup was too much trouble to care for. "He's uncontrollable" monks at the Potala complained, begging us to take him back. Her brother, who had pledged to educate him, said that he, too, had given up. Dismayed, we brought our son home. He was six years old.

Then one day a young monk from Sera Monastery came to interview the oracle who lived just behind our family house. He and other representatives from Sera were searching the houses of Lhasa for the reincarnation of a revered lama. The oracle told the monk that the child had been "born under my territory." The monk asked him for details. As the oracle's shoulders shook and his head rolled back and forth, he said, "In back of me." The monk then wandered into my courtyard near the stables, looking confused.

I happened to be standing on the balcony when I saw this young monk enter. I thought immediately that he might be a horse blanket thief, for there was a lot of that type of thing going on in Lhasa at the time. When he saw me and spoke, he said he was looking for a child who was the reincarnation of a famous lama. I laughed.

"Do you have a child here?" he asked.

I laughed again, refusing to answer. This incomplete response left a suspicion in his mind. He went directly to the Drekhang family and told them what the oracle had said. He also told them of my behavior, saying that he feared I was hiding something.

The Drekhang family were relatives of my wife's, and this monk knew that. Immediately they sent their people to my house, saying, "You have a son here, and we need to discuss this with you."

I was being careful. I answered, "You know my son is here. However, I know nothing about his being a reincarnated lama."

Another lama was then asked to do a divination, and he told the group that the child in my house was indeed the reincarnated lama they were seeking. Two men came from the Drekhang family and asked me for the child. Yeshe Thondup was brought out. He had only been home with us a few days when this occurred. He was presented to the head of the Drekhang family. The dimple in the center of my son's forehead was matched to a description of the former lama, and because of other signs as well, they became certain this was the true reincarnation. Two of the minister's sisters were Sera nuns, and they, too, were delighted that the reincarnation of their revered lama had been found in their household. It was decided that an official recognition ceremony should take place.

The proper date was set. The child was placed upon the throne during the official celebration, which occurred at my house. Then my son went to live at Sera Monastery. We all traveled together, friends and relatives, delivering him to his new home for a full tea ceremony with many donations to the monastery. There was no further trouble with him as there had been at the Potala. My son was officially recognized as Yerba Tsenshab's reincarnation.

Our fifth son, Sonam Gyatso, was at that time two years old and staying with my mother and his uncle at the Shugu estate. Around that time Kunga Gyurme was being carried in his mother's womb. His birth occurred in Lhasa. A year later our daughter was born, and we all went to Black Horse Village for a while.

Sonam Gyatso was recognized a tulku when a very small child. Because he was so young, my brother kept him at Black Horse for a few years. When four years old, Sonam Gyatso met the dogs that had belonged to the former abbot at Ngor. He calmed their barking by saying, "Don't you know me, don't you know me?!" This was taken as a sign.

When the abbot was ill, my father went to Ngor and asked his guru to please live a long life. The abbot said that he might not be able to live much longer. Then he made a little joke, "If I came to your home, would you be able to take care of me?" My father replied, "Of course, if you come to our house by all means we will take care of you. No doubt about it!" At the same time one of the monks, a close friend of the abbot, had a dream and in this dream the abbot was riding horseback wearing white clothes and saying that people hadn't treated him well where he was so he wanted to go back to his own house. Sonam Gyatso was born at Black Horse near the abbot's home.

My first born had already become a monk at Ngor. Later, our third and fifth and sixth sons, too, were given to the monastery. When our first daughter was born, we were very happy. The next child was also a girl, but she survived less than six months. She was the last child born to us.

My daughter was a very religious person, and she later became a nun. She was of good character like her mother. The two were very close even when she was a small child. Later on, she was a great help to her mother during the early years of my imprisonment.

MISTRESS

A problem emerged between my father-in-law the retired Trimon and his son and the son's wife, who was my sister. The Nubling estate, where the son's family lived — my son Kunga Gyurme with them — had been given by Trimon to the Kundaling Monastery. Friends of the family discussed this generous gift, and with the manager of the monastery, an agreement was reached to leave the estate in the family's possession while Trimon was still alive — this only if his son agreed to pay the monastery a sum of five hundred tsangs.

The son became angry and confused. Thinking it bad to have ill feelings between father and son, I spoke directly to the monastery Labrang manager and suggested to them that they shouldn't be asking so much. Although I had gotten along well with this manager before, now he disagreed with me and repeated that the monastery would give back the estate, for the duration of the parents' lives, only if the five hundred tsangs were paid. Later, he spoke privately to my sister's sons, and they agreed to pay the money. But after a few days of discussion and consideration, they changed their minds. Trimon's son told the Labrang that the circumstances were unresolvable, and it was impossible for them to pay.

There were reports of Trimon's strange behavior. This excessive gift was one of the symptoms cited. Events conspired against him. There had been a time when his life was in danger from threat of assassination, events stemming from the time of the death of the Thirteenth Dalai Lama. Perhaps he was unbalanced, perhaps he was too strong-minded. There were those who said he had accepted an enormous bribe. Others reported that he had given all his family's wealth to various monasteries because he himself wanted to be freed of past associations. He had been seen chanting in the streets in the white robes of an ascetic.

I was not in direct contact with him at the time. These rumors circulated during my duty in the far eastern provinces. My sister hinted at the difficulties in her letters.

Trimon's son reported his problem to the government court, and the government appointed Mr. Chopel Thubten and a treasurer minister Lhalu to be in charge of the case. Mr. Chopel Thubten happened to be a special friend of the Labrang manager, and consequently the decision was made in favor of the Labrang.

For Trimon's family, everything seemed lost. Even the son's private house in Lhasa — which was considered part of the estate — was to be confiscated. The Trimon family had to move out immediately and begin renting a smaller place.

Formerly, Trimon's wife had asked that the house in Lhasa be given to the son and his wife, my sister. However, as it was now deemed to be property of the monastery, they had no choice but to leave. The owner of the house was the governor of Shigatse, and even he had no power against the injunction. There was nothing to be done. Later, I built a house for them.

About this time I was living alone in Lhasa; my wife was at the Shugu estate with my brother and our children. Our baby daughter had died. I was involved with another lady, who helped me in many ways. I had known her for a long time, and even later in 1959 when I went to prison she was occasionally able to visit, bringing me things I might need.

The lady I was involved with was a good friend to me. I never felt serious about her. I know she was a source of discomfort for my wife, as

110

indicated by the dream my wife had had many years before. It was clear when they met that my wife had actually dreamed of that lady.

My mistress had formerly been the girlfriend of my cook. Later on, after I left off with her, she and the cook married. She was an ordinary average lady, attractive, considerate, a young woman of good character.

In 1979, after my release from prison, I took a walk one day with the idea of finding my former cook. At the gate to that house I saw a lady standing. As I neared her I recognized the face of my former mistress. We were happy to see each other again. Many years had passed. We went inside to look for her husband, Mr. Nangang. This used to be my sister's house. The house had been divided up, and the cook was now living in one section. I had built a house for him myself in 1956, a nice large place at the back of the main house. That house was converted by the Chinese into an X-ray clinic.

My mistress visited me in prison only at first. She came two or three times, bringing baskets of food. It had been seventeen years since I'd seen her. Nangang, who had been our family cook, had undergone a change in his political ideology, but he was still quite respectful. Our friendship seemed undiminished. My former mistress was also affectionate towards me, though her job at that time as doorkeeper did not allow her to be separated long from her post. The three of us talked and drank tea together briefly.

My former cook was then in charge of the vegetable garden. He, too, was soon required to return to his duties. His garden was the property of the clinic commune, providing fresh food for doctors and the others who worked there.

At one time that whole area had been a suburb of Lhasa with fine large homes. I lived in the center of the city but had often visited friends and family in that suburb. I had designed and managed the building of several large dwellings in the area.

When I built the house for my sister, late in the 1950s, my wife was also staying there with her.

JOURNEY TO INDIA

While I was living in Lhasa, the Fourteenth Dalai Lama's eldest brother, Tulku Thubten Jigme Norbu, graduated from Drepung Monastery. As was traditional, he and the other successful candidates were required to provide ceremonial expenditures. Since he was the Dalai Lama's brother, all the expenses were covered by the Tibetan government.

Mr. Simsur Targyen and I were appointed managers of these expenditures. We set up tents in Gyandraling Park and invited all the lamas, managers, dignitaries from Drepung, and also the geshes who had been Thubten Norbu's classmates. We celebrated extensively with the Dalai Lama's parents and his younger brother Ngari Tulku, as well as with the Cabinet members and other important people.

The following winter, Thubten Norbu became a geshe himself and had a graduation ceremony. Mr. Losang Sangye and I were appointed managers of the celebration. We spent several days at the "many doors" college of Drepung serving tea, rice pudding with fruit, and freshly baked honey sweets to the more than four thousand monks of the college. Each monk was also given one silver coin.

Having fulfilled all our duties, we returned to Lhasa, where we reported on expenses and returned the leftover money and supplies to the government. We had to calculate down to the last detail every intricacy of the overall budget. The day we were to begin this arduous task my colleague told me he felt ill. He asked me to complete the work myself. On my way to work the next day, I got a message that he had died during the night.

I went immediately to his house. His cousin, a young official, gave me the details. My colleague had complained that his stomach felt bad after returning from Drepung. He went to see the Dalai Lama's private doctor, who took his pulses and said it was indigestion. The doctor gave him some medicine, but the medicine seemed only to make him worse. The pain in his stomach increased, and he died. Unfortunately, said the cousin, he hadn't been able to properly explain his illness to the doctor. The illness must have been incurable, the karmic currents being too strong.

Afterwards, the cousin and I finished the budget reports.

At about the same time, we learned of the sudden death of the Dalai Lama's father, which saddened us. Soon, a colleague and I were appointed to negotiate the exchange of properties at the Kundaling Labrang. This took two months.

In the wood-bird year, 1945, Tsipon Shakabpa, his brothers and their sons and daughters, and a few relatives and friends asked if I would like to join them on a pilgrimage to Nepal and India. I agreed. I took leave for two months from work and left my young daughter at my sister's family house.

We traveled in caravan to the border town of Phari, which I had been to twice before. This time the town welcomed us officially, and we spent a few days in celebration with the Shakabpa family and a brother, Trekhang Kenchung, who lived there on a large estate. We crossed the Chumbi Valley on horseback with our mules and servants. Then we crested the high pass, which even at the height of summer is swept by sudden snows.

Slowly we descended the trail through the Himalayas, observing intermittent avalanches from the frozen cliffs. Soon the path was pocketed with clouds of vapor. We passed through forests of fern and coral-colored rhododendron. I had never seen such rich vegetation. My head began to feel thick. Brightly colored orchids and lilies crowded the path, their pungent scents an intoxication. When we paused for a rest, we ate the wild strawberries. Leeches dropped from the trees onto our skin. We removed them with powdered tobacco or ashes.

This was the first time I had traveled outside Tibet.

In Sikkim the orange trees were full in blossom. At the capital, Gangtok, we were visited by representatives of the British government, who offered us use of their motorcars and drivers in order that we might reach Kalimpong. This was a surprise and a pleasure. We left our animals in the care of a livery and descended the final slope to arrive on the plains at Calcutta after crossing the sluggish Ganges. I saw many people standing in the river, praying or bathing in their clothes.

At Calcutta we saw many sights and strange ways of life. We visited the amazing Howrah Bridge. From there we traveled to Bodhgaya. We saw Nagarjuna's cave, we saw the Siwaltsal cemetery, Kushi Nagar, where Buddha meditated under the Bodhi tree, Benares, Vulture Peak, and Lumbini — birthplace of the Buddha. Many sacred sites. I was awed by the beauty of this land and its people, so densely populated that you were forever brushing against someone. At Buddha's birthplace I wished that my wife were with me, knowing what such a visit would mean to her.

We traveled to Nepal and paid homage to Bodhinath and Swayambonath. Then we boarded an airplane, which rose into the sky with such a shudder I feared for our lives. Out the window for a moment I glimpsed

Interpreter, Ponda Yarphel, Shakabpa, Shuguba, in Calcutta, India, 1945.

the fanning red-brown arms of the Ganges — looking like a Vajrayogini. Seeing it from this height, I knew it was indeed a sacred river.

Some of the relatives went back to the Shakabpa house in Kalimpong, but five of us — Tsipon Shakabpa's two brothers, Ponda Yarphel, a Chinese friend, and I — got permits from the British to view military bases. We also visited factories, gold and silver mines, and underground military fortifications. We visited New Delhi, the Taj Mahal, and crossed the continent by train to visit Bombay at the shores of the Arabian Sea, before arriving at Kalimpong.

We visited towns and villages whose names I cannot recall, journeying by airplane, car, and train. We saw many great sights of the world, more than I am capable of describing.

The struggle for independence was gaining force. When we traveled by car, police stopped us to investigate our papers. People had broken the windows of imperialist British shops and smashed British automobiles.

We heard Pandit Nehru speak before thousands, saying there is no need for violence. Independence must be gained through peaceful negotiations. He said that the British will doubtlessly give freedom to peaceful people, that the demonstrations must continue but they must remain nonviolent.

The Indian people listened respectfully and quietly, and we knew that he was a powerful guru. The riots abated.

From Bombay we again went to Calcutta and returned to Kalimpong. Our family business manager also met me there, saying he needed some money to buy things for my brother. My money was all spent, but through Mr. Shakabpa I borrowed some from Mr. Ponda Yarphel. I told our family business manager of the two horses I had left in Phari, and that he might wish to make use of them on his return.

Eventually we made our way back up the path onto the high plateau of Tibet. At Phari, we stopped to make our plans. I was overwhelmed by the immensity and color of the sky, which I had nearly forgotten in those months spent in the lowlands.

I parted with the others to visit my mother, my brother, and my wife at the Shugu estate. They nearly exhausted me with questions. Soon, however, a message arrived from Trimon's son in Lhasa that I had been appointed to replace the *uda*, or military commander, who had retired. I must return immediately, the message said. But since I knew officially I still had a few days of vacation left, I stopped off to see my two lama sons at Ngor, then stayed for a day at my younger sister's house in Shigatse. I visited the Tashilhunpo Monastery before returning to Lhasa.

At Lhasa I was instructed to meet that very day with the Dalai Lama and the Cabinet. The year was 1946, the fire-dog year.

A SECRET EXPEDITION

In my position as uda, I was responsible for the entire Lhasa region. I worked at the Trapchi Magar, which was the post for the Second Battalion, "Kha." After acknowledging my acceptance, I ordered my military costumes made.

On the morning of the day of my inauguration, we visited the Makchikhang military office in the basement of the Potala. We paid homage to the local warlike deities, black and red Dharmapalas. We gave our offerings at ritual ceremonies, then joined the other officers for a general meeting in the military compound. There we met the other captains: the *rugya*, a person who leads the line of marching soldiers, and the *rupon* and *gyapon*, each the head of one hundred soldiers. We exchanged scarves with all of them.

We returned to the upper chambers to meet with the Dalai Lama. Since I was now part of the official staff, we entered the Potala by the main entrance, called the "auspicious road," climbing up long stairways through the halls into the main reception area, where the Dalai Lama was seated in anticipation of our visit.

We each did three prostrations to His Holiness and made body-speech-mind offerings. Downstairs, we also made offerings and gave scarves to Regent Taktra. We offered scarves to the Cabinet, seated ourselves according to rank, and drank tea from silver pots.

The next day my relatives and friends and a few military officials came to congratulate me. We entertained them with a lavish party. I wore my new British-style uniform, and one thousand soldiers lined up to salute me. A military reception was given with full regalia and another party hosted that night. My colleague Depon Surkhang was in attendance, and together we enjoyed tea and chang.

On the first day of the seventh month, there is usually a four-day ceremony called the Shodun at the Norbulinga. During the four days, operas and historical dramas from various traditions are performed, such as Norsang, Nagsa, and Timi Kunden. The morning of the first day the general stands on the platform commanding in a loud clear voice a military parade and salute. All the captains pull out their knives and place them on the ground. The military bands play their British-made horns and bagpipes. In the fire-dog year, I was in charge of this event, including the military salute in which munitions were fired into the air. I was greeted by the Dalai Lama's family in their special tent, and they requested that we share their tea, yogurt, rice, and tsampa delivered from the upper kitchen that prepares the Dalai Lama's own meals. It was a very good year for me, full of leisure.

In the fire-pig year, one of Trimon's sons lost his wife and soon after married the daughter of Rumpa. The wedding ceremony was at Simbu, the house of Tsipon Shakabpa. At eleven, the night of the wedding, January 26, 1947, Minister Surkhang Wangchen, Minister Lhalu Tsewang Dorje, a military general, and Mr. Lose Tundrup Shakabpa requested that I come immediately to the Trapchi military post.

I did so and found that L. T. Shakabpa was already there, preparing to depart. He told me to gather bedding, horses, and provisions for a journey. I sent a servant to get my things from Simbu House, where I had been staying. They told me I needed to engage two hundred cavalry, but they didn't tell me where to go or the purpose of the expedition.

We left the post that night, traveling through the Pembogurla mountain pass just before dawn. On the way, in a narrow passage called Lingpu Dzongsar, someone shot a gun at us and shouted.

"Don't move anywhere!"

Hearing that threat, my soldiers readied their guns, and I dismounted. The soldiers and horses stayed behind in the canyon while I and my aide walked on ahead to see what the trouble was.

The man who had shot at us turned out to be a friend. As soon as he saw me he exclaimed, "Oh, you are so lucky we didn't shoot each other!"

He explained that the ministers had told him they would come back later, and until they did no one should be allowed to pass. The ministers didn't tell him clearly when we would be coming through, which is why his men shot at us.

We climbed up the pass to the top of the mountain, where Minister Surkhang brought out some whiskey, which we drank. Then Mr. Surkhang told me, "I hope Mr. Shakabpa told you that the purpose of

Shuguba's horse, "Zamgyung," given to his son, Ngor Thartse Khen Rinpoche. With Tsering, the cook, at Thartse Labrang, Ngor Monastery, 1956.

this journey is to arrest the ex-regent, Reting Rinpoche, and escort him back to Lhasa."

It was a moonless night. I couldn't see the expression on his face. I was surprised by what he said and told him so. I was aware, however, of the difficulties that had befallen the ex-regent and his chosen replacement Taktra. Earlier an agreement had been reached that Regent Taktra would relinquish the regency upon Reting Rinpoche's request, but Taktra had not done so. There had been several incidents, including an exploding letter bomb — incidents that might be interpreted as a threat to Regent Taktra's safety.

We crossed the mountain pass and entered the Langtang Valley as the sun rose behind the eastern range. We stopped at Lhundrup Dzong for lunch. Minister Surkhang and Lhalu were talking privately, and I heard Lhalu say, as if in argument, "If someone raises his hand toward us, then I will raise my hand toward them!"

Khemsu and Mr. Shakabpa said nothing. I thought about the ex-regent, Reting Rinpoche. . . .

He was born at Dakbo to an impoverished family. At the birth of this child many good omens appeared. Once when he was barely three his mother went outside to collect firewood, and she asked him to look after the cooking pot. She was making soup. The pot began to boil over, and he didn't know what to do. He took a string and tied the iron pot closed at the top. This was a great miracle, and the pot he thusly altered can still be seen.

Soon, investigators came to find out whether or not he was the tulku. Just before they arrived the young boy had driven a wooden peg into solid rock, saying, "This is where my horse is to be tied." He said he was expecting a caravan of guests to arrive and "take him home." It was well known that the Thirteenth Dalai Lama took keen interest in him when he visited Reting Monastery in 1933. The Dalai Lama gave him his divination dice, a most auspicious gift.

With the Thirteenth Dalai Lama's sudden death, the young regent stepped in to lead the search party for the reincarnation. He and a large retinue, including my father-in-law Trimon and Tsipon Shakabpa, made the long journey to Lake Lhamoi Latso in southern Tibet. From the pass they looked down upon the turquoise jewel. Each man in the party stood apart at the lake's edge and began to meditate. Hours passed in which winds, sleet, and penetrating sun rays battered them, but still nothing was seen by any of the men.

The regent returned again and again, accompanied by a few private attendants. Crouching among the rocks he stared for hours into the changing waters of the lake when suddenly a clear vision was presented — the letters "A," "ka," and "ma," which vanished again. Then, he beheld a vision of a three-storied temple with a gilded roof and walls of greenish blue tile. Behind it, a narrow white path led to the foot of a small mountain, where sat a single-storied house with unusual gutter pipes. He wrote down these appearances and preserved them under seal. Later, these details proved extremely useful in determining the location of the home of the Fourteenth Dalai Lama.

The regent was active and well liked. He ordained the Dalai Lama in front of the image of Sakyamuni in Jokhang Temple. It was he who had ceremoniously shaved the young Dalai Lama's head. If anything happened to him at this time it would be very bad:

> *The life span of a bad name will be left*
> *In the earth longer than the life itself.*

The regent had his detractors — those who complained he had broken his vows of celibacy, those who said he indulged in the luxury of exquisite furnishings not befitting a great incarnate lama. There were some who complained that he should not have gone into retreat when he did, leaving the government in the hands of such an old man, such a strong-willed man, as "the tiger." In Lhasa, songs about the regent's rapacity circulated, and wall posters of verse were displayed in the streets:

> *The wolf living between the hills and the valley has a full stomach,*
> *The fox living between two rivers has his thirst quenched,*
> *But the regent who has eaten the mountain is not full*
> *Even if he drink the ocean his thirst is not quenched.*

In spite of his critics, the populace and most of the government officials were devoted to him. I myself felt that he was a powerful protector for the young Dalai Lama, and realized that we must plan carefully not to get into a disastrous situation. We must act wisely to bring him quietly back to Lhasa. Reting Rinpoche was staying at his monastery, three or four days' ride from Lhasa.

I suggested to the general that one of his lieutenants, a man called Gesang, should be transferred elsewhere. As a known intimate of Reting Rinpoche, he might betray the secrecy of our project. We sent him north with twenty-five soldiers to be stationed until further orders.

We crossed the Chakla mountain pass, moving with stealth in the late hours of evening. We arrived at Taklung Monastery and were well cared for, as it was Regent Taktra's monastery. When Reting Rinpoche gave his post to Taktra early in 1941, he expected to get it back within five years. But during the interval, the warmth and admiration had cooled between the two men, and suspicions arose among their followers that each was trying to dispose of the other. These latest events had greatly emboldened "the tiger," who commanded our mission.

On the twenty-seventh of the month, around midnight, we left Taklung Labrang and instead of crossing the river by the Iron Bridge at Pondo Village, we took precautions and crossed at another place downstream. Men with hide coracles waited for us there. With their help we quietly crossed the river and arrived at Reting Monastery just before dawn. Pausing in the forests outside the gates to the monastery, we observed three horsemen approaching. Our soldiers tried to arrest them, but they escaped. We exchanged fire, but the men got away. The three horsemen were, we found out later, representatives from Lhasa loyal to Reting. They had been sent to warn him that his ministers were already under arrest in Lhasa.

Two ministers and the general with a few others, accompanied by one hundred horsemen, proceeded directly to Reting Rinpoche's recreation house, while I and Mr. Shakabpa with sixty soldiers went into the monastery itself. We were soon redirected to the recreation park.

When we arrived, we saw our two ministers and the general sitting with Reting Rinpoche. The atmosphere was tense. Minister Surkhang indicated for me to do three prostrations to Reting Rinpoche, which I did, and received his blessings. He was courteous and unusually solemn.

The two ministers disclosed the nature of their mission. Reting appeared to be considering his options. When the ministers and the general went downstairs, Mr. Shakabpa and myself stayed before Reting Rinpoche. I begged him to come to Lhasa peaceably. I said that we wished him no harm. As he slowly nodded his head, I felt the weight of his doom.

Though well in his forties by now, he had remained boyish and youthful. I recalled having watched the grinning young monk kicking a soccer ball around his yard. . . .

While we were thus engaged in carefully guarding the now placid Reting, his young attendants and bodyguards began acting suspiciously. With agitated glances and spurious movements, they flitted about the room. We told them to stand still. Later we found a closet full of guns and realized they had been trying to reach their weapons.

I went downstairs to tell the two ministers and the general what was going on. Minister Surkhang requested that the young attendants come downstairs. He asked if they had any weapons. One immediately drew a gun from under his robe. I grabbed his wrist and wrested it from his hand, preventing him from shooting.

At the same time, five of our soldiers captured and searched the body-guards, confiscated their guns, and tied them to a tree in the courtyard. The elder attendants of Reting Rinpoche, whom we knew quite well, were extremely depressed, saying that they hadn't yet given Rinpoche his breakfast. They begged us to allow them to bring him some tea. We agreed, but Reting Rinpoche was by that time too frightened to drink.

We decided then to leave with him right away. He asked if he might take his younger assistants and his head cook along. We acquiesced. They were first carefully searched and found to be unarmed.

We packed up Reting's clothes. Minister Surkhang, General Khesu, and Mr. Shakabpa with one hundred cavalry left the monastery with Reting Rinpoche and his assistants. They went directly to Taklung Monastery to await our arrival. Minister Lhalu and I stayed on at Reting Labrang to seal off the recreation house.

Reting Rinpoche had been successful in his import/export business, and his private quarters were full of objects from all over the world. Though his involvement in worldly affairs brought wealth and notoriety to the monastery, it served also to intensify a general dissatisfaction with his purposes. It was felt that as a high lama he should not be so attached to material wealth. His palace was full of unusual items like kites and drapery and Western furnishings. We found an American pistol under his bed, and a closet full of swords, guns, and other devices.

We stayed overnight. The next morning we proceeded to Taklung Monastery to join the others, having left a low-ranking officer with twenty-five soldiers to protect the sealed-off recreation house. On the morning of the twenty-ninth we left Taklung Monastery in a single group with Reting Rinpoche in our charge; crossing the Chakla pass and the Iron Bridge, we stayed overnight at Tse Dzong. On the morning of the thirtieth we crossed the Gola pass, lunching at Lingbu Dzong. There Reting Rinpoche changed into his formal attire. We passed nearby Trapchitang Temple behind the Potala, circling the Potala clockwise and entering at the main gate. Reting Rinpoche had barely said a word.

We had passed some sand dunes from which Sera monks of the Che College fired at us, hurting no one. We made a place by the main entrance of the Potala, in the Sharchinchok, for Reting Rinpoche to rest. All the Tsedron monk-officials were responsible for guarding him. As soon as we arrived, the upper kitchen sent tea and food, and Reting Rinpoche was able to drink two cups. A few of us proceeded to the Parliament, where they told us to go home and rest.

I was to report the next day to the Trapchi army post. I returned home to my wife and my younger brother. They questioned me, but I was unable to answer due to the extreme secrecy of our mission.

The next morning at the Trapchi army post I met with several high officials, who had been appointed to investigate the revolt of the Sera monks.

A few days later, monks from the Che College at Sera set up some old captured cannons and fired them at the Lhasa army post. At that time, the abbot at Ganden, his treasurer, and a few faithful merchants were in the midst of negotiations that had lasted several days, attempting to reach an accord between the government and Sera, which had long been in disagreement. The Che College at Sera was strongly allied with Reting Rinpoche. The government decided that if the monks would return all their arms, they would be paid for them and none of the rebels would be arrested. Pu Lama, the rebel leader, refused, saying that no compromise on that issue would be accepted.

At dawn on the eighth, the Lhasa army post sent troops from the "Kha" Battalion, stationing them east of Sera. A few hundred troops were sent to the western part of the mountain. The two groups then attacked the monastery simultaneously from two sides. Nonetheless, one hundred monks escaped.

We shot at them from the Trapchi post, between Sera and the Potala. We killed eighty monks.

Soon after, accompanied by my lieutenant and several foot soldiers, I approached Sera from the east. Shots were fired, and one of our soldiers was killed. We entered the monastery from the north side of the main congregation hall. From the roof of this hall we could see the monks who had been shooting at us. We fired at them and drove them away. From the north side of the area, the "Kha" Battalion, led by a lieutenant from Shigatse, came and seized the monastery. I saw many monks wounded or killed, lying here and there on the ground.

Four days were spent investigating and collecting their ammunition, which was considerable. The rebel leader Pu Lama and Tzen Nya Tulku, a very high lama, were arrested and imprisoned in the Trapchi military post.

On the twelfth day we returned to our post. I was summoned to the Parliament and informed that the twenty-five soldiers we had left at Reting Monastery to guard the place had been killed by the monks. The government could no longer tolerate this rebelliousness and demanded that the monks loyal to Reting be entirely defeated.

To capture the armed rebels, a plan was devised whereby two army units would approach from two sides. Mr. Shakabpa (Tsipon Shakabpa's younger brother) and General Khesu were to take the main road leading one hundred soldiers from "Cha" and five hundred from "Ja" — the Sixth and Seventh battalions, while I was to direct a cavalry unit of two hundred men through the Drigung Valley to come upon Reting Monastery from above.

My staff included Sholkhang Se, a lay official, and Lobsang Lhalung-pa, a monk-official of the Grand Secretariat of the Dalai Lama at the Potala Palace, the Tsi-Yigtsang. Lhalungpa was in charge of provisions for the horses, which had been borrowed from the Dalai Lama's stables.

At that time my younger brother asked to join me, and I agreed. After the first week, however, he returned, out of concern for his duties as householder.

On the morning of the thirteenth, I met my colleague, Captain Lhathop, and we made ready to depart. With 140 cavalry, we marched around Lhasa from the right side of the temple, crossed the bridge, and spent that night at Tomdo. On the fourteenth day we stayed at Takse, on the fifteenth at Pagmosho, and on the sixteenth at Tangya. By the seventeenth we had arrived at Digung. We had cannons with us, carried on mule back, and seventy trained cannon operators.

Reting Monastery Labrang, c. 1945.

We crossed the Pula pass above Reting and arrived late the next evening at Tsipka. The villagers were hiding in the forest in fear of our arrival. The food in their houses was available for our soldiers to eat.

I sent ten men to search out the people hiding in the forest, some of whom were known to be close friends of Reting Rinpoche. Tsering and his attendants, who had escaped from the monastery, were caught by my soldiers. I told an older man I had known before, named Tisur Sopon, that if he would tell the truth, I would save his life. At first he was so afraid he couldn't talk. I sent him to relax and have tea with my servants. Soon he was able to speak, and told me the following:

"Twenty attendants of Reting Rinpoche and seventy of the monks and templekeepers — around one hundred people altogether — were the ones responsible for killing your twenty-five security guards. They were attacked at night, and each one was shot several times until it was certain no one was left alive. I asked them not to kill Sergeant Nangyela, but someone shot him anyway. During the fight, one of your guards was badly injured, but he continued to kill many people even though his arm was nearly severed. Toward the end he held five bullets in his mouth, and he killed five people, one by one, with those bullets. No one dared come near him. We spent a half day setting up fires to burn down the place where he was. Just before this soldier died, he killed one of the main rebels, a very brave man, who watched as his own brains were splattered all over the wall."

Stealing into the recreation house at Reting Monastery, we found more than forty rifles. At the treasury we discovered fifty new British rifles and one hundred boxes containing one thousand bullets each.

We also found the handguns of the sergeant and our guards who had been killed. Tisur Sopon, the elderly man I'd known before, had been working as the horse trainer to Reting Rinpoche. He was able to help us find the weapons and ammunition we were searching for. We distributed the bullets to our soldiers.

Fifty soldiers were stationed at the narrow roads and by the river. Two hundred village men and women were conscripted to act as porters and guards. Altogether nearly four hundred people guarded the road and the river. That very night rebels and soldiers clashed on the southern road.

Before dawn on the nineteenth, the two generals sent a horseman with a letter saying that Reting Rinpoche was backed by two thousand

Chinese soldiers, who were closing in on us. Since it would be impossible for us to defend the monastery with a few hundred soldiers against so large a force, they suggested that it would be better strategically for me to join my forces with those of General Kheshu and Mr. Shakabpa.

I had a very strong suspicion that the two thousand Chinese soldiers were only a rumor. In consideration of this, I decided that if we had to fight, it would still be better to attack the monastery from two sides as originally planned. I ordered my troops to stay put.

On the twentieth day, the fighting continued in two different places. I sent my messenger out to obtain information. He traveled down the river to the place where the generals were staying at the foot of the mountain. I sent fifty soldiers and Lieutenant Namgye to take the mountain behind the monastery. At the eastern narrow road there was a lot of fighting. The rebels fired heavily; it was difficult to cross the pass. I sent one officer and three machine-gunners to fire back at them through the woods. A few managed to escape.

At the same time Lieutenant Namgye announced his arrival behind the mountain with a trumpet call. I was hiding in a ravine with mules and troops. One lieutenant tried to show off by standing up on a rock, but I made him get down. Just then a bullet flew by, missing him by an inch. Lieutenant Namgye reached the summit as the sound of rebel fire subsided.

We proceeded toward a huge plateau and stationed ourselves at a small town, sending messengers back to the generals to report that the threat of the two thousand Chinese soldiers was indeed only a rumor. We knew exactly how many rebels we had to fight. A few shots were still ringing from the bushes, but we sustained no casualties. I sent two people to guard Reting Rinpoche's possessions in his recreation house, but soldiers who were already there would not allow them to enter. I myself then crossed the river to go to the monastery. Before we reached the other side, rebels began firing at us through the bushes. We hid behind an enormous boulder in the middle of the river submerged up to our noses until well after sunset.

We arrived at Reting Monastery under cover of darkness. The soldiers who were there informed us that they intended to set fire to the place. I told them, "No! One must never burn a monastery." They asked if they could at least burn one old tree, and I said they could if it wasn't too close to the monastery. Having ordered the soldiers to stay alert, I crossed back to the other side of the river and spent the night at the army post at Barugang. However, rebels again attacked us while we were retreating. I had to leave several armed men in their path. That night all night long the sound of guns and bombs inside the monastery disturbed the silence of that once peaceful village. After midnight, reinforcements arrived. Sixty cavalry.

Early on the morning of the twenty-first rebels began firing from the mountain behind the monastery just as the full moon dropped behind the trees. I sighted the rebels with my binoculars. My men positioned three large cannons and awaited my commands. The rebels immediately understood their inferior position and began to flee. The firing rapidly ceased.

All this while the two generals had been staying at Pundo without engaging in battle. When I received a message that they had arrived safely at Reting, I joined them there. At the top of the stairway to the upper stories of the Labrang, I met one of our staff members, who looked worried. He said, "A little while ago we almost had a catastrophe. One of our own soldiers tried to shoot Mr. Shakabpa. I begged the man not to kill Mr. Shakabpa. Finally he was stopped."

Inside, I met General Khesu. "I hope you are not tired," he said. I answered, "No." Mr. Shakabpa was also in the room, but he said nothing. I asked the two generals if they might like to come into another room for a rest. When I asked Lieutenant Wangdu to bring us some tea, he replied angrily, "They don't need it. Leave them alone!"

He continued speaking with a tense, angry face, "We soldiers who despise our lives in order to fight the enemy should be congratulated by the generals. But instead, Mr. Shakabpa threatened the soldiers by firing in the air quite a few times."

I told Lieutenant Wangdu not to worry because Mr. Shakabpa was tired and moreover a short-tempered person. However, he bears no grudges and soon calms down. Again I asked him to bring us a pot of tea, and he complied.

Mr. Shakabpa drank two cups but wouldn't speak. I told the generals that rebels were still in the forest and must be completely defeated before we might retire. I asked them what to do. The reply was that I should send soldiers from my own post to take care of the remaining rebels.

I ordered several sergeants with troops to the scene. Soon a few of my soldiers came back with the head and hands of one of the rebel leaders. It was Reting Rinpoche's personal mule keeper.

We also retrieved ammunition which had belonged to the twenty-five original guards.

Bad feelings seemed to be developing between my soldiers and the generals. Things were growing dangerous in an unpredictable direction. I removed my lieutenants and soldiers who had been stationed at Reting Monastery and placed them a little distance away.

Someone then informed me that the two generals had sent a false report to the Tibetan government, saying that I, Mr. Shuguba, commander of the Trapchi post, had not obeyed them properly. They indirectly blamed me for the soldier who had tried to shoot Mr. Shakabpa.

Despite their report, the Kashag sent me a sealed letter, saying, "We believe that your work is very well done. We reported it to Regent Taktra. We shall not forget your victory over the rebels."

A few days later I received a letter from the government in Lhasa telling me to return immediately with all my troops. I went via Digung. Subsequently, the two generals arrived in Lhasa and reported to Regent Taktra that I should receive military punishment because I had not obeyed them, and that I had allowed the soldiers to steal possessions from the monastery.

I wrote a detailed report about the entire situation, including the conduct of my men. I carried this report in my pocket at all times. I was summoned, and Mr. Thubten Lekmun, the number one aide to Regent Taktra, read the report the generals had sent. He asked for my full report.

I explained all the details, then pulled out my written account and gave that to him. I pleaded that military justice be done. I said that while we were fighting at Reting Monastery the two generals had avoided battle, perhaps out of fear of the rumor that the rebels were backed by Chinese. "In fact," I stated, "they did not fight at all."

During this time, news of the death of Reting Rinpoche surged through Lhasa. Dark rumors persisted about the causes and conditions of his demise. Reting had been interrogated many times. At the final session he admitted he had approved a plan for retaliation against the recalcitrant Taktra, though he insisted he had not approved of any

Reting Rinpoche, c. 1947.

assassination attempts. However, further evidence against Reting erupted in the next few days, based on material written in his own hand — letters he had planned to have secretly delivered which had been intercepted.

A decision about his punishment was difficult for the National Assembly to reach. Some argued that they should follow the legal code developed by King Srongtsen Gampo in the seventh century, which decreed that for revolting against a king the criminal is to be thrown off a high cliff. Others argued that such punishment was not befitting a high lama, a revered tulku such as Reting Rinpoche. No decision was reached. On the night of May 8, 1947, Reting Rinpoche was found dead in his prison room.

He had complained of headaches. He had asked that he be transferred to a room with more light and heat. The doctor who examined him diagnosed the illness as a nervous disorder and gave him some pills. The night of Reting Rinpoche's death, guards reported hearing cries of pain. No wounds were found on the body except for blue marks on his bottom.

Some believe that Reting Rinpoche was poisoned and then dragged or pummeled until he lost consciousness. There are those who say that he willed himself to die, based on his knowledge and skill in advanced practices. Three weeks after we arrested him, Reting's body was cremated. Lhasa, dispirited, mourned.

❋ ❋ ❋

The year the Dalai Lama took his full monastic vows I attended ceremonies at Drepung and Sera. At Sera I saw Lieutenant Gesang, the soldier we had suspected and sent north at the time of Reting Rinpoche's arrest. This man was now serving as a security guard for Regent Taktra. I was astonished that Gesang had been clever enough to get this post. He had no fighting experience whatsoever and was in fact a coward. During the fighting at Sera that continued for weeks after Reting Rinpoche's arrest, the coward Gesang had gotten himself assigned as a Potala guard — to avoid fighting I presumed.

I thought Regent Taktra must be confused to have hired such a man for his bodyguard. I knew other examples of Gesang's cowardice. For example, during the first Sera battle he was discovered hiding in a small hermitage. When questioned, he said he had been searching for ammunition.

A few months later, my third lieutenant and two others who had fought bravely with me at Reting were summoned to the Shoga, Regent Taktra's personal office. The honorable Lieutenant Wangye had been injured in the battle and was unable to come with us. I wrapped his hat and boots in a cloth and took the bundle with me to the Potala to represent him. At the Shoga, tea was served in the normal fashion; however, they treated me as if I were not there.

One of my friends lent me a bowl so that I might drink a cup. Then the Regent Taktra's number one aide, Thubten Lekmun, signaled me to rise. I got up, took off my hat, and bowed. Then I heard the verdict. They said, "Your soldiers were responsible for the destruction of the possessions of Reting Monastery; therefore uda, the central commander, is to be demoted from the rank of captain to the rank of ordinary staff."

They took away all the signs of my commander's rank: my hat and my brocade robe, my knife and my tea cup container, my rainbow boots, and my hanging gold pendant mounted with a large turquoise. Three gyapon, my lieutenants who were heads of one hundred soldiers each, were also discharged that day. Thus we ended our service for the military.

That day, I again saw the cowardly Gesang with Regent Taktra, marking maneuvers with the troops. Someone told me that the soldiers had unanimously congratulated Lieutenant Gesang for fighting so well at Reting. I myself knew that he hadn't been there at all. At this congratulatory ceremony, he was presented with five hundred *dotsek* (one dotsek equals fifty tsang) wrapped in white cloth on a silver tray. When I heard of this travesty, I felt that everything was backwards and out of place and that the present administration of Tibet would soon fall into great turmoil.

After my demotion, I went to a room nearby to put on civilian boots and a civilian hat. I was instructed to leave from the back door of the Potala.

Four of the rupon and gyapon were waiting outside to serve me chang. One man said: "Seeing the government's misconduct it seems that soon 'the breath taken in at the mouth will not be exhaled through the nose.' We should leave."

I tried to console the men. I said that someday the truth will be known. I recalled the warning words the Thirteenth Dalai Lama issued shortly before his death: He asked that all Tibetans, regardless of class, tackle unremittingly the task of ensuring the unity and welfare of the

The Fourteenth Dalai Lama's lay prime minister, Lukhangwa, c. 1947.

country. "If we fail to do so," he had said, "our country is doomed . . . regrets will be useless."

I returned home. Minister Lukhangwa and other friends came to offer their sympathies. Even Mr. Liu, the Chinese ambassador of Chiang Kai-shek, stopped in to offer his condolences and to ask my opinion of the current tumultuous government situation. I replied that the inexperience of the officials of the Shoga, including Reting Rinpoche who was so very young when instated, explains in part the mistakes in judgment.

That year, since I had no immediate new post and not much to do, I spent my time with a close friend whose family I had long known. His wife was part Japanese and part Chinese. Years before in Chamdo I had started up a relationship with her. She was a very beautiful lady. My friend had met her in China and brought her back to Tibet. Now, with my friend's approval, we continued our liaison and eventually had a son together — whom they, having no children of their own, were planning to raise as their own. Soon after giving birth, the beautiful lady died.

. . . during that year we had spent many pleasant afternoons together, the two of us alone or joined by her husband and another friend, playing games of mahjong. This lady had a lovely singing voice. "Life is short," she said, "embrace what you can." She was fond of the songs attributed to the Sixth Dalai Lama. I remember now the words to one song:

> *The young shoots of last year*
> *Have now become trusses of straw.*
> *A young man grows weary and his body becomes*
> *Stiffer than these pillars of bamboo.*
>
> *The lady with the sweet perfumed body*
> *Was my companion as I traveled a dark road.*
> *Twas as though I had found a white turquoise*
> *Shining in the gravel, and held it briefly,*
> *Then cast it aside in my haste.*

CHAPTER IX

Dreams and Visions

N earing the end of the earth-ox year, 1949, when I was forty-five years old, I was appointed a representative to government meetings at which the recent Communist Revolution in China was discussed in terms of the danger it posed to the Dharma-land of Tibet.

One day at a general meeting it was decided that a monk-official and I should visit the Tsang province to make an inventory of grain in all the government storehouses. We were also instructed to collect one million bushels of grain for military provisions. We were given the proper permits and told to depart right away.

We left Lhasa on the first morning of the Festival of Buddha Maitreya, the future Buddha. I hated to go; the whole town was festooned with colorful prayer flags, and people were preparing aromatic delicacies. We stayed the first night in Nyetang, where I gave offerings at the ancient temple.

We crossed the Kampala pass and passed by Tsisum, Chuzenka, and Rinbung, where a great statue of Buddha Maitreya is housed. We traveled through Klung, Nyamorota, Trumpalka, and Lhoku before finally arriving at Shigatse, where I stayed at my sister's house, my colleague lodging elsewhere.

We were to inventory and gather the million bushels of grain, then give it to the Shenyin Chamchen, who was in charge of sending it on to Lhasa. Since it is easier to transport grain by river than by land, we decided to send it from Lhang Pun, on the banks of the Tsangpo.

We traveled north, crossing the Tagla pass, and stayed overnight in the small village of Geting. I had traveled this path before as a young man. Now I felt age gaining on me. It seemed Tibet, too, had aged.

We stayed at the Potang Monastery, where we saw a statue of its founder. We visited several small temples with gilded images of the Buddha. The surrounding hills were inflamed with golden light. We gathered incense bundles in a glade of juniper to leave as gifts for the monks. On departure they threw grain at the heads of our horses, as a blessing to the animals and to their riders.

From there we traveled several days to visit the tanka artist Targye, a friend of my companion. We were invited to stay. Graciously, he fed us and took time to explain many things about how tanka painting is accomplished with brushes of yak and goat hair, the finest being made of sable from China.

"Very excellent brushes," he told us, "have only one or two groupings, mounted onto bamboo stalks."

Days we inventoried huge stores of grain, and at night we played mahjong. Sometimes a family invited us over for the evening. Whenever we had time, we went on pilgrimages to holy places to pray for the benefit of all sentient beings.

During our stay in Lhatse, the high-ranking Kundaling Hototu Rinpoche was invited to the monastery for teachings. When I met with him, he told me of his original intention to go on a pilgrimage to the snow mountain Tisi, but he had heard the rivers were too high and there was no facility for crossing. His treasurer-butler suggested that he stay on at the monastery as they had asked him for teachings many times. I asked if I could attend, and he said yes.

All the monks and many villagers, my servants, my colleagues, and myself — over one thousand in all — gathered for the brief, one-day Lam-rim teaching, which was well received. The next day he gave a long-life empowerment, and I received that as well.

That night I dreamed of rescuing sheep from the butcher. The next day in town Rinpoche was out walking when a low-caste butcher came near him, and Rinpoche called out, "Do not approach me!" at which the butcher fell to his knees, confessed his sins, and promised to discontinue his profession.

Rinpoche was young, wore no special monk's robes, and recited many of the teachings by heart without use of a text. The monks admired him and asked him to stay longer. He was unable to accept. Later, he told me that he would have agreed had they been more insistent.

During that summer spent in Lhatse, I left my mules and horses in the meadow on the other side of the river. Each day I crossed the Iron Bridge. The Lhatse Dzong itself was located on an immense flat rock projecting out from the surface of the mountain. From the dzong, one saw all across the fertile valley and far down the billowing river.

One private room at the dzong housed a statue of the ancient king. Another inner room was sealed off, and no one was allowed to enter. That was Mahakala's room. Mahakala, Lord of Knowledge, is one of the highest protecting deities, fierce in trampling upon hate and greed. There are very many lesser protecting deities whose only function is to worship him, the Lord of Knowledge. Offerings to them are such things as blood-filled skull-cups and the flayed skin of corpses. Mahakala is a four-handed diety who sits in fierce ecstatic union with his consort, Mahakali, inside this sealed room. One can just make out, on the side of the mountain, the image of Padmasambhava carved by the deities themselves.

One afternoon, from the top of the mountain all the way to the southeast of Lhatse, where the goddess Mahakali is said to dwell, a huge thunderstorm raged which sounded like cannon fire. The sound traveled eastward through the entire region. Villagers said it must be a battle between gods and devils. They expressed the wish that the gods should win. I felt certain it would be the devils.

Soon after, we heard a rumor that Chamdo in Kham had been invaded and overtaken by the Chinese.

Deeper into autumn, we traveled to Namring, where we made offerings to the image of Maitreya in the ancient monastery. On top of the temple roof is a platform designed for the three-dimensional Kalachakra mandala, which the Fifth Dalai Lama took with him to the Potala. Inside the Namring Dzong were three human-sized brass statues, which looked completely solid; no joints could be detected. The templekeeper explained that these were made by three Indian craftsmen who were then absorbed into the statues when they had finished making them.

About that time, the Regent Taktra resigned, and the young Dalai Lama took full possession of both spiritual and secular powers. When we heard this news, we did an incense-burning dedication ceremony at the dzong, we erected a prayer flag post, and prayed for many hours.

The incense-burning released clouds of smoke into the sky, which moved in the direction of Lhasa due to the gentle persuasion of the wind.

The year was 1950. I cannot adequately describe the apprehension and confusion in Tibet. As a result of the Communist invasion in the east and the disorder inside the government stemming from the death of Reting Rinpoche and the ambitions of some of Regent Taktra's followers, the Dalai Lama had been coerced to take the throne two years ahead of time, when he was barely sixteen.

Tibet had been without its spiritual and secular leader since the death of the Thirteenth Dalai Lama in 1933. Tibetans believed that with the young Dalai Lama as head of the government, inexperienced as he was, the unity and inviolability of our land might be maintained.

One day the abbot at Namring invited us to a traditional Tibetan dinner of meat, butter, cheese, and tsampa, piled up high in front of each person. It was impossible to finish one's portion, but one had to try. They heaped up cookies and candies before us. After dinner the monastery finance manager opened the storehouse, and one hundred cats came out. He gave them the bones and leftover meat. When the cats had eaten every scrap, they went back into the storehouse. We were told that cats were traditionally kept there as symbols of the wealth deity.

The monastery had stored up much gold and excess grain. Even individual monks there were rich. I told the finance manager of the monastery about a prophesy from ancient times that said people from the Far East would come to take this wealthy accumulation of grain from us. I told them one never knows the future of one's wealth, and that meanwhile one should use excess wealth practically — for distribution to the poor and for spiritual purposes.

The manager said the monastery had provided for soldiers during the Nepali-Tibetan War and was rewarded by the government with a fourth-rank title. Later, I was told that the Chinese Communists took everything from them almost immediately: all of their treasures, the gold, and the grain.

The governor of the dzong invited me many times to visit him. Above the monastery and below the dzong there was a huge storehouse for government surplus. My colleagues and I inventoried the grain. All of it was intact. We sealed off the storehouse again and returned the key to the governor.

We visited him at the dzong, and he pointed out the uninhabited ruins of ancient forts on the hills above his palace. We climbed up there to have a look.

The rocks were grown over and the walls were crumbled away, but from the top of one wall we could see way out across the distance to the caves of the Dzibrigo. Those caves number in the hundreds, and meditators use them to this day.

One day an official arrived from Lhasa saying that the Red Chinese had in fact invaded Chamdo and that the Dalai Lama had been forced to escape. They had heard a rumor in Lhasa that many Chinese had come to this area as well. We replied that we had seen none. I told him that just to make sure he should go to the Tengye Monastery and discuss the situation with the governor.

Soon after, we left by way of Chilung, and four days later arrived at Tengye Dzong. We heard of no danger from the Chinese there.

South of Tengye Dzong we went to see a Sakya monastery, where I met a very old Sakya abbot and saw many beautiful statues and shrines. Then we met with the Tengye Tulku, a young lama who had his own monastery of one hundred monks nearby, which was a branch of the Tashilhunpo Monastery near my home. These one hundred monks were doing well in their studies. They had built new houses which were nice to stay in, except for the water which was bad. The water made your body feel heavier each day so gradually it became difficult to get up or sit down. To counteract this effect, I took many long walks.

We learned more about the Dalai Lama's flight, and that he had set up a provisional government in Yatong, a village in the Chumbi Valley a day's journey from the Indian border. The National Assembly and the Cabinet insisted that the young Dalai Lama go there, against his wishes, to ensure his safety until negotiations could be completed with the Chinese.

By this time it was winter, and the streams were scalloped with ice. The Dalai Lama remained at his outpost until mid-year of 1951, when the Seventeen Point Agreement was signed with the Chinese.

Later, it was reported that at his first meeting with His Holiness, Chairman Mao declared, "All religion is poison."

The plenipotentiary delegates of Tibet agreed to cooperate with the Chinese in repelling imperialist advances — allowing for what was

Shuguba's third son, Yeshe Tenzin, at Rickzin Wangmo's house in Shigatse, 1946.

Shuguba's fourth son, Tsenshab Rinpoche (Yeshe Thondup), in Lhasa, c. 1955.

Shuguba's fifth son, Lama Kunga Rinpoche (Kunga Gyurme), in Lhasa, c. 1955.

Shuguba's sixth son, seated—second from right, Thartse Khen Rinpoche (Hiroshi Sonami), with servants and Kanser Shabtrung on the roof of Thartse Labrang, Ngor Monastery, c. 1955.

termed "a peaceful liberation." Tibetan autonomy was for the moment ensured, in all matters closest to our hearts. Of course we knew that thousands of Tibetans had been tormented or killed already. The stories of abomination and abuse were too numerous and too disturbing to ignore. The Chinese foothold in Amdo had been firmly, and inscrupulously, established. Secretly we feared that this signed document would not bring an end to our troubles.

The day after His Holiness returned, the Red Chinese, enemies of our way of life, were to walk the streets of Lhasa, saying that they were there "to make us happy."

PILGRIMAGES

I continued working on inventory with a monk-official from Shegar Dzong. After a month at Tengye Dzong, a person from Shigatse arrived to tell us to begin making our return. We started back toward Lhasa instead of proceeding farther afield, stopping at Dik for three days, where we visited my butler's family. Then we stayed at a friend's house and completed our inventory in the Hray Dzong, where I had once been governor.

From there we traveled to my father's Nar estate via the Gyaling pass. We descended the ridge to rest in the cave used by the Mahasiddha tailor, Simbupa. I met with my sons. By prearrangement we had agreed to arrive on the same day at the cave, in order to make offerings and prayers for the unity and perseverence of an independent Tibet.

Years had passed, and my sons were grown men. Kunga Gyurme and Yeshe Tenzing arrived, bringing my younger brother. We stayed for two days and two nights, walking about the vicinity and enjoying the wildflowers. We tried to discuss the situation, but none of us knew very much. My elder son, Yeshe Tenzing, was with us only briefly because he was requested to return when a servant arrived informing him that his abbot was ill.

My son, my brother, and myself rode on together to stay for a few days at Payling estate, where my mother was still living. I was aware of the fond affection between my sons and my young brother. My brother had always indulged them, saying, "Let us break the dishes according to the wishes of the children!" His youth and felicity made him popular with children everywhere. And, too, more than a few times he had cured them of their ailments with his medical skills. I had not spent much time with my children. A formal relationship persisted between us. Watching them laugh and play together, teasing each other fondly, I felt more strongly than ever that my own youth had passed.

I returned to Shigatse to stay at the house now belonging to my sister. There my colleague and I did an inventory of the storage house in front of the Shigatse Dzong. Much of the grain had been ruined by moisture from the back wall pressed against the cliffs. We threw out the ruined grain and put the undamaged grain into separate rooms. We sold some of the insect-infested grain for half-price to a local brewer, who said that it produced the most excellent chang.

I was invited to visit the small retreat house belonging to my sister's son, Shiu Tulku, which was nearby. A modest place, it nonetheless contained many excellent images and shrines. I remembered hearing about a powerful man who lived in the area, and I went in search of him. No one could tell me where he might be found. It was believed he had gone into solitary retreat somewhere in the mountains.

Upstream two rivers merge into one at Lang Lang Chung. Many caves are in that place, also the main entrance to the buried sacred place of Padmasambhava, called Sabulung. I stayed for one week on a high mountain ridge at a friend's estate and completed the inventory.

Traveling back toward Gyantse I stayed overnight at a convent to visit the sacred lake. My colleague and I arose before dawn and walked up the torturous path arriving on a promontory. I sat down on a pile of rocks and stared into the reflective water. The lake itself is shaped like a skull-cup surrounded on all sides by large boulders. After looking into the lake for several moments I felt my eyes beginning to tire, and just at that moment I received a very clear vision of a map of the world spread out with all seven continents before me.

Later I doubted my vision and assumed that it was only the illusory effect of the overhanging rocks reflected on the water as the sun began to illuminate them.

My colleague was thinking about the future of the Tibetan government. He said he saw the lake boiling. Other friends described to me various scenes they had seen and the images of people they knew. Once the sun was up, there was nothing much to discover.

As we headed toward the Yungla pass on the way to Rinung near

Gyantse, we passed an aged couple who had come all the way from Kham with a malnourished goat to carry their load. They were traveling to holy places; the sacred mountain was to be their final destination. I wondered if they might in fact die there, so feeble they seemed. Though they were not beggars, we gave each a few small coins.

Nearing the pass I saw something unusual — a chorten with Chinese letters scrawled upon it. This depressed me greatly. I did not even mention it to my companions.

At the top, we said prayers and added our rocks to the cairn. Then we descended into the grasslands.

From there one encounters the monastery called Tsobu, where exist beautiful cast-iron images of the five Buddha-families, each the size of an eight-year-old child. That night, in the monastery, I had an interesting dream. I was a small boy again, crossing a steep gorge of the wintry Salween River, holding tightly to my mother's back, my legs about her waist. She was attached to the cable by a leather strap. The ferryman below pulled on the rope as we crossed, passing very slowly over the pristine waters in which I could clearly see the living forms of rainbow fish and spotted frogs and water snakes and minnows and various other creatures darting from their hiding places among the rocks far below.

Mother admonished me, "Son, hang on tightly or you'll fall!" I remember to this day with great clarity that dream.

We arrived at Gyantse after dark and made our way to the monastery to say a few prayers. Inside the main temple were stacks of statues, the walls painted over with intricate mandalas. Several schools of Tibetan Buddhism were represented by the colleges there. Sixteen schools were enclosed inside the walls of this great monastery.

We traveled then to Duchung Dzong, where I had my first post as governor. On the north side of the river is the Sera Drupe Monastery, above which one finds a cave where Lady Nangsa Obum used to meditate. On one wall of this cave you can see the distinct impressions made by the jewels on the back of her exquisite headdress. She always wore elaborate costumes of jewels and brocade wherever she traveled, even during the long months she lived alone in the cave doing advanced practices. A great yogini, she was once the wife of a powerful lord, warlike and acquisitive. It is said she tamed and humbled him with the strength of her teachings.

146

Women are considered to have a weakening influence on men according to the strictest Buddhist traditions. But it is also understood, according to the same doctrines, that a woman contemplative, if she is any good at all, is often superior to a man.

TRIUMPH

In the water-snake year, 1953, when I was forty-nine years old, I received the Vajrayogini initiation and teachings from our family guru, the abbot of Black Horse Thubten Monastery. My wife, my younger brother, my youngest son, Losang Kunga Gyurme, and my daughter, Ngawang Chodron, also received these teachings.

There was a group of 108 caves near our home, where many yogis had meditated and achieved realizations. A famous lama, Tomcho Gyaltsen, practiced there. My son and I went to one of these caves to do a six-month retreat.

After about a month, I received a letter from the Kashag in Lhasa. They informed me that the fourth-rank accounting minister Mr. Trogawa was resigning from the Tsikhang, and the Dalai Lama had appointed me from among the candidates for his replacement. I was to come to Lhasa at once.

I felt inadequately prepared, having had little experience at higher posts and having spent my youth so foolishly. However, I could not refuse.

I asked my son whether I should go immediately or first complete my retreat. My son advised me to go at once. He said he would finish the retreat for both of us.

I received the announcement in the beginning of the third month and made immediate preparations to return to Lhasa. Once there I went directly to the Potala to pay my respects to the Dalai Lama. Afterwards I attended my inauguration ceremony.

I was one of four tsipon — chiefs of the revenue department. We collected taxes, in-kind, such as grains, from all the Tibetan landowners and government landholdings. We directed the government's expenditures for charitable causes such as temple restoration, renovations, and the various districts, and we managed the staff and governmental salaries. Each dzong had to report to us on its annual yield of wheat, barley, woolens, velvets, carpets, grass ropes, meat, and butter. Every summer we spent two months working on the overall inventories — a difficult task with a great deal of responsibility.

The four tsipon, lay officials, and the four grand-secretaries, monk-officials, held the most important positions after those of the two prime ministers and four Cabinet ministers in the Dalai Lama's administration. My office, the Tsikhang, selected and recommended to the Cabinet lay official candidates for heading various departments, just as the office of the monk grand-secretaries, the Tsi-Yigtsang, did for monk-official candidates — its recommendations being presented directly to the Dalai Lama. Together, these two groups acted as advisors to the Cabinet and chaired sessions of the full National Assembly as well as its Standing Committee.

When the Cabinet called the National Assembly or its Standing Committee to meet, these two groups of high officials conducted the proceedings, recorded the discussions, and prepared the report, which was then presented to the Cabinet. The National Assembly met once a year, or more often as deemed necessary in times of national emergency.

❀ ❀ ❀

Now I will tell you of the time, in the wood-horse year, 1954, when I and another lay official were assigned to head the procession of the week-long celebration held immediately after the lunar New Year, the great prayer festival of Monlam Chemo.

We were to be the *yasor tripa*, or commanding generals. I was the senior official, and the junior official was Dodeba, also of the fourth rank. Each year different officials were chosen for these posts.

On the first day of our duty we went to the chief monk-administrator, who as tradition required, gave us detailed instructions for the festival. The two yasors were required to provide food, refreshments, and resting tents for the staff, using our own funds or money borrowed from friends. We had to supply all the materials for our costumes, which included different kinds of cloth — brocades, fox fur hats, costly rings, and prayer beads.

We also had to provide outfits for two receptionists, four servants, and two grooms: blue and yellow Chinese brocades and special boots for the grooms, heavy coral beads and jade archer's thumb guards, saddles and saddle blankets, saddle cases, and bridles. We provided color-

Tsipon Shuguba, yasor general (left), with colleagues at the Yasor Festival in Lhasa, wood-horse year, 1954.

matched horses for the two receptionists and four servants, along with head and tail ornaments for the horses. And we provided clothing for the *gyersangma* — the ladies who serve chang. They had to be outfitted with five-layered silk blouses, long strings of turquoise and coral, head-dresses, and additional pearl and coral necklaces, needle cases and purses and baskets decorated with pearls, and many different brocades, as well as the chang pitchers and the silver chang serving bowls. Every requirement had to be fulfilled with the highest decorum.

My wife and two sisters organized the clothes and jewelry for the chang ladies. Two young men were hired to assist the chang ladies at the festival itself. We provided their horses. The chang ladies were daughters of some of my official friends. I also hired some friends to assist at the festival: Trimon's son, the younger Shakabpa, and others.

On the twenty-second of the first month of the wood-horse year, we prepared for the procession by serving food to the high-ranking officials. Before the procession could get underway, I made the announcement then my assistant read the instructions aloud to all the gathered participants. Everything was to be done according to specific protocol.

Then I said, "My colleague has clearly read the instructions, and there is no need to repeat them; however, since this is a very important occasion, certain points should be emphasized and double-checked. Tomorrow on the morning of the twenty-third, we will go to the Trapchi Field and line up for inspection — the cavalry forming two lines before the assembly of the government ministers."

Next, a young staff member kneeled before us and chanted: "Horses, saddles, weapons, knives, wooden weapons, spears, arrows, shields, mirror — everything is ready."

On the morning of the twenty-third, after the inspection was completed, the left and the right cavalries lined up parallel and returned to the minister's tent. The procession then began to circumambulate the city of Lhasa. Tens of thousands come to Lhasa to observe or participate in this great festival, inaugurating our new year.

The procession traveled over a mile, ending up at the "Hair of Buddha" willow trees near the main entrance of the Jokhang. Everyone dismounted and went inside. Each did three prostrations and was seated. Gathered there inside the congregation hall were thirty thousand monks from Drepung Monastery — which virtually ruled Lhasa for two months during the New Year's festivities, symbolizing the return of secular power to the religious leaders where it belongs.

The senior monk, Dreba, declared to the monks that day, "At the end of the festival we will throw *tormas* into the fire and take the Maitreya Buddha statue on a float in a religious procession around Lhasa." At that, everyone rose and listened again to the declaration from the senior official (myself), after which the procession left the temple, mounted horses again near the Buddha-hair trees, and proceeded to tents outside the city. There we had a great celebration, with plenty of chang and various offerings given to all the officials.

On the morning of the twenty-fourth, everyone left their tents early and lined up. The procession proceeded to the front of the Potala, paying homage to the Dalai Lama before again circumambulating the town and returning to the main gate. When the important officials dismounted, they did three prostrations toward the Dalai Lama's room, then took three steps backwards and put on their hats before remounting. The procession, lined up four abreast, circumambulated twice around the Barkhor, a route through the city which also circles the Jokhang.

Next, two senior officials, including myself, were served tea, rice, and cookies by our butlers in tents set up at a house near the Jokhang. Important Lhasan citizens congratulated us by offering ceremonial scarves. Later that day the Tunba gave their traditional banquet. We were allowed to relax until the great torma-burning ceremony that evening in which all evil spirits and enemies to Buddhism are symbolically immolated.

The torma-burning ceremony was performed by Lekshe Ling College — the Tantric College of Drepung Monastery. Torma are immense effigies shaped to represent enemies and evil influences. Once they are burned, the Simba soldiers, dressed in uniforms of the soldiers of old with elaborate headgear of peacock feathers and costumes of chain mail, fire their ancient muzzle-loading rifles, and the sound that issues forth is like thunder and lightning. As the torma fire extinguishes itself, thousands of cavalrymen shout a victory cry.

The Maitreya Buddha Festival was held on the morning of the twenty-fifth. Myself and my assistant were invited to sit next to the head monk and the authorities from Drepung, who functioned something like policemen. We were the four responsibles. We watched the horse and footraces, the wrestling matches, and the weight lifting contests in which a heavy smooth stone is lifted to various heights.

In the horse racing contest, the Dalai Lama's horse came in first. Ten of his horses had been entered, one of which traditionally had to win. All other horses attempting to pass it were restrained.

A horse owned by the Surkhang family came in second. Mine, named Ahzomtao, placed thirteenth. Many families competed. Well-trained judges observed the proceedings.

On the morning of the twenty-sixth, the cavalry competed in a contest: shooting guns, arrows, and spears in turn while riding by a stationary target. The right cavalry performed in the morning and the left in the afternoon.

The yasor general (myself) traditionally led the right cavalry. Various families lent the horses. Twenty came from the Gabshi family, twenty-four from Cabinet members, and others from higher and lower officials according to their rank. After awarding prizes, the officials returned to the tent for an elaborate lunch prepared by the Labrang steward. I invited my assistant, my high-ranking friends, ministers' sons, and upper and lower staff members, who had been spectators, to join us in the tent. The chang ladies served chang, and we spent a leisurely lunch hour.

The left cavalry, led by the junior yasor official, took its turn in the afternoon. The Dalai Lama's family and the junior ministers headed the procession. Each had provided twenty-four cavalry, and higher and lower divisions of their horses were raced against one another. After the prizes, were awarded, both the older and younger yasor managers, and the rest of the cavalry, exhibited their competing horses and received their prizes walking slowly from the assembly of ministers to the head of the cavalry. Everyone exchanged scarves, and then a troop of musicians performed while the chang was served. Finally, everyone lined up, took a handful of tsampa from a huge urn, and tossed it simultaneously in the air, shouting, "*Lha-Gyal-O!*" meaning "Victory to the Gods."

On the twenty-seventh, a dedication for ending the festival was held in the pleasure house behind the Potala. The Kalun, the Cabinet, and all the other high-ranking officials gathered and changed into different outfits and hats for the afternoon, according to rank. Rice, tea, and other beverages were served. The Dalai Lama's kitchen sent down tea and sweets.

Streets of Lhasa, Yasor procession of 1954.

Then the distance-archery contest was held. The first, second, and third place winners received as prizes a horse and silk scarves of nine different colors. Fourth place winners received seven different colors of blessing scarves. Fifth place winners received five colors of scarves. Sixth place winners three. The others received plain white silk scarves or scarves of cotton according to their place in the competition.

That afternoon, the younger staff members held various contests. One game involved the practice that when one of the younger officials hit the target, the high Cabinet officials had to drink; and when the young officials missed, they themselves had to drink. Next, the Lhasa officials served rice and food, and the Labrang served butter dates and sweets. Then the Khadruk — the dancing and singing troops — displayed their talents. The cavalry sang traditional victory songs, accompanied by the Lhasa military captain.

Afterward, all were served wheat soup. Any who had dropped ammunition during the shooting contests now had to go collect it in disgrace, showered by balls of tsampa from playful spectators. Then, as all the officials and ministers went on a final march to their homes with everyone singing loudly, the Lhasa New Year's Festival of the wood-horse year, 1954, was over from beginning to end.

DISASTER

In the upper valley of Gyantse in a place near the valley of Nyero close to the Tagri Monastery between two mountains, one finds a white, a yellow, and a black lake. On the fifteenth day of the fifth month of the wood-horse year, the black lake broke through a natural dam, which had held from ancient times. The valley below was flooded, and a large portion of the city of Gyantse was washed out. The flood continued on in a muddy torrent as far as Shigatse. It damaged fields and destroyed possessions and houses. Many thousands of people and animals were drowned.

The Peking government sent $84,000 in aid. The Tibetan government in Lhasa sent eight thousand bushels of grain for food and to use for replanting. Kendrun Lhas and myself were appointed managers of the flood emergency. My staff secretary left Lhasa immediately for Gyantse and met there with the Chinese representative Yin Tranghu, who helped with distribution of blankets, coats, shoes, and hats from the Chinese Army post.

The Lhasa citizens — the aristocrats, the lamas, and the business-men — sent money, grain, cloth, medicines, and other assistance. Many noble families had already fled to India. They sent twenty loads of cotton. The destitute were hired to reconstruct the Gyantse and Shigatse road and were well paid in grain, tea, butter, and money.

It was arduous, time-consuming work unearthing precious objects from the silt and sludge. Months and months passed without much sign of progress. There was not time or energy enough to give each person a proper funeral nor to hire the corpse-slayers necessary for all to be given the traditional Tibetan return. Many families had lost everything and were confused about how to make a new beginning. Hardest hit were the poorer peasant families, whose entire year's salary came from the grain they were about to bring to harvest.

❀ ❀ ❀

When we had finished the work as best we could, we were requested to return to Lhasa. The Dalai Lama was preparing for his Geshe examination, the highest scholastic achievement in our religious educational system. This examination was scheduled to begin in conjunction with the upcoming Monlam Festival. Three of us were to be in charge of the celebration.

Solid gold prayer wheels had to be prepared for the various monasteries the Dalai Lama would be visiting, as well as many new fabric decorations, such as brocades and banners. We opened an office on the roof of the Tsikhang. Our staff, comprised of eighty people, included professional tailors. We decorated the inside and the outside of the temples of Lhasa and its three great monasteries.

Gold butter lamps were fashioned for each temple. We appointed a monk-official to keep constant guard over the goldsmiths to prevent stealing. One time, when the guard went to the restroom, one of the workers caught the head goldsmith stealing gold. He reported to me that the head goldsmith had hidden some gold up his sleeve, intending to replace it with an alloy. He grabbed the head goldsmith's hand just as he was about to mix in the cheaper metal.

I inspected the mixing container, but it contained nothing but pure gold as far as I could tell. Then we had the man shake out his sleeves, and a piece of silver fell out. Just then, the guard returned from the toilet, and we told him to investigate this matter carefully. We took the head goldsmith with us into our office and told him it was not good to counterfeit gold for the Dalai Lama's offering. We added that he would be reported to the high court and punished in order to deter other would-be criminals.

That evening, a mysterious thing occurred. I was on my way to report this to Minister Surkhang when I saw a Chinese jeep leaving his house with the head goldsmith and another minister driving. I thought that the goldsmith might be asking for protection from Minister Surkhang. I met Minister Surkhang in his house, but since he was on his way out to see the new hydroelectric dam project, and since there were three Chinese officials with him, we could only discuss the incident briefly.

Three days later, Chogye Trichen Rinpoche sent to my office a sealed slate letter, which is erasable, with a gift of a fifty-pound block of butter. The slate letter stated that one of the head goldsmith's sons was a novice at his monastery, and since the head goldsmith had confessed and promised not to steal again we should not punish him too severely. In response to this letter, we did not demote the man.

To my dismay, I was reminded of words of the Sixth Dalai Lama: "No one can separate the pure from the impure." I considered myself one of them.

> *You the powerful ones who know how to make profit*
> *Are like the well-planted crop —*
> *Provided you are not hit by morning frost,*
> *And there is as yet no danger from hail.*
>
> *But listen,*
> *A bundle of rice is being arranged.*
> *If not collected it becomes like the powder of bonemeal.*
> *Even dogs and birds will not touch it.*

❊ ❊ ❊

On the eighth day of the second month of the earth-pig year, 1959, the Dalai Lama and his family and top ministers fled in disguise. It took them two weeks to arrive safely in India.

The Dalai Lama left a sealed letter saying that Beijing had not honored the Seventeen Point Agreement.

The letter said, "I have gone temporarily to a foreign country."

I have described already the days and nights of constant bombardment, the shelling of the Norbulinga, dead and wounded lying all about. Those of us left in charge had failed in our attempts to negotiate with the Chinese. I was captured and imprisoned for nineteen years.

The torture and the executions were a way to impress upon our minds that the days of Tibet as we had known it were over.

Shuguba, imprisoned by the Chinese in Lhasa.

CHAPTER X

Prison

They took us to Mr. Osel Gyantsen's, where there were already many prisoners. The Chinese had hired several Tibetans to help identify the others. Hidden from view, they explained who each was. Then they apologized to the prisoners for not being able to serve tea.

The Chinese took me, the younger Mr. Shakabpa, Muling Dzasa, the fourth-rank Losang Tsewang, and Torupba, tied our hands behind our backs, put chains on our arms, and loaded us onto a truck. They took us to our own military prison on the east side of the park, Tsidrunlinga, in Lhasa.

The prison consisted of many houses lined up. We were all put in one small room. The handcuffs became automatically tighter whenever one moved. They became so painful that we screamed all night for them to come and kill us then and there.

❖ ❖ ❖

At dawn, the head of the prison, Yao Ta Pang, and the person who had driven us to the prison, came and released us from the handcuffs. Then they chained our ankles instead.

❖ ❖ ❖

When I was allowed to go to the toilet, I saw that all the rooms were filled with government officials and staff members, lamas, abbots, governors from all over Tibet, military leaders, and noble ladies, including the queen of Nangchen, in eastern Tibet.

We were given rice with a few pieces of preserved wild onion. I was unable to eat anything. Some other pro-Communist Tibetan officials — Tethong Kenchung, Losang Namgyal, Changchen Tse, Wangdu Gyalpo, Ten Chasangpa, and Marlamba came to the door of our room. Tethong Kenchung told us that we had taken the wrong road. The others were silent.

My friend Mr. Shakabpa said to him, "Sir, please give us some bedding." The man didn't reply but wrote something down.

That night our prison guard sent us some Chinese soldiers' overcoats to use as bedding.

✦ ✦ ✦

Later, I was called to talk to some Chinese officials, who said: "In the city of Lhasa, we could control the people's uprisings simply by firing and killing the people, but since we are trying to protect art objects in the temples, we want to control the people another way. Therefore, you must come and tell the people to surrender."

I replied that I couldn't do so because the people wouldn't listen to me. They would only listen to someone like Cabinet Minister Ngabu — who was a known pro-Communist. They sent me back to my room and asked Muling Dzasa to do it.

He told the people to surrender, using a public address system. But the people tore down the poles and wires so no one could hear him.

✦ ✦ ✦

The next day soldiers made Losang Tsewang and Kenchung Thubten Tempa drive slowly through the city in a tank, telling the people to surrender. After three days the rebellions were under control.

That day, they released the foot chains of the two men who had made the announcements, but they did not release them from prison.

✦ ✦ ✦

Later, the Chinese secretary of the Tibetan Autonomous Region, Tim Jin Pao, and some other officials came and asked me, "Who started firing first?"

I replied, "The Tibetans did not decide or order the troops to start, but I heard a shot from behind Pongwari Mountain. Then the Chinese sent up a flare from the Norbulinga immediately after which countless Chinese cannons began firing inside and outside, between the walls of the Norbulinga, killing several thousand people and animals immediately. We then allowed the Tibetans to return fire toward the Chinese-fortified area of the Norbulinga and onto their army truck station."

Continuing the interrogation, they asked me what else I had done. I replied that on the morning after the Dalai Lama fled, when the Lhasa officials came for our daily meeting, we asked them to stay all day instead of leaving after a half-day as they usually did. We did this because we thought that if we let them leave someone might leak to the Chinese the secret of the Dalai Lama's flight, which would gravely endanger his life.

They also asked about the relationship between me and the Dalai Lama. I replied that His Holiness the Fourteenth Dalai Lama is the secular and religious leader of Tibet, and I am a government worker. Therefore, we have a relationship.

Next they asked what had been discussed in the Parliament. I said, "The Parliament told us that during the Lujun conflict the Thirteenth Dalai Lama had to flee to India, but he returned and the Tibetans defeated the Chinese. So likewise, again, the Dalai Lama has had to flee to protect his life. However, we will continue to fight for Tibetan independence."

To this the Chinese responded, "China and Tibet are like head and body. They cannot be separated."

They interrogated me thusly day and night without allowing me to sleep.

❀ ❀ ❀

One day they came for me and for Mr. Lhalu Tsewang Dorje, Kenjung Lhodro Gesang, Khenjung Kesang Nawang, and Mr. L. T. Shakabpa. They removed our foot chains. Mr. Lhalu worried that now they were going to kill us. They put us into two small cars. Mr. Lhalu started to pray.

I tried to console him, "Maybe they won't kill us just yet."

They took us to the front steps of the Potala and filmed us raising our hands in a gesture of surrender as we moved down the steps. They wanted it to look as if we were stepping down from power. They then put us back into the cars and returned us to prison.

We wore no foot chains for three days. Then one afternoon, we were working at our job making charcoal and a soldier shouted, "Who removed your foot chains?"

He put the foot chains back on us.

❀ ❀ ❀

One day all the prisoners' relatives gathered outside the prison fence while the prisoners were lined up along a balcony. We couldn't speak. We could only see each other across the distance. All the relatives were crying. I saw two girls from the Doptra family collapse because they recognized their parents among the prisoners.

161

I thought I saw my wife, but I cannot be certain it was she. Her arm was raised. She was standing toward the back of the crowd. There were perhaps one thousand people there.

❀ ❀ ❀

During the day, while wearing foot chains, we had to dig dirt from the cesspool and carry it on our shoulders to fertilize the vegetable field. To make the fertilizer, we had to mix up the cesspool dirt with our bare feet.

❀ ❀ ❀

During the three years following 1959, droughts, floods, and insect plagues caused many crop failures. Food was scarce. They reduced the prisoners' rations. Each prisoner was given daily one cup of thin rice soup. Thousands of prisoners in all the camps quickly starved to death. In every prison camp horse carts were constantly pulling out loads of dead bodies.

During that period, members of my family brought me food each week. While my wife was still in Lhasa she brought me and Mr. Shakabpa whatever food she could find. I was not allowed to see her face-to-face.

When my wife went back to Tsang province, two of my sisters, a female cousin Ushar, and a nun from Gora Chenmo brought us food several times. My sister Trimon Tse Yangla each week without fail brought tea, soup, fresh tsampa, powdered cheese, sweets, butter, meat, and vegetables. This is how I survived those first three years.

❀ ❀ ❀

Early one morning after I had been imprisoned for three years and seven months, a guard came to me and said, "The Commune of East Lhasa is bringing you to public trial for what you have done."

He took me to another room, where I saw a Chinese man in a black robe with a young lady. When they removed my foot chains, my skin came off, leaving open wounds.

I had a Tibetan shoelace, a ribbonlike belt used at the tops of boots, which I tried to tie around these sores. But they made me drop it.

The guard told the man and the young woman, "Our prisoner's body is healthy and has not been damaged, but he has had no breakfast. Please give him some food."

On the way to the east side of Lhasa they asked me about all the

Shuguba family photo: Lhasa, 1956. Left to right: five servants; two of Shuguba's sisters, Puntsok Drolma and Rickzin Wangmo; Changchi Shakabpa.

familiar places we passed. I explained everything I knew as we traveled along the Ling Gorlam outer road to the Kamdong Trokhang, where the trial was to be held.

When we arrived, I saw one of our relatives' servants, Nayden, stand up and leave. I found out later that he had gone to tell my sister what was happening.

Before the trial, a young lady in the office invited me into a nice spacious room, gave me tea, tsampa, and butter, and told me to eat well. I put butter and tsampa in the tea and ate my breakfast. Then I went into another room, where my sister had just arrived. She was waiting with chang and food, which I ate. She told me she would return that evening with more food. I returned to the other house and waited all day.

By late afternoon, around five hundred people had gathered. Five stood up to interrogate me in front of everyone:

1) the head manager of the Upper Tantric College in Shagar
2) the Dalai Lama's tailors: U Chamba and U Chen Sitar
3) a soldier from the Trapchi post
4) my servant Tundru's wife, Nyima

The manager of the Upper Tantric College began relating a dispute between the college and the Dangduba family, a noble family. He accused my office of unfairly deciding in favor of the family. He said that my office had allowed the family to harvest grain from the monastery's land in Shagar.

I agreed that my office had decided in favor of the family because the college had let that land go unirrigated and unfarmed for many years until the Dangduba family voluntarily began to irrigate and take care of it.

Then they asked me if I had received a percentage of the family's profit from that field.

I replied by reminding them that it had been decided that the family should give 20 percent of their profit to the monastery. This had happened for ten years, but suddenly one year the college sent monks to harvest the grain by force, illegally. Thus, I demonstrated that the monks had in fact acted wrongly, disgracing the teachings of Lord Buddha.

I said, "Don't you remember that at that time, when we were mistreating each other here, the Communists were already gathering in eastern Tibet?" They agreed.

My accuser said, "I have nothing more to say." He left the room.

The two head tailors next interrogated me about an incident, saying: "Although we gave credit to two others — Namgye and Ganden — what kind of bribe did you receive?"

I replied that my bribe had been a piece of bread and a leg of lamb.

Then they asked me what bribe I had received for withholding punishment from Namgye. I replied that he had tried to give me ten tsangs (one to two dollars) and one kata, which I had refused; but he left it with me anyway. I explained that I told Namgye I had already reported his case and that he would have to come to the office for a hearing.

One of the tailors, U Chen Sitar, cried out aggressively, with a clenched fist: "I made most of your clothes!" The other tailors in the audience tried to calm him by saying that I was not such a bad person. They said, "Do you remember that his high office gave us good tea everyday?" The conversation ended.

Nyima, the wife of my servant, said, "You loaned me a large sum, twenty do-ze, and each year for ten years we had to pay you back at 100 percent interest. How much did you get from us?"

I said, "Yes, over ten years I received two hundred do-zes from you."

She pushed at me angrily but didn't really hit me. That was the end of her interrogation.

My fourth interrogator was a soldier from the Trapchi army post where I had once been commander. He said, "Do you remember when we were bringing the Regent Reting to Lhasa? I suggested we take the Pundo route, but you didn't listen and took the Gola pass route instead, didn't you?" I said yes. He was silent. Then a Chinese man came up from the crowd and tried to kick me, but the young Tibetan work leaders prevented him.

The trial lasted two hours, during which time I had to stand leaning forward from the waist with my arms hanging down. (If one tried to support oneself by placing the hands on the knees, one was thrashed.) It was very painful for my back, but I received no other physical punishment. A lady cried out from the crowd, "These self-claimed nobles are nothing but evil people!"

I said, "Yes, indeed, I am a most evil person."

The trial was over, and I was ordered to return to prison.

❀ ❀ ❀

In one corner of a small building my sister and my cook's wife — the kind lady who was once my mistress — were waiting for me with tea, chang, and food. The cook's wife gave me a towel and soap, but I mistakenly left it behind at our parting.

By dusk, two prison guards were escorting me along the outer road around Lhasa back toward the prison. On the way, my nephew met me.

"Grandpa," he cried, placing a package next to my foot. Then he ran away.

The guards asked me who he was, and I told him it was my cousin's son. I asked if I could take the package with me, and they said yes. The package contained some food and five packs of cigarettes.

At the guarded prison gate my escorts told me to go inside. They left to go home for the night. Inside the gate, the Chinese warden, Yao Ta Pang, inquired if I was all right and if the people had punished me severely.

I told him they hadn't hurt me.

He asked what I had in my hand, but when I started to show him he let me keep it without even bothering to look at it closely. He sent me inside to watch a film with the other prisoners.

❋ ❋ ❋

After that I didn't have to wear foot chains. I was assigned to laundry work, for which I was paid a small wage.

Lhalu Tsewang Dorje was head laundryman. There was so much laundry we had to work hard all day without resting, stopping only once to eat.

To wash the quilt bedding, we had to wash the inside quilts and then the outside sheets separately, dry them, then sew them up again before the evening pickup. The winter's cold made our task especially difficult.

I had this job for two years. Our wages every month had to be paid back to the people's government. Mr. Lhalu received extra credit for his work.

One day, in the inside pocket of a Chinese lady's jacket I was to clean, I found a dirty sanitary napkin cloth, which I washed and dried in the sun. The prison-warden happened to walk by and see that piece of cloth. He asked who had washed it. When I said that I had, he took it.

That evening when the woman came to pick up her jacket he scolded

166

her severely and charged her five dollars. She was extremely embarrassed and cried for a long time.

I felt very sorry for her and wished I had thrown it in the garbage so she would not have been scolded.

The warden told me that in the future I should not wash this type of thing, but I should bring it to him.

I thought to myself that the warden appeared harsh externally, but since he always performed his duties diligently and tried to make sure we had enough to eat, inside he was actually a good person.

❁ ❁ ❁

One day during visiting hours my daughter came to see me, and I asked about my wife. My daughter replied that my wife had died on the evening before her scheduled trial, which was to take place in Black Horse Village.

A friend of my wife's had told her the trial would be very bad. There were people visiting from another village who had said that three people had been killed at a trial in their village, due to the animosity of the accusers. The worst was to be expected.

My wife prayed and then died in meditation that night.

The next morning they found her dead though she had been in good health.

I assume she left her body yogically through the advanced practice of Phowa with which she was familiar.

She was my wife, and I grieved heavily. There was nothing to be done.

My daughter cried without stopping, and I tried to comfort her. She asked me if she could stay in Lhasa to be near me, but I told her she must return to Tsang to live with my daughter-in-law and her daughters. I thought that this would be best for her so that she would end her grieving and not be too lonely.

I regret having sent her back to Tsang. I found out later that she became very sad there and finally had a nervous breakdown. One day she burned her hand in a candle flame. They tried to restrain her, but she escaped and damaged a family shrine. Thereafter, she roamed the fields, avoiding people. Three years later she was found dead.

If I had allowed her to stay in Lhasa, perhaps this would not have happened.

Ngawang Chodron (Shuguba's daughter), nineteen years old, in Lhasa, 1956.

❀ ❀ ❀

During the four years I spent at that military prison many prisoners died. The ministers Thubten Rabyung and Trashi Lengba died in the hospital. One day Mr. Tsarong Dzasa dropped dead without warning or apparent cause. The head of the Chinese doctors came to do an autopsy but found no evidence of poisoning.

Tsecha Jamdopa, the head doctor Loden Sherab, and the fourth-rank Drangdopa also died during this time. When Kentrung Chopel Thubten became very ill, he was released to his home and he died there.

One day my good friend Mr. Shakabpa had severe stomach pains and was sent to the hospital. They treated him and he returned to the prison, but again he became ill. They sent him home, where his sister cared for him, but soon he died.

❀ ❀ ❀

1963: mid-winter. A guard accompanied several of us on a transfer to Trapchi Prison — my former army post outside Lhasa. Myself, along with a secretary, Gyamtsho Tashi; a general, Lhodro Gesang; a "Kha" Battalion lieutenant named Ganden; and another secretary, Khungram, were transported by truck. When we arrived, three people of different ages checked our personal effects after which I was sent to room number eight.

In that small room were Ungese Tulku, a high lama; Tsawa Tulku, the Sera Tantric College abbot; a Chinese man, Tang Ten Pao, who was in charge of the garden; Karma Shang Kuten, an oracle; a Chinese prison guard named Wang Ping, who was the head of our unit; a translator; and two others besides myself — nine altogether living in one room.

In that prison rooms one through twenty were twenty-by-thirty or twenty-by-forty feet in size. Eight to nine people lived in each.

During the day the prisoners could go out into the yard to get some sun. Since rooms one through twenty all faced into the yard, I met people from the other rooms — some people I knew and some new Chinese prisoners.

These twenty rooms formed a prison block, which was surrounded by eight other blocks arranged in a square; there were approximately eight hundred prisoners in all.

One day while on a march, I caught a glimpse of my younger brother, Sonam Wangyal, who was living in one of the other prison blocks. I had

169

heard that he had been arrested at Shugu, where he headed our family estate. I was unable to find out more about him. I never saw him again.

❀ ❀ ❀

Twenty of the prisoners of our block were the survivors of a group of eighty high government officials who had been together in Chunju Prison, where I was first imprisoned. The other sixty had died of starvation and various other causes during the three-year drought which followed the Chinese takeover.

During my four years at Trapchi Prison, Secretary Gyamtso Tashi, the abbot of Sera Tantric College, and Lieutenant Ganden all died in the hospital.

❀ ❀ ❀

One day at Chunju, a huge newly made stone mill for grinding grain was brought in. Twelve prisoners were to set it up in the courtyard, harness themselves up, and drag the stone around like mules in order to grind tsampa for the prisoners.

The prison guard allowed these twelve to compose songs and sing them while they worked; but later they were accused of composing reactionary songs in Tibetan, and they were punished.

❀ ❀ ❀

In Trapchi, I was assigned the job of watering and composting the fields and picking vegetables. Other Trapchi prisoners were building a new prison in Sang Yi near Sera Monastery, which was finished in 1964.

On January 29, 1964, eighty of us were transferred there. They gave each of us a mattress and sent kitchen equipment, food, and a white pig for meat. They transported us in two military trucks, and we arrived in the late afternoon.

At the new prison we met Prime Minister Lobsang Tashi, Lhalu Tsewang Dorje, Jangra Nawang Tsebe (my wife's cousin), Canche Ngawang Trakba, Mondrang Thubten Chotar, and others. They arrived from a different prison accompanied by Chinese soldiers with bundles of rice, wheat, salt, oil, mattresses, and a felt carpet for each of us.

Although the prison was large and newly built, there were as yet no partitions or floors, so we had to sleep right on the sandy ground. Every day we brought gravel in from the mountains, and gradually we built a nice concrete floor. When this construction was completed, ten people were housed in each room.

Our next job was to make a huge number of sun-dried bricks at the east end of the prison. We also cut stones at the front of the mountain and carried them on our backs. This produced painful sores and blisters as if we were animals.

When we had gathered enough bricks and stones, we built a fence, then partitions in the new prison and an individual cell prison with back-to-back rooms. On the east side of the outer prison fence there was a large, sixty-acre sandy field and a stream once used by a queen, Srongtsen Gampo's wife, for washing her hair. Tibetans believe that the stream is sacred water. We made a reservoir from that stream to use for the prison water supply.

❀ ❀ ❀

Below us was an old field, no longer farmed or irrigated but with good soil. We carried dirt in baskets on our backs from that old field to a new field, where we planted "hair of Buddha" trees, willows. Around that area we built a barbed wire fence.

I worked one entire summer guarding the new field to keep the trees safe from pastured cows.

❀ ❀ ❀

Fruit trees were brought in from Shanghai. Pear, apple, and peach trees were flown into Lhasa and distributed throughout different departments. The prisoners got the leftovers. We got twenty peach trees and one hundred pear and apple trees, which we planted as soon as they arrived.

Alongside the eastern mountain range, we made an irrigation ditch which carried water into the prison's fields. However, at one point the Dode Commune cut off some of our water supply since its members were building their own reservoir. After that, our prison had a hard time getting enough water for its trees.

Mr. Mendo Lobsang Wangdu and I were appointed to take care of the orchard. We went out after breakfast, and the cook brought lunch to us.

We had to carry water on our shoulders from the reservoir up and down hills quite a long distance in order to water the fruit trees. Although the work was difficult, there was a kind of freedom in it, and we were, for the time, relatively content.

As the saying goes: One's own freedom is happiness, but the other's freedom — the freedom to do something bad to you — is always viewed as suffering.

❀ ❀ ❀

During these years, we planted over one hundred native rose bushes to harvest their rose hips. Carefully, we tended them, hauling the water up from the reservoir.

I was taught to graft apple and peach trees together. When the trees began bearing fruit, we harvested them and packed several sacks full for the Chinese officials and the prison guards. We also distributed three peaches and seven or eight apples to each prisoner.

❀ ❀ ❀

A prison guard brought one of my former servants with his eight-year-old child to see me while I was working in the fruit orchard.

I could see the child had inherited his grandfather's features. I had been good friends with the man.

We were given no freedom to converse but could only look at one another. Then the guard led them away.

Later, I found out that my former servant was now manager of the prison hospital.

❀ ❀ ❀

Through the summer of 1969 thunderclouds covered the sky, and a tremendous amount of hail fell. The storms caused a flood which broke the concrete-based reservoirs, endangering prison camps.

All the prisoners at Sang Yi, the new prison, had to work hard placing sand bags to hold back the rivers. We were able to prevent the waters from reaching the prison. But at Trapchi, the waters flooded badly. Hospital personnel and sick persons were moved to our prison until their own could be rebuilt.

The day after the flood, the prison guards took us to work on the fences around the fruit trees and told us to bring big stones from the reservoir to use for repairing the fence. However, the manager of the neighboring Dode Commune (formerly my sister's estate) stopped us, saying, "All those stones belong to us!" His commune had built the reservoir.

172

After that, members of the Dode Commune immediately started work rebuilding their reservoir. They made it a little smaller than it had been before the floods damaged it. Thus they reestablished their rights to ownership.

❄ ❄ ❄

One day a Tibetan staff worker asked me if I was studying the new Lhasa newspaper. I replied that every evening a group of us read it together. He asked me what was the news. I told him about the huge meteor that had just fallen into China, and I mentioned the old proverb: "A meteor portends a bad omen which cannot be prevented." We both felt it wasn't a good sign.

During that year, 1969, the Chinese Minister Chung Nze Lin, vice-chairman of the People's Republic of China and minister of foreign affairs, died. Mao appointed Ho Ku Pung to replace him. At the end of that year, Du De, another high-ranking deputy minister, died. Then we heard that Mao himself was ill.

Also, during that summer there was a big earthquake in China, which destroyed many towns and factories and killed one hundred thousand people. We read this in the newspaper. A prison guard told us that a group of one thousand miners had perished in the earthquake.

Thus, many Chinese people had suffered in that year, proving clearly to me that the proverb about the meteor was true.

❄ ❄ ❄

Once in 1970, my niece, my nephew, and his four sons came to see me during the prisoners' visiting hours. One of these grandnephews had just returned from college in the Chinese province of Tin-Jin. The other was about to leave for college by plane, but he decided to visit me first. The third was returning to agricultural college in the Tibetan village of Kongbo. Another was studying medicine in Lhasa.

The guard asked me if we were relatives, and I said yes, so he gave us a little time to relax and converse.

Later, the other prisoners asked me why so many Chinese soldiers had come to see me. I explained that they were not Chinese soldiers but my relatives. All had been wearing Chinese uniforms.

❄ ❄ ❄

173

In 1976, the fire-dragon year, thirty-four of us were transferred to rooms outside the prison where the guards used to live. I felt strong, but I had grown old in prison. I was now seventy-two.

This was a better situation for us, where visitors could visit directly in our houses. We were also allowed to go to Lhasa during the day as long as we returned at night.

The guards took us sightseeing to show us everything that had been accomplished during the time that we had been in prison. We were shown agricultural improvements at Pembe Lungtang which allowed the production of many thousands of bushels of grain. This area was formerly the Lhangtang, Kartse, and Sala estates of the Takse District, which had formerly been divided between the government, private owners, and monasteries. Several thousand miser and tuchung laborers had worked the land.

Pembe Village, the place of my wife's birth, was in an area where many monasteries had been established by ancient masters of the Kadampa tradition. The giant chortens had mostly been destroyed. Tsekhang Gompa, which had housed several hundred monks, and similar monasteries were all now in ruins. Ganden Chokor, the largest monastery, which was located in the middle of the village, had become a people's commune. The few lamas and monks remaining had been living as lay people, and they, too, worked for the commune, tending the fields.

The village beyond, in the district of Lhun Drub, had been demolished, and a large dam had been built across the valley from one village to the other. In summer, when the reservoir is full, water is still available through the old irrigation ditches. They told us that with this water, enough land could be irrigated to grow thousands of bushels of wheat, much of it for export to China. We know that barley is the staple crop of Tibet. Barley is our food. It is suited to our climate and our altitude.

They also showed us the upper and lower town communes, a large meeting house, a school, factory, hospital, dairy, brick and pottery factories, an experimental ranch for breeding horses and cows, and a center for wildlife preservation studies that houses a few wild deer.

They showed us around for three days, giving us a good reception and food wherever we stopped.

❀ ❀ ❀

At the hospital there was a famous Tibetan doctor who had treated many village people. He could not only cure physical pain but also read the patients' minds.

Our prison guide's right eye had become inflamed and gave him considerable pain. That doctor drew a lot of blood with a needle. The pain subsided, and eventually the eye was cured.

❀ ❀ ❀

When we had finished our tour of the Pembe Commune, we returned to the prison in Lhasa. Next, they took us to Yugay, Lhunze Dzong, the Nyame People's Commune, Nedong, and Chungye. We drove over the new bridge near Lhasa, then got out of the truck to look at the bridge. The bridge has two lanes for automobiles and enough room for people and animals to walk across as well.

South of the bridge, at the foot of the mountain, we saw a lot of military buildings and a commune which used to be a private school. I knew the former owners well.

In the valley below, where there used to be a number of small monasteries, only an airstrip was to be seen built on the plateau. Two airplanes recently purchased from Russia were being used to transport people back and forth between Lhasa and Chengdu.

Airport soldiers asked for our permits to visit. Our guide explained that we were prisoners.

From the airstrip we took the main road to the former Keshung estate. There we saw that the summer's excessive rainfall had covered the grain "up to the neck," making harvesting difficult.

Next we visited Tachinang, Mendroling, the estates of Namseling and Chimba, and the commune of Netong, which is near Tsetang Commune.

We stayed overnight at the guest house of Netong Commune. The next morning we went to Yalung Village built by King Srongtsen Gampo.

The ancient king's castle and its temple, which I had visited years before, had been completely destroyed. There was no sign of any of the buildings. The rock had been completely smashed to bits or carried off.

Nearly all the monasteries in Yalung Valley were severely damaged.

Next we went to Yuge Lhundze Village via the mountain passes. The

175

few monasteries still standing were being used for people's communes — the temples had become storage houses. All the monks and lamas were gone.

In the district of U Gye, the Lhundze Dzong itself is nothing but ruins.

In Nyeme Village we met the head of the commune, Rigzing Wangyal. We shook hands with him, ate dinner, saw films, and stayed overnight at his house.

The next day we visited a new waterworks project. The monastery there was being used as a storage unit. We saw a thousand-bushel field. To the northeast of Nyeme Village we saw another thousand-bushel field whose crop had been entirely destroyed by hail. We heard that at night the villagers there often heard the sounds of horses hooves and bells and other disturbances made by the angered local spirits.

The Communists had insisted on building a cattle ranch and an extensive hydroelectric plant, which were to be exhibited next on a two-day tour. I was too tired to go and asked to be excused.

❀ ❀ ❀

On the side of Shedra Mountain, the big chorten was now half-destroyed. Near the site of the Fifth Dalai Lama's birthplace, the monastery of Riwo Dechen was destroyed beyond all recognition. The surrounding fields that year, planted only with wheat, were all infested with black insects. The grain looked all right from the outside, but when I took it in my hand, it crumbled to dust.

At Changkim Shiga, a formerly private estate, we met an elderly man who had once been a peasant farmer there. He showed us his three rooms and many large sackfuls of grain which he said were enough provisions for his lifetime. "In the old regime," he said, "I was the first person up in the morning and the last to bed at night. I worked very hard, but even then I rarely had enough to eat or enough clothes to keep out the cold. Those in their expensive, luxurious houses who called themselves nobles recklessly and wastefully spent their lives from generation to generation." Thus he made his speech.

They showed us their harvest. We examined everything. I noticed that the average worker's clothing was not really better than before.

❀ ❀ ❀

We visited the Shokhang and Pulungpa estates, which were now being used to breed cattle. We saw four calves and their red bull father. We watched villagers building an irrigation ditch, and we stayed overnight at the Nedong guest house. The next morning we went around the side of the mountain, traveling on rubber wheels across the newly paved road. We saw that the famous monastery of Lilung Sheba was in ruins. Everything was gone from the "copper red mouth," where there had been so many precious Buddhist objects.

We visited Ukha, where there was a large hydroelectric project scheduled to begin producing electricity on the first day of the tenth month. This project seemed better built than the one near Lhasa.

On our return to Lhasa we were again taken on another tour, this time to the Kongbo region. We crossed the Lhasa river at the bridge and passed to the foot of Ganden Monastery. Instead of crossing the pass we took a military road around the mountain.

We were taken to a people's printing press, then to paper and match factories. We crossed a bridge to the former Chomo District, now the People's Commune Minority College. I saw my grandnephew, who was studying there. When I asked him if he knew where my younger sister was — my older sister was his grandmother — he was silent, so I thought she must be dead. I had heard that she'd been taken to a prison labor camp.

We went to the Student Union, where the president of the college, Lobsang, made a little speech: "We have eight hundred male and female students, most of whom are now home on vacation. We have classes in agriculture and dairy science, manufacturing, cement studies, mathematics, and athletics."

He showed us the fruit orchards and the buildings which the engineering students were constructing. The president of the college said that they hoped eventually to have over one thousand students.

Next we visited a wool manufacturing plant, which employs two thousand Chinese and a few Tibetan workers. There the wool is washed, dyed, and woven. Various types and qualities of woolen clothing and blankets are produced.

A little way beyond the place was a large fruit and apple market managed by an old friend of mine — a Chinese gentleman who used to work as a translator for the Tibetan government. He told me that if I had come to visit ten days earlier I could have seen my younger sister, who had just died. He told me my grandniece took very good care of her.

We came to a lumberyard in the lower valley of Kongbo, where all the workers were prisoners. Above that lumberyard, there were apple orchards worked mostly by the women. That was where my younger sister had worked.

The guide, a guard from our prison who was leading the tour, told me that if she were still alive he would have allowed me to see her. He drove out to the orchard, returned, and said that indeed since she had died just ten days before there was no reason to visit there.

❈ ❈ ❈

We stand in the evening cold, snow collecting on our shoulders. Our guards explain that from here a road leads up over a high pass to Po. The way back to Lhasa is difficult right now, they say, because it is snowing on all the passes. Several trucks have reportedly fallen from the road.

I am thinking of the numberless times I crossed that pass alone on horseback in just such conditions.

At a guest house, some Chinese women ask for our opinions about developments in Tibet. We say much has been done in a short time.

The next morning we thank them for their hospitality and proceed on our way.

❈ ❈ ❈

Next we are taken on a tour of Lhasa. We visit the Potala and the three great monasteries. I knew that the very famous image of Lord Buddha at Ramoche Temple had been utterly destroyed. Friends told me they collected ashes from that statue. The guards didn't take us to Ramoche because it was being used now for the commune's storage house.

❈ ❈ ❈

In the Jokhang we visit the most sacred image of Sakyamuni, said to contain relics of the Buddha. It was brought into Tibet by Srongsten Gampo's queen in the seventh century.

I put my hand under the statue's garments to feel the knee. It is covered with gash marks where they tried to chop up the bronze statue with axes. I scrape a little dust off the knee to take with me.

Many of the altar niches of the courtyard are now used for storage, so there is nothing much to see there. The original eleven-headed Chenrezig statue — called the "self-manifesting from clay" — was destroyed in the early days of the "Cultural Revolution." A Tibetan sculptor recently made a replacement. Since I'd heard that some of the famous old pillars had also been replaced, I wondered if some of the sacred texts buried under the pillars had been lost. Many of the upstairs and downstairs rooms are now permanently blocked off.

❀ ❀ ❀

We view the Dalai Lama's private living quarters at the Potala, his private temples, and a famous image of Chenrezig, which had been a favorite of his. Most of this is intact and has been left the way it was the day he departed for India.

A room previously used for altar ceremonial preparations is now a luxurious reception area. We rest there and are served tea and fruit. Then, we are driven to Drepung Monastery.

The congregation halls, the Dalai Lama's government rooms, most of the books and images are intact, but the monks' private rooms and fraternity halls have all been ruined. At the foot of the monastery a field of destroyed buildings has been made into an orchard, under the care of six or seven older monks. There are a few templekeepers and a few people in retreat, but the eight thousand monks who had lived there previously are all gone — murdered or departed.

At Sera, too, the congregation halls, statues, and art seem intact, but only six or seven elderly monks inhabit the immense place.

❀ ❀ ❀

On the tenth day of the tenth month, the Chinese National Holiday, we were taken to the Norbulinga to see the Dalai Lama's private buildings, the Gesang Potang, the Takden Minggyur Potang, and the Chenze Potang, which has two lady templekeepers. During that day, all the people of Lhasa put up tents and have picnics in the Norbulinga park. The walls that had been destroyed by the shelling have by this time largely been repaired.

My relatives come to picnic in the park, but though they call to me I am not allowed to go over and talk with them.

Our guard brings us tea and cookies. We are taken back to prison.

179

Far right: Shuguba on release from prison, 1979, in front of the Potala in Lhasa with (left to right) his nephew Shiu Chogyen Rinpoche, his sister Tsering Dekyi, and his grandnephew.

***

On the twentieth day of the tenth month of the earth-horse year, 1978, all the prisoners are gathered in the courtyard.

Our prison guard, Nyimala, reads a list of prisoners' names: Umgese Tulku, Phuntsok Nyamgye Lhagyeri, Pembe Tulku, Pobun Kenchung Nangar, Shide Kenchung Thubtenpa, myself, Rimshi Mendoba, Shatrase Ganden Paljor, Rimshi Lantonpa, Pema Dorje, Ponshose, Tangbise, Tsidrung Lobsang Tenzin, Losempa Tulku, Pembapu Dutu. These people are to be released from prison and transferred to the Chebsi Trazo, the Chinese Office for Tibetan People, which will provide us each with a job in their administration and a room housing two or three people.

Belongings that had been taken from us nearly twenty years before are displayed on a table: watches, medicines, jewelry. We aren't allowed to take back anything which had once been a mark of rank. A blue sheet and enough padding for making a quilt are given to each prisoner.

The Chinese Office for Tibetan People sent a car with two people to transport us in small groups away from the prison house.

***

People who had sided with the Chinese and had not gone to prison were working in the Chinese Office for Tibetan People. Thirty-one in all. I have memorized their names.

***

Each month we were provided rice, flour, tea, and butter by the office of Shingra next to the Jokhang. Another office provided us with meat and vegetables. A kitchen was built next to the meeting hall. The cook and his daughter, members of our group, brought us Tibetan tea — one thermos for each person — each morning. We were given excellent tsampa, some of which we traded with the monks at Drepung for rice.

In the mornings we ate tsampa in buttered tea, at noon we were given lunch, and in the evenings the kitchen prepared us each another thermos of tea, some meat and vegetables, Chinese steamed bread, and rice. Each person had to collect his share from the kitchen himself. Some people borrowed a small churning stick for the tea.

Saturday afternoons everyone but the pig and sheep keepers and the doorkeepers went home by public car. Monday mornings the car picked them up at a certain place to return them to their jobs, where they stayed all week.

During the day, myself and the other released prisoners were to study culture and the developments in the local and national areas based on what we read in the Chinese-run Lhasa newspapers. We were required to attend group discussions in which we were encouraged to express our thoughts and impressions. The meetings lasted two hours.

Sometimes all of us were asked to gather in our meeting hall with the Chinese president of our committee, Rin Dun, and the secretary and vice-secretary, to listen to their reports and speeches.

After dinner every night we watched Chinese dance and music performances, which youth groups and people from other offices also attended. The older members were not required to attend, but if we did, we got an extra thermos of tea, a few sweets, and cigarettes.

Outside this building, fruits and vegetables were grown. One day the office told me and my colleague to help care for the fruit trees since we'd had experience working in the orchards in prison. The five people already assigned to this task didn't need our help because they were doing a fine job on it. There wasn't anything for us to do, but we gave them a few suggestions, pointing out, for example, that since the trees were not planted on a slope, too much water might damage them.

Shuguba (seated) with his grandniece Dekyi Drolkar, in Lhasa, 1979, upon release from prison.

Center: Shuguba at Ewam Choden Tibetan Buddhist Meditation Center in Kensington, California, 1989, with Takhang Khenchung (his wife's cousin, left) and Lama Kunga Rinpoche, right.

CHAPTER XI

Epilogue

If you really intend to practice, your homeland is the
devil's prison — cast it all behind you.
— Milarepa, eleventh-century

Since I've been living in the United States with my son, my mind has been related to that of my son. The food and shelter are of a high standard, and my health has been generally good. I have met many people, Western students and new friends, who complain that I cannot communicate with them. I feel badly that I didn't learn English as a young man. Generally I am happy to be here, oriented toward Buddhist practice, which is my job. Ewam Choden Meditation Center is a good place for practice.

Much of my time is spent in the meditation room, reading sutras and other Buddhist texts. I try to improve my mind. I try to recognize and eliminate the three poisons: greed, hatred, and ignorance, or fear. I try to overcome my inner problems.

I am thinking now about the young Dalai Lama. Nearly every day I used to see him at the Potala. Every other day there were meetings and public interviews with him. I saw him passing in the hallways. He was always kind to me. I gave him a cream-beige horse, and in return he gave me one of my favorite horses — the blue-haired horse with red tips on the mane. I thought of this horse when the Dalai Lama asked me my age. My speaking had become difficult for I was breathing unevenly.

The Dalai Lama made me pull my chair close to him. We sat facing each other knee to knee. He asked me to tell him about what happened after he left Tibet. He asked me about prison. He told me to write my story, to say the truth about everything, not to try to protect anyone. Do not exaggerate, he said, just speak the truth.

I am looking now at a color photograph of myself in that room with the Dalai Lama, and I am remembering the sound of his voice. I am the only one left of the imprisoned high officials of his original government. His Holiness had many questions. My young friend Peggy Day arranged the visit. She is here in this picture smiling, holding onto my arm.

The blue horse is a big-sized horse; my son Kunga Gyurme used to care for my horse while I was away. He was very fond of that horse. Generally in Tibet we believe that horses are in particular agreement with higher deities. They are here as protectors, as special protecting friends for mankind.

We spoke together for nearly one hour. The Dalai Lama greeted me formally, calling me "Kuno." He bowed and touched his forehead to mine in affectionate greeting. I hadn't seen him for over thirty years.

There is a special kind of deity with a horse head, called Tadrin. Horses are highly respected in Tibet, as are cows in India. Horses can save your life, or tell you when it's time to die. In battle, a horse is your best friend. Horses are powerful and respected gifts. They are believed to know things that men cannot know. They have unusual powers.

The Chinese, too, loved horses and had many fine breeds. When the Chinese made the roads for the use of buses, trucks, and automobiles, the dust rose high into the air and the sound of engines could be heard for miles. Few roads were paved, so a lot of dust and mud was generated. But the man on horseback could still get over the old pathways, climbing straight up the side of a mountain.

These are words from a prayer written by Kunga Zangpo, founder of Ngor Monastery:

> In the cities of earth may the airs come lightly,
> Fanning the white prayer flags garlanded like a rosary.
> Gracefully-swaying clothes and ornaments of precious stone,
> May all possess them.
> For each inhabitant of the city may prosperity increase.
> The sky gleams with clouds forked by silver lightning.

186

On the earth below, the delighted peacocks dance.
Gently rain feeds the earth, persistent in spring are the showers.
For everything that lives this is my prayer:
May the joy that is spontaneous grow and increase.

There are four tones in the Tibetan language: There is a falling tone, and a mountain tone — that is, rising then falling. There is a flat high tone — the masculine one. And a rising tone, which is feminine.

I am in my room. These are tanka paintings hanging on the walls. None of these was brought with me from Tibet. All were given to me since I came to the United States. One of the tankas is a picture of White Tara — a long-life deity. Next to her is Manjushri, the personification of wisdom. And this is a photograph of His Holiness. Beside it are sixteen *arahats*, at the center of which sits the Vajrayogini. If one carefully meditates on the Vajrayogini, it is possible to obtain the pure land. One can reach to that land in one's lifetime. This is a significant practice.

I don't dream much anymore. When I do, they are not terrifying dreams, they are peaceful dreams. In one dream, I am inside a large beautiful house, a type of country farmhouse with two floors. The upper story is for the use of the family, and the lower story sometimes houses favorite horses. In this dream my horses were sleeping below, and my wife was with me. We were both young, in our twenties, and very happy in that house. I was walking about in the house, looking carefully at everything.

My wife's name was Tsering Chodsom. She was born in Pembe Village. Her father was a Tibetan finance minister as I later became. Her father came to the house of Trimon from outside. My wife's mother was the daughter of a military minister. Her father, mother, and uncle had all passed away, and she was alone in the house. Then a man from Shakabpa estate came to her and married her and became part of the Trimon family. My wife was born the second daughter. They also had seven sons.

The next picture is of the great teacher, Sakyamuni Buddha, who lived many hundred centuries ago. On the other side is Chenrezig, with four hands. He is a unique tutelary deity for the land of snows. This here is Green Tara. One prays to Green Tara for protection from the eight fears.

This is a picture of my son, who died recently, born Sonam Gyatso. And this is his young daughter Chinzalee. Generally, my son Sonam Gyatso's health was not good for most of his life. I understand the nature of the disease and that anyone who gets that disease has very little chance to live. When I heard of that disease in him, I knew that he would lose his life in a matter of time. I also felt that he was not very old and my life had been long and the fact that I am still alive and he is not makes me sad. I have seen so many of my children pass on in their youth. The sadness comes from a feeling of that. I regret the loss of all of my children who have died. However, I look forward to the survival of my two remaining sons, Kunga Gyurme and Yeshe Thondup.

I did talk with Sonam Gyatso a few days before he passed away. I had given him some Tibetan medicine to be used for his health. During this last conversation I asked if he had been able to take that medicine and he said no. I was disturbed and said to him that he should have used that medicine also. I asked him why he didn't, and he replied that he was in the process of taking treatment from the Western doctors and he felt that for the time it would be important for him to continue what he had started. He felt that it would not be necessary to take Tibetan herb medicine as well. From my own point of view I think he should have tried the Tibetan treatment. I regret that he neglected it.

Tibetans believe that suffering is a prelude to compassion. We are aware of three types of suffering: The suffering of change, which is sometimes viewed as happiness. The suffering of suffering, which is extreme pain or grief. And the cosmic or universal suffering, which is based on the knowledge that all things are related and all things must pass.

It has been said that knowledge was the industry of Tibet: Knowledge of how to live in peace and serenity. Knowledge of how to die.

This plant is a coffee plant; these are the coffee plant flowers. Since I have been here in America I have had much opportunity to experiment with plants and flowers, trying to improve their growing conditions. That is a medicine. I keep the Tibetan medicines in glass jars. There are medicines for various illnesses. . . . This one helps a stomach problem, indigestion. This one helps the liver. This is useful for *lung* — when a person feels agitated and nervous. The white ones help rahula sickness. This here is a medicine for the eyes; it helps with eyesight, blindness. It is a precious medicine, expensive.

This is a picture that was taken in Tibet. This picture is myself, a long time ago, with my son Kunga Gyurme, "Kungula" we called him when he was very small. His mother is not in this picture. She was at Black Horse at the time, and the picture was taken in Lhasa. The belt we wear symbolizes mortality.

I remember the day I was released. That was the day the Chinese prison guards brought some of my belongings, such as my wristwatch, which they handed back to me. Also they did say that any objects and ornaments that were precious, or made of precious metals such as gold, I could not have, because those things had been confiscated by the government, by the Chinese.

There were quite a few Tibetan prisoners released when I was. Among those some were set up as a committee in an office for rehabilitation. I was one of them. At the beginning I was set up in that office, and they told us to go meet with our relatives, whatever relatives we still had in town. I was able to talk with my sister and her sons and her daughter and their children, who were the part of my family still alive. I did then enjoy my family in Lhasa.

It is indeed true that while I was in prison I believed that my destiny would be to die in prison. When I was released, it became clear that I might be able to die outside prison.

This is a picture of Mt. Everest and the monastery at the bottom of the mountain. A picture of a chorten there, or a stupa, which is a monument to hold sacred objects such as things belonging to great departed lamas.

I enjoy the view from the library at Ewam Choden. I can see across the bay to Mt. Tamalpais: the mountain that looks like a sleeping lady. Some days the water is covered in mists and fogs, and it reminds me of the snows of Tibet.

This picture was taken in China. In Beijing. A white chorten in

Tsering Dekyi, Shuguba's sister, in Lhasa, 1979. Photograph by Fred Ward.

China. In Tibet we do not toss away any papers because generally they are prayers and scriptures, and so we collect them. Then they are used or worn or placed inside a chorten in order that the power of the words might increase and radiate out. I was told that the Communists shredded many fine prayer books printed in the traditional and laborious manner of hand woodblock printing. They used the scraps as shoe linings or in paving roads.

This is my hat. When I went to India, I bought this hat and I often wear it. It was very helpful in Tibet when the sun was bright. In the language of Tibet this hat is called *chingsha*. We Tibetans have many kinds of hats. A large gilded traveling hat, made of wood covered in brocade, is particularly useful in protecting from *nyima*, the sun.

The Dalai Lama is the leader of the Yellow Hat Sect, the Gelugpas. Two of my sons, Kunga Gyurme and Sonam Gyatso, are monks of the Sakya school, the White Earth Sect, and my son Tsenshab, who lives in Switzerland, is part of the Gelugpa Sect, the Dalai Lama's order.

The Dalai Lama is known to be a Great Adept, a Master of the Kalachakra Tantra, which is the spiritual technology of the Wheel of Time. Whoever knows the Wheel of Time has a hand in destiny.

Members of the Yellow Hat Sect were reformers, and the Dalai Lama himself always had very progressive ideas about the direction Tibet should be going. Unfortunately, he was so young when he was forced into exile he had no time to initiate reforms. Left to ourselves, I believe we would have overcome our obstructions. Many young people, such as my sons, were interested in reform. They never had a chance to implement their ideas. The invasion changed everything. Since then, the Dalai Lama's message has been one of patience and great forebearance. He says the Chinese will eventually tire in their role of subjugating our people. It might take ten years or it might take fifty. We must be steadfast in our aims to reclaim our land. He says that the Chinese will eventually come to see that they were wrong.

Mahatma Gandhi died in 1948. His achievement was to free India from over two hundred years of domination by England. Tibet too will one day achieve liberation.

191

Festival at Sakya Monastery, c. 1950.

When the Chinese took over Tibet, they opened to the people the elaborate parks and gardens through which the Dalai Lama once strolled in privacy. The Norbulinga means "garden of jewels." Families now go to these formerly sacred places to picnic, drink chang, and play *bas*, a gambling game like dominoes. I have heard it said that six thousand monasteries were destroyed. Over one million people have died. It is clear today we were not invaded we were conquered.

This is a picture of America. A map. This is a picture of the Potala Palace. The name Potala means "high heavenly realm." And these are the three Dharma kings.

This is an offering to the foreign god, Jesus, given to me by a friend.

This is a Hindu statue given to me by my daughter-in-law, Laetitia, mother of Chinzalee, the wife of Sonam Gyatso. It is a deity, a horse that rides on the clouds, is flying on the clouds in the sky. The horse's feet are in the clouds.

My son Sonam Gyatso was a great scholar. When he died, he was in the process of translating one of the books of the *Abidharma*. The book he was working on was called "Three Experiences: The Jewel That Pleases" — esoteric hermeneutical teachings of Tibetan psychology and metaphysics. It tells of the path traversed by all those gone to well-being in the three times. It tells how there are accomplishments and powers to be attained, ordinary or common powers, and a supreme consummation, the attainment of Buddhahood. Interferences, interruptions, impediments, and evil circumstances arise both from inside and outside oneself.

This is a picture of the young Dalai Lama with his two tutors.

This is the name of the Fourteenth Dalai Lama of Tibet.

This is a name for Tibet, translated "bod." We call ourselves the *bodpa*.

Wisdom, here, is represented by the bell. The method, leading to immortality, compassion, is represented by the *vajra*, a scepter.

The Fourteenth Dalai Lama and Hiroshi Sonami (Sonam Gyatso) in Japan, c. 1960.

These are the flowers of the juniper tree, and these are lotus flowers. One, two, three, four, five, six, seven, eight petals, in English.

This is a picture of the green bird we have in Tibet — I don't know the name of it but it makes beautiful singing. It doesn't know anything about the human language. I used to have two birds that could speak human languages, but one day I dropped the cage on the floor and they escaped. They were lovebirds. So small, fitting in the palm of the hand. They learned how to say *father, mother, son,* in Tibetan. When I dropped the cage, the door opened and they flew away.

At Black Horse Village we had a small dog named Park Tro that was a favorite of my sons. The children were happy there; they were fed a kind of chang soup and they liked that. They had a nurse. And their uncle, who was kindhearted, let them do as they wished.

I am father of nine children. Two are yet living. One child, a girl, died shortly after birth.

These are various small statues around here such as 'Tara, Vajrayogini, and Chenrezig.

This is a red sandalwood rosary, called a *tengwa* in Tibetan. Also it can be used as a *chupshe*, or counter. If you circle it around ten times, you make one thousand prayers.

This paper comes from inside a Tibetan dumpling, a momo. At this year's New Year Festival we ate the oracle soup. My momo said "Travel."

I have seen Tibetans living in this country, and they seem to have a good livelihood and are doing good studies. I feel that Tibetans living abroad are still fighting for the freedom of Tibet.

For nineteen years in prison I was self-contained. I did not allow anything to influence me from outside. Observing my mind the first day I saw that it felt as if a terrific weight had dropped.

I remember the broad-rimmed red hats worn by gentlemen's servants. I remember the yellow-billed swans in the gardens of the Jokhang, and on Mapham Lake under the sacred mountain. We also had many other waterfowl, such as cranes, ducks, and geese.

This is the White Mahakala. The history of the White Mahakala practice is such: In ancient times, Chenrezig paused in front of the infinite Buddha Amitabha and promised not to become enlightened but to work untiringly for the good of all sentient beings. He took this oath: If I fail in my work, may my head be split into a thousand pieces.

Chenrezig stayed for countless years on the mountain called Potala, laboring day and night for the benefit of all. After such a long time he thought that because of his great effort, and the time spent, the suffering of sentient beings must surely be lessened.

He looked down and discovered that the quantity of sentient beings was about the same, and because it was a degenerate time, their passions and evil deeds were even greater than before. He sighed despairingly, "I am not able to rescue even one sentient being." Thus breaking his oath his head flew into one thousand pieces.

His guru, Amitabha, appeared before him, saying, "It is bad of you to become so discouraged. To expiate your mistake, you must take an even greater oath." He reached out and magically assembled the thousand pieces into eleven heads.

Chenrezig thought to himself, "I have spent such a long time in fruitless effort, how can I ever gather up my energy again?" He was so tired, so discouraged, that for seven days he was unable to move and remained unconscious.

Finally, he recovered and said to himself: "Degenerate sentient beings have short lives and bad luck. Easily hurt, easily sick, they are subjected constantly to adverse conditions and sufferings. They exhaust their energy in order to eat and drink each day. They have no leisure to meditate. They are dogged by negative forces, unable to maintain their vows; they engage in destructive and immoral acts. Even true Dharma practitioners and other spiritual people are caught in confusion. . . ."

With sudden understanding, the eleven-headed Chenrezig decided that these unfortunate degenerated sentient beings needed a deity they could experience immediately, without taking too much time. One who protects them in life and in death, who brings them wealth and companions, and devastates their enemies. He took an oath then and there to devote himself to accomplishing such common and supreme abilities. Having completed that thought, he manifested a dark blue HUM in his heart from which issued a six-armed Mahakala, the deity with the strength to accomplish all deeds and wishes. At the same time there were tremendous earthquakes and lightening storms.

Then the once-born, and the deity-born, and the Tathagatas of the three times said, "Well-done! Such concern for sentient beings!" And they gave him all the empowerments.

This is my television; in Tibetan it is called *sukton lungting*, meaning, "to see pictures." There are many things to see. The language I do not understand. Lots of people are talking. I see a lot of scenery, landscapes in other countries, beautiful things that are a joy to watch. Sometimes it shows pictures of nature such as deer, musk, wild animals, and other creatures in the countryside. Animals out enjoying themselves. I like to watch before the evening meal what is called the "Wheel of Fortune." The wheel they use is similar to a prayer wheel.

My son Kunga Gyurme teases me about my girlfriends — four ladies who are kind enough to pay attention to an old man. There is the young Bhutanese girl, who is very beautiful. A Bhutanese princess. She helps me with my daily tasks. She took me to a department store one day. I was amazed by the lifelike manikins. (Once I was foolish enough to try to kiss her, but she only laughed.)

On my walks around Kensington, I stop to exchange greetings with a charming elderly lady whose voice is soft as a breeze. She tends her flowers and has a small black dog with her always.

There is the one who helps to write this life story. She asks many questions, some of them difficult to answer. We hold hands and enjoy exchanging words in our own languages, such as those for horse and airplane and eye.

Peggy Day has been my friend for years. Some days she takes me to the Bay, where I watch from a bench as she rides her sailing board on the water. She is lovely in the face, and her spirit is calm and refreshing. Her gentle strength reminds me of my wife.

My son Sonam Gyatso asked me before his death to tell him about what happened to Regent Reting Rinpoche. I could not tell him. It seemed to me then that nothing could be accomplished by going into it again. Now, I have told all that I have to tell. I think perhaps some of us made mistakes. I think perhaps there are many unclarified subjects for Tibetans, for the peoples in the world today.

I hope that Tibet under the present aggression of Communism will be better in the future. I hope it will be inevitably changed and that soon Tibetans will be enjoying Tibet again as before.

I was delighted to come to the United States of America because I felt there was a true freedom here. I learned about this country before I came here. I had learned about the history of the United States and its democracy, and I read about it in the newspaper. Under the Communists, the oppression was very bad. Living under oppression was so bad that I began to envy the freedom that other countries had.

This book is part of the *Kangyur*. I read from the *Kangyur* daily. This book here, this big book with pictures, is about King Gesar — a story of warriors in which wealth is exchanged. It tells of how in ancient times the warriors went out to bring wealth into Tibet from Persia. They are interesting stories of battles with bows and arrows, swords, and spears. No guns are used. There are many horses pictured in this book, with the names of the types of horses. This is a picture of the son of the king. These are metals. This is blue, blue sky. These are the thirty warriors of King Gesar. The king is said to have been the personification of Manjushri, born as a Tibetan.

From one book I discovered that the horse as a power was supreme for thirty centuries, and during the last one hundred years the horse has gradually been replaced by mechanical machines. Horses now run on wheels, as the prophesy stated. There are trains and cars and airplanes. Before the invasion, all Tibetans rode. There were only three automobiles in the country, no buses, trains, or airplanes. Change came swiftly.

This is a clock. You can put it on the table. Above is a picture of King Srongtsen Gampo. There were many statues of him in Tibet. Someone took a photograph of one of those statues.

This is the altar. These are long-life prayers. The six longevities: long-life mountain, long-life tree, long-life water, long-life person, long-life crane, long-life prayers. *Tsering jungdruk* they are called. Auspicious signs.

❀ ❀ ❀

Tomorrow they take me to another place so that I might make a slow recovery from this illness. My right side is paralyzed. I cannot swallow food so they have cut open a place in my belly and inserted a tube there through which liquid nourishment travels directly into my intestines. This is less painful than when the tube was placed down my throat.

I cannot speak words in response to questions, though I find that in reciting mantras aloud I have no trouble. My sons ask am I in pain, and I try to make it plain that I am not.

This place I now am in is a hospice in a town called Pleasant Hill, and it is indeed not an unpleasant place in which to be ill. It all began with the rahula sickness. His Holiness Sakya Trizin called again today.

I always felt a fondness for specially-trained horses that do a fast canter. I chose the smoothest horse. I love those comfortable riding horses. My last ride was in 1959, the last day my horses were kept at the Norbulinga. All those horses were confiscated. Three of my horses were *gyangbo*, the color of wild ass, one was *tawo*, brown, and all four of them were well trained, well mannered, and young — two- to three-year-old males. The names? One was "The Comet" and another "The Auspicious Good Omen."

I was staying in Lhasa, and everything seemed all right. Then my son Kunga Gyurme came and told me that living in the United States was interesting and since two of my sons were there, perhaps I'd like to go for a visit. I have been liking it here for ten years.

I believe I have contracted the wind disease. I have been sick for a month.

I remember the yellow-billed swans in the gardens of the Jokhang. I wake at the first light and see that the night nurse has put on the face of a horrific deity. My son Yeshe Thondup comes and reminds me that this is the festival day for ghosts and demons,

Chinzalee Sonami (Shuguba's granddaughter) with Shuguba at Ewam Choden, Kensington, California, 1987.

Halloween. At evening, children pass from house to house begging sweets. My grandaughter Chinzalee arrives looking like a small dakini in her jewels, her tasseled slippers, and her bracelets of silver bells from India. Streamers of colored ribbon are woven into her hair.

She speaks quickly, laughing in high-spirited health. The rooms are full of sick people, very old people, most of whom seem to suffer much more than I. They cry out at night.

My hands look as if they belong to someone else, bent and elongated like the long white hairs that grow from my chin. I am certainly old enough to die.

It is night. I am alone with the silence. I begin my prayers.

JAMYANG KHEDRUP SHUGUBA DIED ON OCTOBER 31, 1991.

Lama Kunga Rinpoche and Tsenshab Rinpoche (with Gonpo, the dog) at Ewam Choden, 1991.

Lama Kunga Rinpoche's
Postscript

Lama Kunga Rinpoche was born in Lhasa in 1935, son of the noble family of the Shugu estate. In 1979, he returned to Tibet, for the first time since his escape in 1959, to retrieve his recently released father and bring him back to the United States. Rinpoche urged his father to write down all that had happened to him. Assisted by Lucy Du Pertuis, Ph.D., Rinpoche translated into literal English Shuguba's original autobiographical account, hand-written in Tibetan. He acted as translator and advisor in the completion of this book. He has coauthored two published translations of Milarepa's songs, as well as numerous Tibetan poems, prayers, and stories — revised excerpts of which are included in the preceding pages. Rinpoche's postscript was compiled from conversations with him in Kensington, California, 1994–1995. — S. C.

❀ ❀ ❀

In 1978, the Chinese Premier Hua Guofeng decided to release some prisoners in Tibet and in China. My brother Tsenshab Rinpoche, who was then staying in Hamburg, Germany, phoned me as soon as he received news that thirty-four prisoners had been released in Tibet. A friend of my brother's worked at the local newspaper, and he had seen a partial list of names on the wire service. Subsequently, an article was printed in the *London Times* and the *New York Times*, on November 16, 1978.

Soon, the Office of Tibet in New York sent out a notice listing all the names. My father's name was unclear (as "Shagaba Janying Kedup"), but the description of his former office was fairly accurate. Tsenshab tried to find out exactly who this person was — to see if it might indeed be our aged father, imprisoned in Tibet for over nineteen years.

I began writing letters to various persons. I wrote to my friend Dick Blum and to Congressman Ron Dellums. I wrote to the U.S. Embassy in Beijing, asking them to locate the man we believed to be our father. The process took many months. The Chinese said at first that they couldn't locate him. I kept writing letters, sending the Chinese various newspaper accounts. Finally, they found him, living in Lhasa with his sister. My brothers and I were very excited to find out that he had survived all those years.

I discovered that a photographer named Fred Ward would soon be visiting Tibet. I was introduced to him by my friend Lewis Lancaster, a professor at the University of California, Berkeley. Fred came to see me, and I asked him to attempt to visit my family in Lhasa and to please take a picture of my father.

When he returned and showed me the photograph he had taken, I was very happy to see the faces. There was my father with his sister and some nieces and nephews. We had not had communication with any of them since 1959 when Tsenshab and I escaped the invading Chinese. We still didn't know the fate of other family members. We didn't yet know that our mother and our uncle and our sister had died, as well as many others.

My brothers and I unanimously decided to do everything we could to bring my father out of Tibet, in order that he might live in Switzerland or in the United States to be near his sons.

I decided to travel to Tibet right away, before the situation changed. I applied for a visa to enter through Nepal. The Chinese gave me permission, saying that any Chinese citizen can come to visit relatives. I flew to Kathmandu, Nepal, and in June several of us boarded a bus headed for Lhasa. There were many others who had been allowed visas for visiting their families.

Previously, after seeing the photograph of my father, I had written to him to ask if he would like to come to America for a visit. I sent him my photograph. He wrote back:

> *You my sons have gone through a lot of difficulty in order to be able to ask me, an old man, to come to the United States, offering to supply all the expenses and such. I was overwhelmed with sadness and happiness as if meeting you from my grave. Also I am overwhelmed after so many years of separation, that you, as my children, did not forget me. However, there is little chance for your request to come to pass. I am very old now, the journey would take a long time. The journey would prove too difficult for me.*

Shuguba in Kensington, California, at Ewam Choden, 1986.

The three of you, my sons, should meet with us here. You are still young. You should come to see me and our relatives, also to see the new Tibet. If you come here, the local Chinese government will have a good policy toward you, not bothering you about what happened in the old times. The policy is better now. You should not have any doubts about that. You can come and take a look, and then you can go back.

Here I have an easy situation with an opportunity to enjoy the people of Tibet. The Chinese have given me a title of chapsi totsok.* One of my four sisters, Tsering Dekyi, is still alive, as well as her children. Don't worry, I'm happy now. They've given me a place to stay. My sister and her son, Shiu Chogyen Rinpoche, are together here, and we three live happily now in Lhasa.

In Danak Village (Black Horse) lives my daughter-in-law, Tseten Drolma,† and her children. Some of the Trimon relatives, are still alive, here in Lhasa. I showed your picture to all the relatives, and they were so happy. They ask for you to come see us.

Tashi Delek — August 1979

The bus I boarded in Nepal dropped me off at the station in Lhasa. I had sent a telex from the border. Four days were spent traveling the uneven Chinese-made road. When we arrived, I saw that Lhasa was dirty, dusty, filthy. Some of my cousins met me at the station. Together we boarded a minibus. Everything looked so different. And I was different too — wearing a jean jacket and jeans from Sears. We were let off at the place where I was to meet with my father. When the bus pulled up in front, I saw that he was not at the door. The street was full of people awaiting my arrival. They gave me jars of incense and cups of chang to drink. Then an old, old man came out the door with a very old lady. I saw that it was my father and his sister. We embraced and exchanged katas. Everyone was crying and laughing. People filled the street. I met the members of my family as well as some old and some new friends.

I felt exhausted from the journey, but nonetheless I spent a lot of time trying to reacquaint myself with my relatives. Food was rationed,

---

*Indicating that they have forgotten previous crimes and former rank and made him a member of a reform group with a small salary.

† The daughter-in-law had been blacklisted and branded with what is called "the hat." By 1994, she, too, had been given the title chapsi totsok.

Shuguba in Kathmandu, Nepal, 1980, with son Tsenshab Rinpoche and nephew Shiu Chogyen Rinpoche.

but the Chinese had given a little extra to my family for a reception and a share for me. They also gave packages of candies and cigarettes, even though I don't smoke. They told my family to make me comfortable.

I was able to convince my father that he should come to live with us, his sons, that he should come back with me to the United States.

Many people at that time were still having "the hat." By that I mean they were labeled as political criminals with severely reduced rights. They were "untouchables" — not allowed to work, treated with severe disrespect. They were not allowed to talk or associate with any members of their own family or the community.

Some people were afraid to talk to me, but they wanted to talk, they tried to talk. Every day I listened to the sad stories. Some asked for a piece of my clothing to remember me by. In any town, they were so desperate to meet with us Tibetans who had been abroad. They had no hope.

I spent four months in Tibet. I had to be careful not to express my anger in front of any Chinese. Visiting Gyantse — I had never been there before — people broke down the door to my guest room. I was sleeping at night, and about forty people came in and surrounded me and said, "Do something. We are suffering so much. What are you going to do? We heard that you came here today, and we wanted to talk to you."

I said, "I am not such an important person, but I want to tell you not to worry. The important thing is that His Holiness is alive, he is healthy, and he is working hard for you. We Tibetans who are living abroad have not forgotten you." I set up my tape recorder and asked them to tell me everything. I was so tired, but I let them tape their stories all night. I promised to send the tapes to the Dalai Lama. In every town it was like that. By the time I left, I had to carry two duffel bags full of mail out of Tibet to be delivered to people living in exile communities.

One of the reasons I stayed so long in Tibet was that I had difficulty obtaining a visa for my father. I myself had a current U.S. passport, so the Chinese instructed me to ask for a "leave of absence" for him to visit the United States. When we got the acceptance, it seemed everything was in order and it was time to go. However, the Chinese wanted me to exit through Beijing, where all the papers were kept. I said no, I wanted to exit through Nepal. Very difficult, the Chinese official said. After that, I myself traveled back to Nepal to talk to the U. S. Consulate there. I asked them to request that all the documents be sent from Beijing to Nepal. They promised me they would try, but they said it might take a while.

For three weeks I lived in Kathmandu until finally the papers arrived. Then I traveled back to Lhasa and spent two more months there. The Chinese in Peking had released my father's papers for travel, but the local Chinese government in Lhasa was also required to give its agreement. Eventually the officials told me yes, but they said, you still must talk to the city division. If the city division says OK, then there is still the police department, which has to give its approval as well.

I went to each of the different departments, waiting for four hours or more at a time to get the proper signatures. Often the officials told me I would have to come back the next day. Lhasa had been divided up into ten communes. The commune people were also required to approve. The people in our commune said it was fine. They were simple people, they didn't even read the document. Finally, I got all the papers and letters together, and we were allowed to depart. I had also asked that my cousin be allowed to travel with us to Nepal.

We hired a Chinese jeep to take us to the border. We traveled three days. The young Chinese soldier was kind and a very good driver. He offered to let us stop off in Shigatse for one night. There we made a pilgrimage to Tashilhunpo Monastery. We said our good-byes.

At the border, after crossing the pass, the Chinese guards had to make a call to Lhasa for approval. Our driver dropped us off before the bridge. He couldn't cross. As he started on his return, we hugged him and gave him a kata, wishing him well.

Tsenshab was waiting for us in Nepal. We spent one month there with him in Kathmandu. My father's daughter-in-law and her daughter visited us later. They had been allowed to come to Nepal to visit a sister who had been living in Nepal for some time. From Kathmandu we flew to Bangkok, then to Japan. We crossed the Pacific Ocean to land in San Francisco.

At the San Francisco Airport we had to hire a taxi because my friends had mixed up the dates due to an error in the telegram I had sent from Kathmandu. They had been there to pick us up the day before.

We drove across the Bay Bridge and up the freeway to Ewam Choden in the hills of Kensington above Berkeley. I showed Pala ["Father"] his room, which was all prepared for him. He went every-

Local school, 1994, Black Horse Village (Tanak). Tibetan is no longer taught, only Chinese.

where in the house, slowly looking everywhere at everything, upstairs, downstairs, like a cat. He said he was very happy to see the shrine and the many Tibetan books.

Then we all relaxed.

We have been happy and grateful that Pala's health was so good for such a long time. He seemed happy here — meeting new students and making lots of friends. He got up early every day. Each morning he circumambulated Ewam Choden through the streets of Kensington. A half hour walk. All the neighbors knew him.

Soon after his arrival, I began asking him about his experiences, and he started writing things down. He attended our group meditations and teachings. He read through the entire 108 volumes of the *Kangyur* once, and, by the time he died, he was halfway through his second reading. He lived here eleven years. In the afternoons we made tea and lunch; then he'd take a nap. He watched TV in the evenings. On the days he received a social security check, we cashed the check and bought a six-pack of Dos Equis or some German beer, and we drank it together.

❖ ❖ ❖

Tibet today: My last two trips have been short ones. I visited Tibet very recently (April 1994) for about a week. I had visited also in 1984, traveling with a group of students and friends. We stayed only a month, traveling to Lhasa from Beijing. Our impression of Tibet wasn't too clear. We traveled in the company of a Chinese liaison. Whenever we tried to converse with other Tibetans, there was always a Chinese person listening. However, by 1984 things seemed a little better than they had been in 1980. People weren't so desperate. Communications were opening up a little. I didn't have to carry out as many notes with me.

This last visit, 1994, I could see that China has really converted Tibet to its own culture. There are more Chinese people there now than Tibetans. To my own eyes, the towns of Shigatse and Lhasa are ten times bigger than before, and there are ten times more Chinese in them. What the Chinese are doing is cultural genocide. The streets in Lhasa are lined almost entirely with Chinese businesses. There are Chinese civilian shop owners even in the villages. They are taking over the occupancy of all services. Most of the jobs are filled by Chinese people. The Tibetan farmers and city people are becoming jobless. It is harder and harder for Tibetans to find work. They just aren't being hired.

The Chinese have also introduced alcoholism to Tibet by opening clubs — called *arkhang* — which serve hard liquor, have pool tables, and play recorded music. Every street in Lhasa or Shigatse now has one of these bars. Young people spend their days playing pool.

At first, all Tibetans tried to work. Work permits were given to them to go on with their work as before. Then, the Chinese opened gambling shops. Tibetans are the only ones who go to those gambling shops.

Many more Tibetans are becoming homeless every day. They lose their money and their jobs by gambling and playing mahjong. I saw very few Tibetans who were working and making it. Those mostly owned shops or restaurants. The communes seem to be breaking down.

On the outskirts of town, land is rented to Chinese people for growing wheat or vegetables. No longer is barley primarily what is grown. However, a few Tibetans are still growing barley. Rickshaws are in use by Chinese and Tibetans, but you need a permit to own one. Some Chinese are able to obtain a large number of permits, and they then sublet those permits to others, especially to Tibetans, for a price.

The schools are a problem; they are mostly run by Chinese now. Tibetans have few books and no supplies. No Tibetan language or history is being taught. In fact, in the schools, Tibetan is discouraged. They say you won't get a job unless you speak Chinese.

The University of Lhasa is just a name. Mostly it offers Chinese language and Chinese subjects. The monasteries seem to be opening up a little. Of the monasteries that were not completely destroyed, there are a few selected monasteries where monks are now allowed back in.

The smartest Tibetan children are sent to China for six to seven years of training. By the time they are finished they have been indoctrinated into the Chinese method and lifestyle. They don't want to come back to live and work in villages. If they do come back, they have been taught that the Tibetan system is no good. The Chinese are taking more and more Tibetan students this way. They even take the nomads and turn them into scientists and musicians (that's what they tell me). It's true they are educating some people, but those people cannot then go back into their own culture. A few are waking up and protesting. They realize they have been tricked.

During this last visit, I saw many changes. Tanak Village [Black Horse] is the site of a hydroelectric plant. Yamdrok Tso, the sacred turquoise lake, is being drained and dammed for another hydroelectric plant. You see and hear the tractors digging a tunnel through our sacred mountain, Chomol-hari, to make way for the artificial reservoir. This is a very secretive project. They are digging something out. They are putting bundles of something into large packages and stacking them onto special trucks. They ship this substance off to China. We suspect it's gold or uranium.

If the Chinese have found a source of wealth in Tibet, they will not let go until they have torn it all out. The Chinese claim they have helped "these backward people." They aren't helping Tibetans; they are helping themselves. Of course, the Chinese have pointed out that there was inequality in our culture before, some people were very wealthy, some of the monasteries, too, and others were poor. From the middle path point of view we do see such inequality as a negative and a contributing factor in our downfall.

Tibet's tragedy is similar to what happened to the Native Americans. The Chinese have no respect for our culture. They are taking what they want. There has been famine, which was unknown to us before. They have made poor housing and bad roads. Electric power that works inter-mittently. The hydroelectric dams they are building will benefit the Chi-nese mining industry, not Tibetans.

After all they have done — after all the deaths and destruction, after the slogans and promises of a better life — the Chinese have not brought Tibet anywhere near to a modern living standard. Tibetans have not been trained to care for electrical power or to repair the roads. The improvements are hollow in Tibet today. There is the shadow of mod-ernism, the gesture only.

Tibet was isolated from the rest of the world before 1959, looking inward rather than outward culturally. We were naive. We were ignorant of world politics; most of us were ignorant of the politics in our own country.

We need other nations to monitor what China is doing to Tibet. The United Nations must become involved. We need representatives from other nations living there, watching.

The Dalai Lama wants Tibet to be declared a nuclear-free zone of peace. The Chinese have talked of selling land to Germany for a toxic waste dump. Much of Tibet's wildlife has been killed off; there has been a lot of deforestation. Nomads have fewer and fewer yaks and sheep and goats. Many have sold their herds to the Chinese for fast money. Then they have no means of making a living.

We have a long way to go. If the Chinese were to leave Tibet, say within the next ten years, Tibetans would have to consider carefully what to do. We cannot go back to the old ways, but we must maintain our spiritual practices. We need to understand how to best utilize the resources of our land. We need to look at other cultures, to see how other people live. Especially cultures that have gone through similar experiences. There are many small countries that have undergone tyranny and have gained independence. We can learn from them.

I believe that the people of Tibet cannot hold out much longer. Things are really bad. Tibet now is like the Native American community — dispirited. You can see it from the airplane. Towns are isolated, dusty, poor, sad.

When I was visiting Tibet this last time, the Chinese National Assembly met, and this assembly was televised in Tibet over the Chinese-owned network. The heads of Tibetan local government were asked about such difficulties as joblessness, the price of food, housing, education, and so forth. Tibetans are now telling the truth. The Tibetan heads of government are finally blaming the Chinese authorities, saying to them, "we can't do this anymore to our people."

— Lama Kunga Rinpoche

[NOTE: The documents following Lama Kunga Rinpoche's family photographs (taken in Tibet) represent a sample of the bureaucratic exchanges involved in bringing Tsipon Shuguba to the United States, beginning with the Chinese government's official press announcement about the release of prisoners.]

Shuguba (center) with grandniece Dekyi Drolkar (left), sister Tsering Dekyi (right), and grandnephews in Lhasa, 1979.

Remaining members of Shuguba family in Tibet, 1984. Photograph by Lama Kunga Rinpoche.

Left: Lama Kunga Rinpoche with cousins at Black Horse Village, 1994.

TIBET RELEASES 'REACTIONARY' PRISONERS, SECRET AGENTS
OW150720 Peking NCNA in English 0700 GMT Nov 78 OW

[Text] Lhasa, 15 Nov (HSINHUA) --All important prisoners who were
members of the reactionary group of the upper strata in Tibet were set
free on November 4 by the public security organ of the Tibet Autonomous
Region as an expression of leniency.

The 24 criminals released included officials of the former Tibet local
government, living buddhas and former commanders of local rebel forces.
Among them were Lhagyari Namgyal Gyagso, prince of Loka and dzasak of
the former Tibet local government; Shagaba Janying Kedup, former
commander of the rebel forces and tsipon of the former Tibet local
government; Kanchung Lacha of the former Tibet local government Tubdan
Danba; general administrator of Nagchuka district of the former Tibet
local government Menduiba Losang Wandui; deputy general administrator in
charge of grain of the former Tibet local government Shadra Gendan
Baljor; deputy general administrator of Ari district of the former Tibet
local government Lang Dung Benma Dorje; pogbon of the former Tibet local
government Changrag Ngawang Tsebal; former living buddha of Daipung
monastery Gyalsei Ngawang Losang; former living buddha of Peinpa
monastery, Pienpa Ngawang Losang; commanders of district rebel forces Bu
Dondub and Jangkang Gedor.

Also granted leniency and released at the same time were ten secret
agents who had sneaked into Tibet at the orders of foreign reactionaries
and the secret services of the rebels now in exile abroad.

TIBETAN COMPATRIOTS IN EXILE URGED TO RETURN TO PRC
OW150722Y Peking NCNA in English 0705 GMT 15 Nov 78 OW

[Text] Lhasa, 15 Nov (HSINHUA) --All Chinese compatriots of Tibetan
nationality now living in exile abroad, including those of the upper
strata who fled the country, are welcome to return to China if they so
wish.

This was announced by Tien Pao, vice-chairman of the Revolutionary
Committee of the Tibet Autonomous Region, on November 4. He was
addressing a meeting at which all the important criminals in detention,
who were members of the reactionary group of the upper strata in Tibet,
were set free as an expression of leniency. Tien Pao called on all
Tibetan compatriots now living in exile abroad to "acquire a clear
understanding of the excellent internal and international situation and
see through the scheme of the social-imperialists and reactionaries to
commit aggression and subversion and split our motherland. They should
extricate themselves from their predicament of living on alms and
suffering discrimination, and return home to participate in the
country's socialist construction."
"All patriots belong to one family whether they come forward early or
late," Tien Pao stated. "We welcome all those who are willing to come
back and we will not hold them responsible for their past misdeeds and
will provide them with appropriate jobs and means of production and
livelihood."

RELEASED TIBETANS ADDRESS MASS MEETING
OW150848Y Peking NCNA in English 0826 GMT 15 Nov 78 OW

[Text] Lhasa, 15 Nov (HSINHUA) --All 24 important prisoners in detention
who were members of the reactionary group of the upper strata in Tibet
were released as an expression of leniency at a mass meeting held here
on November 4. At the meeting, Benma Doje, deputy director of the Public
Security Bureau of the Tibet Autonomous Region, announced the decision
to grant clemency to these 24 criminals and issued them certificates of
release. They included dzasak of the former Tibet local government and
prince of Loka, Lhagyari Namgyal Gyagso, and former commander of the
rebel forces and tsipon of the former Tibet local government, Shagaba
Janying Kedub.

Shagaba Janying Kedub, former commander of the rebel forces and tsipon
of the former local government, said at the mass meeting: "Chairman Hua
and the party Central committee have given us the chance of turning over
a new leaf. Remorse grips us when we recall our past crimes. From now on
we will follow the Communist Party with determination, turn over a new
leaf in the true sense of the word and contribute to the construction of
a socialist new Tibet."

The releases were all granted citizenship rights and appropriate
arrangements were made for them according to their specific conditions.
Thirteen of them, including Lhagyari Namgyal Gyagbo and Shagaba Janying
Kedub will be given jobs and chances to study by the United Front Work
Department of the autonomous region.

In 1959, the reactionary group of the upper strata in Tibet violated the
agreement on the peaceful liberation of Tibet, worked hand in glove with
the imperialists and foreign reactionaries in staging a counter-
revolutionary armed rebellion. The released criminals were all chief
culprits and masterminds who plotted, organized and took part in the
rebellion. Since the rebellion was put down and the democratic reform
carried out, the public security organization in Tibet has followed
Chairman Mao's policy of "combining punishment with leniency and
combining reform through labor with ideological education" and of
"giving a way out." In the spirit of revolutionary humanitarianism, it
has done patient and meticulous work over a long period of time in
educating and reforming these criminals who committed crimes against the
motherland, the people and the revolution. Four groups of such criminals
had been given lenient treatment and set free since 1963 on the merit of
the repentance they had shown and the good services they had performed.
Now most of the remaining 24 criminals, after 19 years of education and
reform also pleaded guilty and were willing to turn over a new leaf.
Therefore all of them were accorded lenient treatment. . . .

Before they were discharged, the prisoners were each issued a new suit,
bedding, a hand bag and other daily necessities and 100 yuan R.M.B. as
pocket money. Their wrist watches, fountain pens and wallets which the
Public Security Department kept for them during their imprisonment were
returned to them. . . .

Mr. Yeshe Thondup
1, Seestrasse
CH-8700 Kuessnacht
Zurich, Switzerland

Kuessnacht, 23.11.1978

To
His Excellency
The Ambassador
The Embassy of China
3015 B e r n

Dear Sir,

      Recently I read in the newspaper that your government has freed some important prisoners of the former governing body of Tibet, among which is also my father, TSE PON SHUKU PA, Jamyang Khedrup. I was very happy to hear this excellent news.

      Now, I would like to address myself to you with the heartfelt request, whether a meeting with my father can be arranged. It is since 19 years that I and my family have not seen or heard from my father. Needless to say that we are most anxious to meet him. He should be very old by now and I wish to see him before he passes away. Please, would you let me know as soon as possible as to what arrangements must be made to meet my father.

      For your kind assistance I express my sincere thanks.

Truthfully,

Yeshe Thondup

THE OFFICE OF TIBET
801 Second Avenue, New York 17, New York. MU 6-7294

December 12, 1978

Lama Kunga Rinpoche
Ewam Choden
254 Cambridge
Kensington, Ca 94708

Dear Rinpoche:

It was my pleasure speaking to you recently on
the phone. Enclosed is the detailed text concerning
the release of Tibetan prisoners in Lhasa recently
by the Chinese. I think you should solicit the help
of your Senators and also write to Mrs Patricia
Derian who is Assistant Secretary for Human Rights
and Humanitarian Affairs at the State Department,
Washington, D.C.

I would very much appreciate hearing from you if
any progress is made. You are aware there are
other Tibetans in this country would also like to
be reunited with their parents and loved ones.

With my very best wishes,

Tenzin N. Tethong
Acting Representative

I, Tsepon Wangchuk Deden Shakabpa, born in Lhasa, Tibet
on January 7, 1907 am now a retired Tibetan Government
official presently in the United States on a visit with
my children. On November 5, 1978 Peking news report disclosed the release of officials and supporters of the old
Tibetan Government held as prisoners since the Communist
Chinese takeover of Tibet in 1959. The news report also
stated that the Peking Government would permit these released prisoners to visit their relatives who are living
abroad. Among those released is Jamyang Khedup Shugu,
the father of Losang Kunga a close relative of mine who
is an American citizen and is presently residing at Kensington, California.

Jamyang Khyedup Shugu was married to my uncle Kalon Trimon Norbu Wangyal's daughter, Tsering Chonzom in 1926.
They had six sons and one daughter. Their three eldest
sons died in Lhasa. In 1959 during the Tibetan Uprising
in Lhasa, Jamyang Khedup Shugu was arrested. His three
younger sons, all lamas, fled to India. Their eldest
son, Yeshe Dhondup was a lama in Sera monoastery and now
lives in Switzerland. The second son, Sonam Gyatso, was
the abbot of Ngor monastery and is now living in California. The youngest son, Losang Kunga was a lama in
Ngor monastery. Their daughter, Ngawang Chondon is living
in Lhasa. Implementing his rights as an American citizen,
Losang Kunga is presently requesting the United States
Government to assist him in his efforts to invite his
father and sister to visit him and his brother in
the United States. I guarantee, as a close relative
of Losang Kunga and his brothers, that the information
I have given is correct; and I hope that the U.S.
Government will give him all the assistance he will
need to invite his father, Jamyang Khyedup Shugu and
his sister, Ngawang Chodon to visit him after a sepa-
ration of twenty years.

Tsepon W.D. Shakabpa

Jan. 7th 1979

254 Cambridge Avenue
Kensington, CA 94708

February 9, 1979

Office of the People's Republic of China
Chinese Embassy
2300 Connecticut Avenue, N.W.
Washington, D.C.   20008

Dear Sirs:

I am a United States citizen, born in Tibet. I am writing to inform you
that on December 29, 1978 I filed with the United States Immigration
Office in San Francisco, CA for an Immigrant Visa for my father,
Shugu Jamyang Khedrub. My father was one of the 34 political prisoners
recently released from prison in China. To the best of my knowledge
he is now residing in Lhasa.

Although I have filed for an Immigrant Visa for my father and I am
awaiting notice of approval, I would appreciate any suggestions for
further action that you may be able to give me. If you can offer any
advice as to what I can do in this interim period, please let me know.
I will be deeply grateful for any help you can offer. I enclose a
self-addressed stamped envelope for your convenience.

                                        Yours sincerely,

                                        Losang Kunga Gyurme

LKG:led

Congress of the United States
House of Representatives

RONALD V. DELLUMS
8TH DISTRICT, CALIFORNIA

DISTRICT OF COLUMBIA COMMITTEE

CHAIRMAN, SUBCOMMITTEE ON FISCAL
AND GOVERNMENT AFFAIRS

ARMED SERVICES COMMITTEE

WASHINGTON OFFICE:
1417 LONGWORTH BUILDING
WASHINGTON, D.C. 20515
(202) 225-2661

DISTRICT OFFICES:
201 13TH STREET, ROOM 105
OAKLAND, CALIFORNIA 94604
(415) 763-0370

3357 MT. DIABLO BOULEVARD
LAFAYETTE, CALIFORNIA 94549
(415) 283-8125

2490 CHANNING WAY, ROOM 202
BERKELEY, CALIFORNIA 94704
(415) 548-7767

DONALD R. HOPKINS
DISTRICT ADMINISTRATOR

March 5, 1979

~~Shuikupa Jamyang Khedub~~ LOSANG KUNGA GYURME
254 Cambridge Ave.
Kensington, Ca. 94708

Dear Mr. ~~Khedub~~: GYURME

I have been checking with a number of people in the State Department
about your father, and have the following suggestions from them:

1. You might write to the following places, inquiring the whereabouts
    of your father, and enclosing a photocopy of the approved visa
    petition, as soon as you receive the notification from the U.S.
    Immigration and Naturalizations Service:

Revolutionary Committee	Consular Affairs Department
Lhasa	Ministry of Foreign Affairs
Tibetan Autonomous Region	Beiking (Peking)
Peoples Republic of China	Peoples Republic of China

    You may send the letters registered, return receipt requested in
    order to make certain that they get there.

2. If you locate your father, send him the photocopy of the approved
    visa petition as soon as you receive it so that he may show it to
    local officials as evidence that he will probably be able to come
    here as an immigrant. Also request from your father the address
    and contact person at the local level so that you can address a
    letter to them confirmed your wish to have your father come here
    and also enclosing a copy of the approved visa petition.

3. Send a letter to the American Embassy in either Hong Kong or China
    telling them of your interest in having your father join you and
    enclosing a copy of the approved visa petition. Please let me know
    when you get the approved petition and I will be able to tell you
    which is the correct office to send the letter to. As you may be
    aware, the recent normalization of relations with China still have
    our consular offices in a state of some confusion, but it may be
    resolved by the time you receive the approved visa petition.

Should you have any questions meantime, please feel free to call on me.
I will have a letter prepared from Congressman Dellums to send to the
Revolutionary Committee in Lhasa, and will send you a copy as soon as
it is finished. Should you not want this letter sent, please call me.

Sincerely yours,

Nancy Snow
Administrative Aide

P.S. I have been told that it would be best for you <u>not</u> to mention the
source of your information that your father was released from prison.
According to the State Department, that information was transmitted to
them by the Foreign Broadcast Information Service, that is, you could
have learned of your father's release from that source.

URS CORPORATION
473 JACKSON STREET
SAN FRANCISCO, CALIFORNIA 94111
TEL: (415) 434-1111

Richard C. Blum
VICE CHAIRMAN

July 2, 1979

Mr. David Denny
Embassy of the United States
Peking, People's Republic of China

Dear David:

As you may recall, when we were in Peking I discussed
the fact that a friend who is a Tibetan Lama living in
Berkeley, was interested in helping his father immigrate
to the United States. He has not seen him in over twenty
years and inasmuch as his father is quite elderly, it
would be a fine act of humanitarianism if the family could
be reunited. Enclosed is some correspondence with Senator
Cranston's office concerning this matter.

Thank you so much again for your hospitality when we were
in Peking. It was an eventful, successful trip. We are
only sorry that it was so short. Please let me know what
might be done.

Yours very truly,

Richard C. Blum

RCB/bae

Enclosures

Chinese free East Bay man's father in Tibet

By Jon Kawamoto

A tiny news item back inside the Nov. 15 edition of The Examiner, telling of 34 Tibetan prisoners being released by the ruling Chinese government, meant little to many people. But to an East Bay Buddhist, it renewed hope that his father is still alive. He hasn't heard from him for 19 years.

Lama Kunga Rinpoche's prayers were answered last week when he received word from his older brother in Switzerland that their 73-year-old father, Shul Kupa Jamyang Khedub, was among those freed after being imprisoned by the Chinese during their takeover of Tibet in 1959.

Rinpoche's father was imprisoned because of his government role as an accountant for the then-ruling Dalai Lama.

"I was really overwhelmed by the news that my father is still alive," said Rinpoche, clasping his hands in a grateful prayer.

The 40-year-old Tibetan Buddhist teacher fled his homeland with thousands of others during the takeover and now lives in Kensington. He said he intends to bring his father to the Bay Area to live with him and also hopes his mother, sister and a brother, who stayed behind, are still alive in Tibet.

Until he read his brother's letter, he had reconciled himself to the belief that his family had died during the 19 years since the Chinese purge.

"There was no correspondence allowed and I was afraid for years that the Chinese would try to get me," he said. "All I could do was pray. But, until now, I had given up

hope. It's been such a long time."

Tibet, the largely mountainous region whose Himalayan peaks now form China's southern border, was run by the Dalai Lama (the reincarnation of Buddha to Tibetans) and noble families such as Rinpoche's for centuries. But the age-old processes crumbled in the upheaval and 100,000 Tibetans were killed.

Immediately after Rinpoche's father was imprisoned because of his ties with the old government, Rinpoche fled with his older brother to neighboring India.

"I was still in a monastery when my father was imprisoned," he said. "I knew, as did my brother, that we had to leave — and not as monks because the Chinese would then surely arrest us. So I went dressed in secular clothes."

For two weeks as they searched for paths through the steep Himalayas, Rinpoche and a band of other Tibetan refugees lived on handsful of water and scraps of barley flour cakes they begged from nomads. Hiding by day and walking by night, the group traveled 200 miles before reaching India.

"We were fearful and confused those two weeks," he said. "We always thought they would find us. Just total fear and confusion — I can't describe it."

Instead of finding refuge in India, however, Rinpoche said he and the others encountered total culture shock as they shifted from one refugee camp to the next for four years. Compounding the shock of another lifestyle was the frustration they felt for their loved ones.

When the Chinese gained con-

trol of Tibet, they limited freedom of movement, confiscated radios and weapons, labeled nobles and monks parasites and encouraged children to denounce their parents and masters. It was a purge Rinpoche remembers painfully.

"All of us wanted to communicate with our families or with someone who would tell us whether they were still alive, but we all feared the Chinese government. We just prayed for their safety."

In 1963, at the behest of a Tibetan monk who fled to the United States instead of India, Rinpoche arrived in Farmingdale, N.J., 35 miles east of Trenton. He eked out a living by teaching classes in Tibetan Buddhism and Tibetan language.

He arrived in Kensington in 1972 after accepting a similar teaching job at the California Institute of Asian Studies in San Francisco.

"I love the weather and the people in the Bay Area," he said, gazing at the Bay view from his home. "I want to bring my father here so he, too, can be happy.

"Even though there was no reason given for the prisoners' release, the action shows a compassionate change on the part of the Chinese. It appears as if Chairman Hua Kuo-feng is getting rid of the bad misunderstanding between the Chinese and Tibetans. I'm not bitter about the past, just hopeful for the future."

Rinpoche gazed at a torn, fuzzy photo of his father, mother, uncle and niece, taken before the takeover.

"I hope they are all still alive," he said softly.

San Francisco Examiner, December 18, 1978.

Interview with
Lama Kunga Rinpoche

LAMA KUNGA RINPOCHE: In Tibetan culture, whenever we have emotional identifications within ourselves — strong feelings of confusion, desire, or anger — we know that it is very good at that time to turn to the spiritual teachings. They are an antidote to strong feelings.

I think that emotional problems are the same here and in Tibet. Always it is something occurring within your own mind. However, in Tibet, techniques have been developed for counteracting those forces. Here in America, whenever I have those kinds of feelings, I try to relax and think about the spiritual knowledge that I have received from my teachers. I try to read more and study further, and that works for me instead of, say, going out and going to a movie to escape. Or eating or drinking more. Those things don't work for me.

It does help somewhat, when you have an emotional upset, to visit friends or take a walk on the beach. Smokers pull out another cigarette and drinkers drink more, substituting those things immediately. But that's kind of like taking aspirin for a headache, which temporarily stops the pain. The long-range solution is to sit down and contemplate, to utilize the philosophies of the mind developed over centuries by spiritual practitioners.

Emotional problems are things that have really stirred us up inside our brain or our heart. They are internal, not external at all, coming from the most secret part of our life. So we need a special method — to my own understanding — we need a method based on spiritual practice and spiritual knowledge.

All the teachings are basically oriented toward solving confusion: mental pollution and mental disorders. The aim of all Tibetan Buddhists is to clarify the inside of our brain and heart. Even to go beyond brain and heart to *who we really are*. Brain is only a substance, a chemical thing. When we die, our brain is nothing. Mind, however, is different. We go through different layers of meaning, from a philosophical point of view, to try to explore the structure of the mind and consciousness. We try to discover what is making the problem, what makes joy and what makes us upset. We drill into the source of suffering and the source of happiness, drilling into that source philosophically, scientifically, and analytically. We investigate many different views of masters and teachers, their teachings and their writings, trying to solve the anxieties of humankind.

You believe, then, that an approach to solving some of our large-scale problems such as violence, aggression, materialistic greed, and injustice, is to teach people how their minds work?

We should be asking ourselves to settle down, to be content, to limit our needs in certain areas, to study the philosophy of the mind, and learn something about it. And then we can share some of our wisdom with our own generation.

Theoretically, one could say that it might help to eliminate problems. But in truth, it is difficult to know, because we are talking about a mass society, millions of people. . . . It takes time and space. On the other hand, technology is a positive development which could help to satisfy some people's desires for wisdom.

The technology such as this tape recorder is good — a machine into which we can converse and people can hear it later. Also, technologies such as certain medical techniques, and technologies for exploring space, these things are quite wonderful.

In my country Tibet people have developed a science or a technology of spiritual things, but our science of material things is poorly developed. It should have been taught at the monastery along with spiritual matters. Both things hand in hand. We as monks in the monasteries received a lopsided education. So, a combination of those two sides might be better. Who knows but that the highest level of Western science and the highest level of the philosophy of mind will meet together one day, and then there will be a kind of "big bang" of enlightenment.

Are you in disguise here in America, are you necessarily wearing a mask of sorts because this culture is so different?

I try to reveal my true nature as much as I can. My monk's robe was maybe not quite my true nature. So I gave up my monk's robe to be as true as possible. I do not want to disguise any aspect of myself. I like to reveal myself as clearly as possible. My problem is a human one. To try to be as true to myself, as honest, as is possible. Not to conceal anything. I try show what I am.

As I said I am a human being and I have worldly desires, which are the desires of average people. Therefore for me, for my own individual sake, it was not right to disguise those desires by wearing the robes. On the other hand, if I were still living in a monastery in Tibet I would have had more training, and the living conditions there are so different that I would have felt right in that role. The emphasis of our two cultures is different. But I do acknowledge that I am freer here, in many ways. And though I am freer 100 percent in what I can do, I still try to limit myself, to watch myself as much as I can.

What can you say about the type of freedom we have in the West — does it strengthen one?

For myself, I think it is very good. I feel I have accomplished more here than I would have done in a small corner of Tibet. I feel that it is possible for me to explore more spiritual pathways here, and meet different types of people, and find my own simple small way of accomplishing things. I have a feeling of independence here, which I like. At least I feel — it might not be right — but I feel that I myself have benefited from this freedom.

What aspect of Tibetan culture have you brought with you to the United States, and is there anything that you have permanently left behind?

To tell the truth, I am still very attached, very rooted in my own country. I am a tree that has several roots, and some of the older roots are not severed. The old ground is still there. At the same time, the new roots are growing, and yet I feel that I have not completely lost anything.

I was fortunate to have been born into such a nice family. They were very peaceful, loving people. My parents were kind. They loved each other, and they were spiritually oriented. I was introduced to the positive side of Tibetan culture that way. Also, I spent much of my childhood in a monastery until the age of sixteen, and there I learned more of the best of Tibetan culture.

Culturally, my background is religious. So, since I've been in America, I've been teaching and establishing this Tibetan Buddhist meditation center. As you know, the old Tibetan way of life is deteriorating because of the political situation — the art objects, manuscripts, philosophical disciplines are very important and must be saved. As I said, most of Tibetan philosophy teaches how to deal with mind and body together — how to let them cooperate peacefully and how not to be overwhelmed by greed and negativities. I am concerned to preserve these documents. I am hoping to make these teachings available to people here at the center, and eventually we can have translation projects here, so the manuscripts can be read in English. English is a good language. Indeed, it is used widely across the world now.

Would you say that you do not regret leaving the monastery, leaving Tibet?

Regret? In a sense of giving up my monk's robe, turning into a lay person, no. Perhaps, though, in a sense of neglecting my monastic duties, or not following the rules, there is perhaps some sort of guilty conscience in me. But that all has to be sorted out with confessions and prayers. I feel that it is not a big issue.

Other than that I have no regrets about leaving my country because I was forced to do so.

Following is a quote from the Fourteenth Dalai Lama.* I wonder if you might comment on it: "We Tibetans are grateful to the Chinese for the opportunities they have given us to practice patience, tolerance, and forgiveness. They provided us with a supreme test of courage. On the other hand, it is almost time for them to leave."

[Laughter] I think that is really well said. I myself, as part of Tibet, feel the way he feels about the country and the people. We learned so much from that aggression and hatred. All the negative things. We learned mistrust, we learned depression, yes. We have gone through all the depths of *samsaric* woe. And I think, in a sense, that we do see the Chinese as our teachers. You know, you read in all the books that they are wise men. And so now it seems it is time for the wise men to act wisely. A wise man knows that all of mankind should be treated fairly and equally. Tibetans are part of mankind. Tibetans now need a rest from the Chinese. Tibetans wish to be free and happy. We've suffered. We've lost our jobs and our families and our houses and our way of life. If that is what they hoped to accomplish, they have in fact achieved it. Generations of Tibetans have been born outside Tibet. The future is unknown. Now it is time for China to leave Tibet, and leave it peacefully.

Interviewed by Sumner Carnahan
1987 in Kensington, California

*From the *Snow Lion Newsletter*, Spring 1987

Selected Bibliography

Ash, Niema. *Flight of the Wind Horse: A Journey into Tibet.* London: Rider & Co., 1990.

Avedon, John F. *In Exile from the Land of Snows.* New York: Alfred A. Knopf, 1984.

Bernstein, Jeremy. "Our Far-Flung Correspondents: A Journey to Lhasa." *The New Yorker,* December 14, 1987, 47–105.

Beyer, Stephan. *The Cult of Tara: Magic and Ritual in Tibet.* Berkeley: University of California Press, 1973.

Bryant, Barry, in cooperation with Namgyal Monastery. *The Wheel of Time Sand Mandala: Visual Scripture of Tibetan Buddhism.* San Francisco: Harper San Francisco, 1992.

David-Neel, Alexandra. *My Journey to Lhasa.* Boston: Beacon Press, 1927; reprint Harper & Row, 1986.

David-Neel, Alexandra, and Lama Yongden. *The Secret Oral Teachings in Tibetan Buddhist Sects.* San Francisco: City Lights Books, 1967.

Evans-Wentz, W. Y., comp. and ed. *The Tibetan Book of the Dead: Or, The Afterdeath Experiences on the Bardo Plane,* according to Lama Kazi Dawa-Samdup's English Rendering. Boston & London: Shambhala, 1993. Reprint.

The Fourteenth Dalai Lama of Tibet. *Freedom in Exile: An Autobiography of the Dalai Lama of Tibet.* San Francisco: Harper San Francisco, 1990.

___. *Ocean of Wisdom: Guidelines for Living.* Santa Fe, N. M.: Clear Light Publishers, 1989.

___. *My Land and My People.* New York: McGraw-Hill, 1962.

Fremantle, Francesca, and Chögyam Trungpa, trans. and commentary. *The Tibetan Book of the Dead: The Great Liberation through Hearing in the Bardo* by Guru Rinpoche, according to Karma-Lingpa. Boston & London: Shambhala, 1992.

Goldstein, Melvyn C. *A History of Modern Tibet, 1913–1951.* Berkeley: University of California Press, 1989.

Goodman, Michael Harris. *The Last Dalai Lama: A Biography.* Boston: Shambhala, 1987.

Harrer, Heinrich. *Seven Years in Tibet.* New York: E. P. Dutton & Co., 1954.

Hopkins, Jeffrey, and Anne Klein, trans. and ed. *Khetsun Sangpo Rinbochay's Tantric Practice in Nyingma.* London: Rider & Co., 1982.

Johnson, Russell, and Kerry Moran. *The Sacred Mountain of Tibet.* Rochester, Vt.: Park Street Press, 1989.

Lama Kunga Rinpoche, trans. "The Secret Biography of Tsangyang Gyatso, the Sixth Dalai Lama of Tibet, written by Lhundrub Dargyay." Unpublished manuscript.

Lama Kunga Rinpoche and Brian Cutillo, trans. *Drinking the Mountain Stream: New Stories & Songs by Milarepa.* Novato, Calif.: Lotsawa, 1986.

___. *Miraculous Journey: Stories & Songs by Milarepa.* Novato, Calif.: Lotsawa, 1978.

Lhalungpa, Lobsang P., *The Life of Milarepa.* New York: Viking Penguin, 1992.

Lhalungpa, Lobsang P., trans. Takpo Tashi Namgyal, *Mahamudra: The Quintessence of Mind and Meditation.* Boston: Shambhala, 1986.

___. (In collaboration with His Holiness the Fourteenth Dalai Lama). *Tibet: The Sacred Realm.* New York: Aperture, 1983.

Norbu, Thubten Jigme. *Tibet Is My Country.* New York: E. P. Dutton & Co., 1961.

Normanton, Simon. *Tibet: The Lost Civilization.* London: Viking Penguin, 1988.

Olson, Eleanor. "Tibetan Art: Tibetan Life and Culture." Newark, N.J.: Newark Museum, n.d.

Rockwell, John, Jr. "A Primer for Classical Literary Tibetan." From the Naropa Institute, Boulder, Colorado, 1985. Working draft.

Shakabpa, Tsipon W. D. *Tibet: A Political History.* New York: Potala Publications, 1984. Reprint.

Snellgrove, David, and Hugh Richardson. *A Cultural History of Tibet.* New York, Washington: Frederick A. Praeger, 1968.

Sogyal Rinpoche. *The Tibetan Book of Living and Dying.* San Francisco: Harper San Francisco, 1993.

Sonami, Hiroshi (Ngor Thartse Khen Rinpoche). *Tibetan Mandalas: The Ngor Collection.* Tokyo, Japan: Kodansha, 1985. Limited edition.

Sonami, Hiroshi, and S. B. Aldridge, trans. "Three Experiences: The Jewel That Pleases, Ngor-chen dKon-mchog lhun-grub (1497–1557)." Unpublished manuscript.

Taring, Rinchen Dolma. *Daughter of Tibet.* London: John Murray, 1970.

Thurman, Robert A. F. *Life and Teaching of Tsong Khapa.* Ithaca, N.Y.: Snow Lion, 1986.

Trungpa, Chögyam. *Shambhala: The Sacred Path of the Warrior.* New York: Bantam Books, 1984.

___. *Cutting Through Spiritual Materialism.* Berkeley, Calif.: Shambhala, 1973.

___. *Born in Tibet.* Baltimore, Md.: Penquin Books, 1971.

Venerable Lama Lodö. *The Quintessence of the Animate and Inanimate: A Discourse on the Holy Dharma.* San Francisco: KDK Publications, 1985.

List of Photographs

Index

About the Authors

Sumner Carnahan is the author of *The Time Is Now* (1983) and *Thirteen* (1995) from Burning Books, as well as works of short fiction published in magazines and anthologies. Her reviews and profiles have appeared in the *San Francisco Chronicle*. Dramatic compositions based on her stories were premiered by composer Laetitia Sonami in Amsterdam and in New York City. Carnahan has received acknowledgments for her writing, including recent commissions from New American Radio. In 1987, the National Endowment for the Arts designated *The guests go in to supper*, which Carnahan originated and edited, as one of the "best independent press books" of the year. Born in Corpus Christi, Texas, Carnahan received an M.F.A. from Mills College, and she studied classical Tibetan with Hiroshi Sonami (Ngor Thartse Khen Rinpoche). Since 1989 she has lived in New Mexico.

The son of Tsipon J. K. Shuguba, **Lama Kunga Rinpoche** was born in Lhasa, Tibet, in the wood-pig year, 1935. At the age of seven Rinpoche was recognized as a *tulku* — a reincarnation of Sevan Repa, heart disciple of the great sage Milarepa. Rinpoche entered the monastery and by age sixteen was ordained a monk. At the time of his escape from Tibet in 1959, he was vice-abbot (Thartse Shabtrung) of Ngor Monastery, Sakya tradition. Geshe Wangyal, under the auspices of the Fourteenth Dalai Lama in Dharamsala, brought Rinpoche and three other young lamas to the United States in 1962. Founder and resident lama at Ewam Choden Tibetan Buddhist Meditation Center, Rinpoche has recorded songs of Milarepa on the Lovely Music label for composer Eliane Radique, and he has authored, with Brian Cutillo, two translations of Milarepa's stories and songs: *Drinking the Mountain Stream* (1978) and *Miraculous Journey* (1986), published by Lotsawa.